THE UNIVERSITY OF CHICAGO

ORIENTAL INSTITUTE PUBLICATIONS

VOLUME 113

Series Editors

Thomas A. Holland

and

Thomas G. Urban

ORIENTAL INSTITUTE PUBLICATIONS • VOLUME 113

ORIENTAL INSTITUTE HAWARA PAPYRI

DEMOTIC AND GREEK TEXTS FROM AN EGYPTIAN FAMILY ARCHIVE IN THE FAYUM (FOURTH TO THIRD CENTURY B.C.)

by

GEORGE R. HUGHES† *and* RICHARD JASNOW

with a contribution by

JAMES G. KEENAN

THE ORIENTAL INSTITUTE OF THE UNIVERSITY OF CHICAGO
CHICAGO • ILLINOIS

Library of Congress Catalog Card Number: 96-67506
ISBN: 1-885923-02-3
ISSN: 0069-3367

The Oriental Institute, Chicago

Series Editors' Acknowledgments

We thank Professor Robert D. Biggs, Thomas Dousa, and Steve Vinson
for their assistance in the production of this volume.

Printed by BookCrafters, Chelsea, Michigan

TABLE OF CONTENTS

LIST OF ABBREVIATIONS

BM	British Museum
ca.	*circa*, about, approximately
cm	centimeter(s)
cont.	continued
Demot. Nb.	*Demotisches Namenbuch.* By Erich Lüddeckens et al. Wiesbaden: Dr. Ludwig Reichert Verlag, 1980–
ed(s).	editor(s)
e.g.	*exempli gratia,* for example
et al.	*et alii,* and others
fig(s).	figure(s)
Glossar	*Demotisches Glossar.* By Wolja Erichsen. Copenhagen: Ejnar Munksgaard, 1954
i.e.	*id est,* that is
l(l).	line(s)
O.I.	Oriental Institute
no(s).	number(s)
n(n).	note(s)
P.	Papyrus
pers. comm.	personal communication
p(p).	page(s)
pl(s).	plate(s)
sc.	*scilicet,* that is to say
s.v.	*sub verbo, sub voce,* under the word
vso.	verso

LIST OF FIGURES

LIST OF PLATES

LIST OF TABLES

PREFACE

Professor George R. Hughes had worked on the Oriental Institute Hawara papyri for a number of years. However, both heavy administrative responsibilities and his involvement with other complicated projects, such as the publication of the Hermopolis Legal Code, prevented him from spending as much time as he wished on these magnificent texts. During the last years of his life increasingly poor health and, particularly, his deteriorating eyesight, made it very difficult for him to continue study of the papyri. In September of 1992 Professor Janet H. Johnson suggested that I work together with Professor Hughes to complete the publication. Professor Hughes, with whom I had earlier read through several of the texts, agreed to this arrangement. I began at that time, but sadly, it was not possible to finish the manuscript before his death in December 1992. Professor Hughes had prepared preliminary transliterations and translations of all these papyri, including the Rendell Papyrus published in the *Appendix*. These form the basis of the editions presented here, though I have naturally checked the transcriptions repeatedly against the originals. I have also furnished the discussions, commentaries, and glossaries. It is a great loss to scholarship that Professor Hughes, with his profound knowledge of Demotic legal documents and ancient Egyptian law, was not able to prepare the commentary on these texts. The few notes that he left have been incorporated, but at no time could I consult with him concerning the manuscript.[1] I am well aware, therefore, that this publication is not what it could have been had Hughes been able to finish it.

It remains for me to thank those who helped Professor Hughes and me to produce this volume. First, I should like to thank Professor Janet H. Johnson, who made the publication possible, and who also greatly encouraged Professor Hughes to continue his work on Demotic even when plagued by ill health. Professor James G. Keenan of Loyola University most obligingly assumed the task of editing the Greek dockets and the Greek document P. O.I. 25260 (= Chicago Hawara Greek Papyrus 7C). It is a pleasure for me to offer to him my gratitude for his contribution and also for useful comments on various drafts of this manuscript. I am also deeply indebted to Mr. Thomas Van Eynde, who took the excellent publication photographs of the papyri. Dr. Karen Wilson, Director of the Oriental Institute Museum, encouraged and expedited my project; Dr. Raymond Tindel, Oriental Institute Museum Registrar, provided ideal and hospitable conditions for the study of these awkwardly large documents; Laura D'Alessandro, Conservator of the Oriental Institute Museum, skillfully unrolled the Greek Papyrus O.I. 25260 and also helped to prepare the papyri for photography; Jean Grant, Photographer of the Oriental Institute Museum, took the publication photograph of the *scriptura interior* of the newly unrolled Greek Papyrus O.I. 25260 (pl. 42); and John Larson, Oriental Institute Museum Archivist, provided information and correspondence pertaining to the Hawara papyri. It is impossible to ascertain the names of all those who may have aided Professor Hughes in connection with the Hawara papyri over the years. I am certain, however, that he would have wished to thank the following for assistance and information: Sir Eric Turner, T. C. Skeat, Ursula Schneider, Barbara Hall, Robert Hanson, Charles Nims, and W. Erichsen. I myself am also grateful to Professor Adam Bülow-Jacobsen, Dr. Willy Clarysse, Christina Di Cerbo, Professor Erich Lüddeckens, Dr. Peter Lacovara, and Mr. Kenneth Rendell. Carol Andrews offered helpful remarks and corrections. I conclude by thanking the editors of the Oriental Institute Publications Office, Thomas Urban and Thomas Holland, for bestowing so much care and attention upon the manuscript.

Richard Jasnow
Johns Hopkins University

---

1. For this reason comments in the first person employed throughout the manuscript refer to the undersigned.

BIBLIOGRAPHY

Allam, Schafik

    1981   "Quelques aspects du mariage dans l'Égypte ancienne." *Journal of Egyptian Archaeology* 67: 116–35.

    1991   "Egyptian Law Courts in Pharaonic and Hellenistic Times." *Journal of Egyptian Archaeology* 77: 109–27.

Andrews, Carol A. R.

    1988   "The Sale of Part of a Pathyrite Vineyard (P. BM 10071)." In *Pyramid Studies and Other Essays Presented to I. E. S. Edwards*, edited by J. Baines, T. G. H. James, A. Leahy, and A. F. Shore, pp. 193–99. London: Egypt Exploration Society.

    1990   *Ptolemaic Legal Texts from the Theban Area*. Catalogue of Demotic Papyri in the British Museum 4. London: British Museum Publications.

Bakry, H.

    1968   "A Statue of Pedeamun-Nebnesuttaui." *Annales du Service des Antiquités de l'Égypte* 60: 15–25.

Beinlich, H.

    1991   *Das Buch vom Fayum*. Ägyptologische Abhandlungen 51. Wiesbaden: Otto Harrassowitz.

Bernand, Étienne

    1975   *Recueil des inscriptions grecques du Fayoum, Tome I: La "Méris" d'Herakleidès*. Leiden: E. J. Brill.

Bogaert, Raymond

    1987   "Banques et banquiers dans l'Arsinoïte à l'époque ptolémaïque." *Zeitschrift für Papyrologie und Epigraphik* 68: 35–75.

Bonnet, Hans

    1952   *Reallexikon der ägyptischen Religionsgeschichte*. Berlin and New York: Walter de Gruyter.

Boswinkel, E. and Pestman, P. W.

    1978   *Textes grecs, démotiques et bilingues*. Papyrologica Lugduno-Batava 19. Leiden: E. J. Brill.

    1982   *Les Archives privées de Dionysios, fils de Kephalas*. Papyrologica Lugduno-Batava 22. Leiden: E. J. Brill.

Botti, Giuseppe

    1969   "Frammenti del papiro demotico n. 8698 del Museo Egizo di Firenze." *Mitteilungen des Deutschen Archäologischen Instituts, Abteilung Kairo* 24: 73–77.

Breasted, James Henry

    1933   *The Oriental Institute*. University of Chicago Survey 12. Chicago: University of Chicago Press.

Bresciani, Edda

    1986   "Iconografia e culto di premarres nel Fayum." *Egitto e Vincino Oriente* 9: 49–58.

Bülow-Jacobsen, Adam

    1982   "Three Ptolemaic Tax-receipts from Hawara (P. Carlsberg 46–48)." *Bulletin of the Institute of Classical Studies* 29: 12–16.

Calderini, Aristide and Daris, Sergio

1978 *Dizionario dei nomi geografici e topografici dell'Egitto greco-romano, Volume 3*. Milan: Cisalpino-Goliardica.

de Cenival, Françoise

1968 "Un Document inédit relatif à l'exploitation de terres du Fayoum (P. Dém. Lille, Inv. Sorb. 1186)." *Revue d'Égyptologie* 20: 37–50.

1972 "Un Acte de renonciation consécutif à un partage de revenues liturgiques Memphites (P. Louvre E 3266)." *Bulletin de l'Institut Français d'Archéologie Orientale* 71: 11–65.

1973 *Cautionnements démotiques du début de l'époque ptolémaïque (P. dém. Lille 34 à 96)*, Société d'histoire du droit. Collection d'Histoire Institutionnelle et Sociale 5. Paris: Éditions Klincksieck.

1975 "Acte de vente d'une ânesse, de l'an 9 de Ptolémée Épiphane (P. Inv. Sorbonne n° 217a)." *Revue d'Égyptologie* 27: 56–61.

1978 "La Deuxième partie du P. dém. Lille 18: Déclaration de petit bétail (P. Inv. Sorbonne 1248)." *Enchoria* 8/2: 1–3.

1984 *Papyrus démotiques de Lille (III)*. Mémoires Publiés par les Membres de l'Institut Français d'Archéologie Orientale du Caire 110. Cairo: Institut Français d'Archéologie Orientale.

1985a "À propos d'une nouvelle lecture de *Mythus Glossar n° 997*." *Enchoria* 13: 201–05.

1985b "Les Nouveaux fragments du mythe de l'oeil du soleil de l'Institut de Papyrologie et d'Égyptologie de Lille." *Cahier de Recherches de l'Institut de Papyrologie et d'Égyptologie de Lille* 7: 95–115.

1986 "Comptes d'une association religieuse thébaine datant des années 29 à 33 du roi Amasis (P. démot. Louvre E7840 bis)." *Revue d'Égyptologie* 37: 13–29.

1988 *Le Mythe de l'oeil du soleil*. Demotische Studien 9. Sommerhausen: Gisela Zauzich Verlag.

Chauveau, Michel

1991 "P. Carlsberg 301: Le Manuel juridique de Tebtynis." In *The Carlsberg Papyri 1: Demotic Texts from the Collection*, edited by P. J. Frandsen, pp. 103–27. Carsten Niebuhr Institute Publications 15. Copenhagen: Museum Tusculanum Press.

Clarysse, Willy

1975 "The Suggenes Komon and the Hawara Embalmers." *Zeitschrift für Papyrologie und Epigraphik* 17: 253–54.

1976 "Two Notes on Eponymous Priests." *Enchoria* 6: 1–5.

1980 "Philadelpheia and the Memphites in the Zenon Archive." In *Studies on Ptolemaic Memphis*, by D. Crawford, J. Quaegebeur, and W. Clarysse, pp. 91–122. Studia Hellenistica 24. Leuven: Fondation Universitaire de Belgique.

1984 "Bilingual Texts and Collaboration between Demoticists and Papyrologists." In *Atti del XVII Congresso Internazionale di Papirologia, Volume 3*, edited by M. Gigante, pp. 1345–53. Naples: Centro Internazionale per lo Studio dei Papiri Ercolanesi.

1987 "Noms démotiques en -*ỉw*, -*m-ḫb* et -*ỉ.ỉr.dj-s*." *Enchoria* 15: 11–24.

1993 "Egyptian Scribes Writing Greek." *Chronique d'Égypte* 68: 186–201.

Clarysse, Willy and Lanciers, Eddy

1989 "Currency and the Dating of Demotic and Greek Papyri from the Ptolemaic Period." *Ancient Society* 20: 117–32.

Clarysse, Willy and van der Veken, G.

1983 *The Eponymous Priests of Ptolemaic Egypt*. Papyrologica Lugduno-Batava 24. Leiden: E. J. Brill.

Clarysse, Willy and Winnicki, J.

1989   "Documentary Papyri." In *The Judean-Syrian-Egyptian Conflict of 103–101 B.C.: A Multilingual Dossier Concerning a "War of Scepters,"* by E. van't Dack, W. Clarysse, G. Cohen, J. Quaegebeur, and J. K. Winnicki, pp. 37–81. Collectanea Hellenistica 1. Brussels: Pulblikatie van het Comité Klassieke Studies, Subcomité Hellenisme. Koninklijke Academie voor Wetenschappen, Letteren en Schone Kunsten van België.

Cockle, W. E. H.

1988   Review of *Yale Papyri in the Beinecke Rare Book and Manuscript Library II*, by Susan A. Stephens. *Enchoria* 16: 169–73.

Corcoran, Lorelei Hilda

1988   "Portrait Mummies from Roman Egypt." 2 vols. Ph.D. dissertation, University of Chicago.

1992   "A Cult Function for the So-called Faiyum Mummy Portraits?" In *Life in a Multi-Cultural Society*, edited by J. H. Johnson, pp. 57–60. Studies in Ancient Oriental Civilization, no. 51. Chicago: The Oriental Institute.

1995   *Portrait Mummies from Roman Egypt (I–IV Centuries A.D.) with a Catalog of Portrait Mummies in Egyptian Museums.* Studies in Ancient Oriental Civilization, no. 56. Chicago: The Oriental Institute.

Crawford, Dorothy J.

1971   *Kerkeosiris: An Egyptian Village in the Ptolemaic Period.* Cambridge: Cambridge University Press.

Cruz-Uribe, Eugene

1990   "A Note on the Early Demotic Grain Formula." *Enchoria* 17: 55–68.

1992   "The Lake of Moeris: A Reprise." In *Life in a Multi-Cultural Society*, edited by J. H. Johnson, pp. 63–66. Studies in Ancient Oriental Civilization, no. 51. Chicago: The Oriental Institute.

Daressy, Georges

1914   "Une Stèle de Hawara." *Recueil de Travaux* 36: 73–82.

Dawson, Warren and Uphill, Eric

1972   *Who was Who in Egyptology.* Second revised edition. London: Egypt Exploration Society.

Derchain, Philippe

1978   "Miettes (suite)." *Revue d'Égyptologie* 30: 57–66.

Devauchelle, Didier

1983a   "Notes sur les inscriptions démotiques des carrières de Tourah et de Mâsarah." *Annales du Service des Antiquités de l'Égypte* 69: 169–82.

1983b   *Ostraca démotiques du Musée du Louvre, Tome 1: Reçus.* Bibliothèque d'Étude 92. Cairo: Institut Français d'Archéologie Orientale.

1983c   "Les Graffites démotiques du toit du temple d'Edfou." *Bulletin de l'Institut Français d'Archéologie Orientale* 83: 123–31.

1986   "ḤḎ: deben ou kite?" *Enchoria* 14: 157–58.

1987   "Notes sur l'administration funéraire égyptienne à l'époque gréco-romaine." *Bulletin de l'Institut Français d'Archéologie Orientale* 87: 141–60.

Drower, Margaret S.

1985   *Flinders Petrie: A Life in Archaeology.* London: Victor Gollancz.

Edgar, C.

1938   "The Stolistae of the Labyrinth." *Archiv für Papyrusforschung* 13: 76–77.

Edwards, I. E. S.

1971   "Bill of Sale for a Set of Ushabtis." *Journal of Egyptian Archaeology* 57: 120–24.

El-Amir, Mustafa

1955   "Note on '*t ḥyrt*' in Boundaries of Ptolemaic Houses at Thebes." *Annales du Service des Antiquités de
            l'Égypte* 53: 135–38.

1959   *A Family Archive from Thebes*. Cairo: General Organisation for Government Printing Offices.

Erichsen, Wolja

1950   "Zwei frühdemotische Urkunden aus Elephantine." In *Coptic Studies in Honor of Walter Ewing Crum*,
            edited by M. Malinine, pp. 271–86. Bulletin of the Byzantine Institute 2. Boston: The Byzantine Insti-
            tute.

1954   *Demotisches Glossar*. Copenhagen: Ejnar Munksgaard.

1958   "Ein neuer Typ einer demotischen ehegüterrechtlichen Urkunde." In *Proceedings of the IXth Interna-
            tional Congress of Papyrology, Oslo, 19th–22nd August, 1958*, edited by L. Amundsen and V. Skån-
            land, pp. 320–27. Oslo: Norwegian Universities Press.

Eyre, Christopher

1992   "The Adoption Papyrus in Social Context." *Journal of Egyptian Archaeology* 78: 207–21.

Felber, Heinz

1991   "Augustus Ζεὺς ἐλευθέριος im demotischen und die Etymologie von ⲢⲘⲍⲈ." *Göttinger Miszellen* 123:
            27–36.

Foraboschi, Daniele

1967   *Onomasticon alterum papyrologicum: Supplemento al namenbuch di F. Preisigke*. Testi e Documenti
            per lo Studio dell'Antichità 16, Serie papirologica 2. Milan and Varese: Istituto Editoriale Cisalpino.

Franke, Detlef

1984   "Probleme der Arbeit mit altägyptischen Titeln des Mittleren Reiches." *Göttinger Miszellen* 83: 103–24.

Gagos, Traianos; Koenen, Ludwig; and McNellen, Brad E.

1992   "A First Century Archive from Oxyrhynchos or Oxyrhynchite Loan Contracts and Egyptian Marriage."
            In *Life in a Multi-Cultural Society*, edited by J. H. Johnson, pp. 181–205. Studies in Ancient Oriental
            Civilization, no. 51. Chicago: The Oriental Institute.

Glanville, Stephen R. K.

1939   *A Theban Archive of the Reign of Ptolemy I, Soter*. Catalogue of Demotic Papyri in the British Museum
            1. London: The British Museum.

Grenfell, Bernard and Hunt, Arthur S.

1907   *The Tebtunis Papyri, Part II*. University of California Publications, Graeco-Roman Archaeology 2. Ox-
            ford: Oxford University Press.

Grunert, Stefan

1984   "Theorie und Praxis im ptolemäischen Eherecht." In *Grammata Demotika: Festschrift für Erich Lüd-
            deckens zum 15. Juni 1983*, edited by H.-J. Thissen and K.-Th. Zauzich, pp. 61–69. Würzburg: Gisela
            Zauzich Verlag.

Habachi, Labib

1977   "Hawara." In *Lexikon der Ägyptologie, Band 2*, edited by W. Helck and W. Westendorf, cols. 1072–74. Wiesbaden: Otto Harrassowitz.

Hagedorn, Dieter

1976   "P. Hawara 322 und der Stratege Claudius Protogenes." *Zeitschrift für Papyrologie und Epigraphik* 21: 165–67.

1991   "P. Ashm. 1984.77 Rekto." *Enchoria* 18: 37–42.

Harrauer, Hermann

1987   *Griechische Texte IX: Neue Papyri zum Steuerwesen im 3. Jh. v. Chr.* Corpus Papyrorum Raineri Archeducis Austriae 13. Vienna: Verlag Brüder Hollinek.

Hoogendijk, F. A. J. and van Minnen, P.

1991   *Papyri, Ostraca, Parchments and Waxed Tablets in the Leiden Papyrological Institute.* Papyrologica Lugduno-Batava 25. Leiden: E. J. Brill.

Hughes, George R.

1956   "Are There Two Demotic Writings of *šw?*" *Mitteilungen des Deutschen Archäologischen Instituts, Abteilung Kairo* 14: 80–88.

1958   "The Sixth Day of the Lunar Month and the Demotic Word for 'Cult Guild.'" *Mitteilungen des Deutschen Archäologischen Instituts, Abteilung Kairo* 16: 147–60.

1975   "The Demotic Egyptian Archive from Hawara, Part 1." *The Oriental Institute News & Notes* 22: 2–3.

1976   "The Demotic Egyptian Archive from Hawara, Part 2." *The Oriental Institute News & Notes* 23: 2–3.

1980   "On Two Demotic Egyptian 'Memoranda.'" *Serapis* 6: 63–68.

Husson, Geneviève

1976   "Note sur la formation et le sens du composé προνήσιον." *Chronique d'Égypte* 51: 167–68.

1983   *Oikia.* Université de Paris 4. Paris-Sorbonne, Série "Papyrologie" 2. Paris: Publications de la Sorbonne.

Janssen, Jac J.

1968   "The Smaller Dâkhla Stela." *Journal of Egyptian Archaeology* 54: 165–72

Jasnow, Richard

1982   "Two Demotic Papyri in the Oriental Institute." *Enchoria* 11: 17–22.

1990   "Demotic Texts from the Carnegie Museum of Natural History." *Enchoria* 17: 89–96.

Johnson, Janet H.

1986   "The Role of the Egyptian Priesthood in Ptolemaic Egypt." In *Egyptological Studies in Honor of Richard A. Parker*, edited by L. H. Lesko, pp. 70–84. Hanover: Brown University Press.

1994   "'Annuity Contracts' and Marriage." In *For His Ka: Essays Offered in Memory of Klaus Baer*, edited by D. P. Silverman, pp. 113–32. Studies in Ancient Oriental Civilization, no. 55. Chicago: The Oriental Institute.

Jordan, D. R.

1988   "A Love Charm with Verses." *Zeitschrift für Papyrologie und Epigraphik* 72: 245–59.

Kaplony-Heckel, Ursula

1963   *Die demotischen Tempeleide.* Ägyptologische Abhandlungen 6. Wiesbaden: Otto Harrassowitz.

Kessler, Dieter

1989   *Die heiligen Tiere und der König, Teil 1: Beiträge zu Organisation, Kult und Theologie der spätzeit-lichen Tierfriedhöfe.* Ägypten und Altes Testament 16. Wiesbaden: Otto Harrassowitz.

Kramer, Bärbel

1991   *Das Vertragsregister von Theogenis (P. Vindob. G 40618).* Corpus Papyrorum Raineri 18; Griechische Texte 13. Vienna: Verlag Brüder Hollinek.

Kurth, Dieter; Thissen, Heinz-Josef; and Weber, Manfred

1980   *Kölner ägyptische Papyri (P. Köln ägypt.), Band 1.* Papyrologica Coloniensia 9. Cologne: West-deutscher Verlag.

Lewis, Naphtali

1972   "ΝΟΗΜΑΤΑ ΛΕΓΟΝΤΟΣ." *The Bulletin of the American Society of Papyrologists* 9: 59–69.

Lüddeckens, Erich

1960   *Ägyptische Eheverträge.* Ägyptologische Abhandlungen 1. Wiesbaden: Otto Harrassowitz.

1978   "Die demotischen Urkunden von Hawara." In *Das ptolemäische Ägypten,* edited by H. Maehler and V. M. Strocka, pp. 221–26. Mainz am Rhein: Philipp von Zabern.

1985   "Noch einmal zum *Demotischen Namenbuch,* Lieferung 1 und 2." *Enchoria* 13: 73–78.

Lüddeckens, Erich et al.

1968   *Demotische und koptische Texte.* Papyrologica Coloniensia 2. Cologne and Opladen: Westdeutscher Verlag.

1980–   *Demotisches Namenbuch.* Wiesbaden: Dr. Ludwig Reichert Verlag.

Maehler, Herwig

1983   "Häuser und ihre Bewohner im Fayûm in der Kaiserzeit." In *Das römisch-byzantinische Ägypten,* edited by G. Grimm, H. Heinen, and E. Winter, pp. 119–37. Aegyptiaca Treverensia 2. Mainz am Rhein: Philipp von Zabern.

Malinine, Michel

1953   *Choix de textes juridiques en hiératique "anormal" et en démotique (XXVᵉ–XXVIIᵉ dynasties), Première Partie.* Paris: Librairie Ancienne Honoré Champion.

1974   "Un Vente de prébendes sous la XXXᵉ dynastie (P. Moscou n° 135)." *Revue d'Égyptologie* 26: 34–51.

Mattha, Girgis and Hughes, George R.

1975   *The Demotic Legal Code of Hermopolis West.* Bibliothèque d'Étude 45. Cairo: Institut Français d'Archéologie Orientale.

Meeks, Dimitri

1979   "Les Donations aux temples dans l'Égypte du Iᵉʳ millénaire avant J.-C." In *State and Temple Economy in the Ancient Near East,* edited by E. Lipiński, pp. 605–87. Orientalia Lovaniensia Analecta 6. Leuven: Departement Oriëntalistiek.

Menu, Bernadette

1972   "Un Contrat de prêt démotique conclu sous le règne de Ptolémée IV Philopator (P. Marseille, Inv. n° 297)." *Revue d'Égyptologie* 24: 120–28.

de Meulenaere, Herman

1977   "Derechef Arensnouphis." *Chronique d'Égypte* 52: 245–51.

de Meulenaere, Herman and Quaegebeur, Jan

1982 "Bijoutiers thébaines et memphites: Notes de prosopographie thébaine, 2ème série Nr. 9." *Chronique d'Égypte* 57: 209–18.

Milne, J. G.

1913 "The Hawara Papyri." *Archiv für Papyrusforschung* 5: 378–97.

Mooren, L. and Swinnen, W.

1975 *Prosopographia Ptolemaica VIII: Addenda et corrigenda aux volumes I (1950) et II (1952)*. Studia Hellenistica 21. Leuven: Fondation Universitaire de Belgique.

Mueller, Dieter

1975 "On Some Occurrences of the Verb 'to Seal' in Coptic and Egyptian Texts." *Journal of Egyptian Archaeology* 61: 222–26.

Nims, Charles F.

1948 "The Term *HP* 'Law, Right' in Demotic." *Journal of Near Eastern Studies* 7: 243–60.

1958 "A Demotic 'Document of Endowment' from the Time of Nectanebo I." *Mitteilungen des Deutschen Archäologischen Instituts, Abteilung Kairo* 16: 237–46.

1960 "Demotic Papyrus Loeb 62: A Reconstruction." *Acta Orientalia* 25: 266–76.

1968 "A Problem of Syntax in Demotic Documents." In *Festschrift für Siegfried Schott zu seinem 70. Geburtstag*, edited by W. Helck, pp. 94–98. Wiesbaden: Otto Harrassowitz.

Obsomer, Claude

1992 "Hérodote, Strabon et le mystère du labyrinthe d'Égypte." In *Amosiadès: Mélanges offerts au Professeur Claude Vandersleyen par ses anciens étudiants*, edited by C. Obsomer and A.-L. Oosthoek, pp. 221–324. Louvain-la-Neuve: Université Catholique de Louvain.

Parker, Richard A.

1972a *Demotic Mathematical Papyri*. Brown Egyptological Studies 7. Providence: Brown University Press.

1972b "An Abstract of a Loan in Demotic from the Fayum." *Revue d'Égyptologie* 24: 129–36.

Peremans, W. and van't Dack, E.

1977 *Prosopographia Ptolemaica, I: L'Administration civile et financière, n° 1 à 1824*. Studia Hellenistica 6. Leuven: Fondation Universitaire de Belgique.

Pernigotti, Sergio

1984 "Dagli archivi demotici del Fayum." In *Atti del XVII Congresso Internazionale di Papirologia, Volume 2*, edited by M. Gigante, pp. 727–32. Naples: Centro Internazionale per lo Studio dei Papiri Ercolanesi.

Pestman, Pieter Willem

1961 *Marriage and Matrimonial Property in Ancient Egypt*. Papyrologica Lugduno-Batava 9. Leiden: E. J. Brill.

1963 "Les Documents juridiques des 'chanceliers du dieu' de Memphis à l'époque ptolémaïque." *Oudheidkundige Mededelingen uit het Rijksmuseum van Oudheden te Leiden*, New Series 44: 8–23.

1967 *Chronologie égyptienne d'après les textes démotiques (332 av. J.-C.–453 ap. J.-C.)*. Papyrologica Lugduno-Batava 15. Leiden: E. J. Brill.

1968 "Eine demotische Doppelurkunde." In *Antidoron Martino David Oblatum Miscellanea Papyrologica*, edited by E. Boswinkel, B. van Groningen, and P. Pestman, pp. 100–11. Papyrologica Lugduno-Batava 17. Leiden: E. J. Brill.

Pestman, Pieter Willem (*cont.*)

1969 "A Greek Testament from Pathyris (P. Lond. Inv. 2850)." *Journal of Egyptian Archaeology* 55: 129–60.

1972 "A Note Concerning the Reading *ḥḏ sp-2*." *Enchoria* 2: 33–36.

1977 *Recueil de textes démotiques et bilingues.* 3 vols. Leiden: E. J. Brill.

1980 *Greek and Demotic Texts from the Zenon Archive.* Papyrologica Lugduno-Batava 20A. Leiden: E. J. Brill.

1981a *L'Archivio di Amenothes figlio di Horos (P. Tor. Amenothes).* Catalogo del Museo Egizio di Torino, Serie Prima-Monumenti e Testi 5. Milan: Istituto Editoriale Cisalpino-la Goliardica.

1981b "Nahomsesis, una donna d'affari di Pathyris: L'Archivio bilingue di Pelaias, figlio di Eunus." In *Scritti in onore di Orsolina Montevecchi*, edited by E. Bresciani et al., pp. 295–315. Bologna: Cooperativa Libraria Universitaria Editrice Bologna.

1983 "Some Aspects of Egyptian Law in Graeco-Roman Egypt: Title-Deeds and ὑπάλλαγμα." In *Egypt and the Hellenistic World*, edited by E. van't Dack, P. van Dessel, and W. van Gucht, pp. 281–302. Studia Hellenistica 27. Leuven: Fondation Universitaire de Belgique.

1985a "Registration of Demotic Contracts in Egypt: P. Par. 65, 2nd Cent. B.C." In *Satura Roberto Feenstra sexagesimum quintum annum aetatis complenti ab alumnis collegis amicis oblata, Volume 1*, edited by J. A. Ankum, J. E. Spruit, and F. B. J. Wubbe, pp. 17–25. Fribourg: Editions Universitaires Fribourg.

1985b "Remarks on the Legal Manual of Hermopolis." *Enchoria* 12: 33–42.

1987 "'Inheriting' in the Archive of the Theban Choachytes (Second Century B.C.)." In *Aspects of Demotic Lexicography*, edited by S. P. Vleeming, pp. 57–73. Studia Demotica 1. Leuven: Peeters.

1992 *Il Processo di Hermias e altri documenti dell'archivio dei Choachiti (P. Tor. Choachiti).* Catalogo del Museo Egizio di Torino, Serie Prima-Monumenti e Testi 6. Turin: Ministerio per i Beni Culturali e Ambientali. Sorprintendenza al Museo delle Antichità Egizie.

1993 *The Archive of the Theban Choachytes (Second Century B.C.).* Studia Demotica 2. Leuven: Peeters.

Pestman, P. W. et al.

1981 *A Guide to the Zenon Archive.* Papyrologica Lugduno-Batava 21. Leiden: E. J. Brill.

1985 *Textes et études de papyrologie grecque, démotique et copte.* Papyrologica Lugduno-Batava 23. Leiden: E. J. Brill.

1989 *Familiearchieven uit het land van pharao.* Zutphen: Uitgeverij Terra Zutphen.

Petrie, W. M. Flinders

1889 *Hawara, Biahmu, and Arsinoe.* London: Field and Tuer, "The Leadenhall Press."

Pierce, Richard Holton

1972 *Three Demotic Papyri in the Brooklyn Museum.* Symbolae Osloenses, Fasc. Supplet. 24. Oslo: Universitetsforlaget.

1975 Review of *Embalmers' Archives from Hawara*, by E. A. E. Reymond. *Bibliotheca Orientalis* 32: 26–28.

Porten, Bezalel

1992 "Aramaic-Demotic Equivalents: Who is the Borrower and Who the Lender?" In *Life in a Multi-Cultural Society*, edited by J. H. Johnson, pp. 259–65. Studies in Ancient Oriental Civilization, no. 51. Chicago: The Oriental Institute.

Preisigke, Friedrich

1922 *Namenbuch.* Heidelberg: Selbstverlag des Herausgebers.

1925 *Wörterbuch der griechischen Papyrusurkunden, Band 1.* Berlin: Selbstverlag der Erben.

Quack, Joachim F.

1991 "Über die mit ⁽nḫ gebildeten Namenstypen und die Vokalisation einiger Verbalformen." *Göttinger Miszellen* 123: 91–100.

Quaegebeur, Jan

1973 "Considérations sur le nom propre égyptien Teëphthaphônukhos." *Orientalia Lovaniensia Periodica* 4: 85–100.

1979a "De Nouvelles archives de famille thébaines à l'aube de l'époque ptolémaïque." In *Actes du XVᵉ Congrès International de Papyrologie, Quatrième partie: Papyrologie documentaire*, edited by J. Bingen and G. Nachtergael, pp. 40–48. Papyrologica Bruxellensia 19. Brussels: Fondation Égyptologique Reine Élisabeth.

1979b "Documents égyptiens et rôle économique du clergé en Égypte hellénistique." In *State and Temple Economy in the Ancient Near East II*, edited by E. Lipiński, pp. 707–29. Orientalia Lovaniensia Analecta 6. Leuven: Departement Oriëntalistiek.

1984 "La Désignation 'Porteur(s) des dieux' et le culte des dieux-crocodiles dans les textes des époques tardives." In *Mélanges Adolphe Gutbub*, pp. 161–76. Montpellier: Publication de la Recherche-Université de Montpellier.

1987 "Aspects de l'onomastique démotique: Formes abrégées et graphies phonétiques." In *Aspects of Demotic Lexicography*, edited by S. P. Vleeming, pp. 75–84. Studia Demotica 1. Leuven: Peeters.

Quaegebeur, Jan and Rammant-Peeters, Agnes

1982 "Le Pyramidion d'un 'danseur en chef' de Bastet." In *Studia Paulo Naster Oblata II: Orientalia Antiqua*, edited by J. Quaegebeur, pp. 179–205. Orientalia Lovaniensia Analecta 13. Leuven: Peeters.

Quaegebeur, Jan; Clarysse, Willy; and van Maele, Beatrijs

1985 "Athêna, Nêith and Thoêris in Greek Documents." *Zeitschrift für Papyrologie und Epigraphik* 60: 217–32.

Ranke, Hermann et al.

1935–77 *Die ägyptischen Personennamen*. 3 vols. Glückstadt: J. J. Augustin.

Ray, John

1976 *The Archive of Ḥor*. Texts from Excavations 2. London: Egypt Exploration Society.

1977 "The Complaint of Herieu." *Revue d'Égyptologie* 29: 97–116.

Reekmans, T.

1948 "Monetary History and the Dating of Ptolemaic Papyri." In *Studia Hellenistica* 5, pp. 15–43. Leuven: Bibliotheca Universitatis.

Rendell, Diana and Rendell, Kenneth

1979 *The Ancient World 3100 B.C.–800 A.D: Early Writing from Mesopotamia and Egypt*. Newton: The Rendells.

Reymond, E. A. E.

1968 "A Dispute in the Hawara Necropolis." *Chronique d'Égypte* 43: 55–77.

1973 *Embalmers' Archives from Hawara*. Catalogue of Demotic Papyri in the Ashmolean Museum 1. Oxford: The Griffith Institute.

1984 "Papyrus no. 219 de la Bibliothèque Nationale de Paris." *Zeitschrift für ägyptische Sprache und Altertumskunde* 111: 18–24.

Riad, Henri

1958   "Le Culte d'Amenemhat III au Fayoum à l'époque ptolémaïque." *Annales du Service des Antiquités de l'Égypte* 55: 203–06.

Ritner, Robert

1984   "A Property Transfer from the Erbstreit Archives." In *Grammata Demotika: Festschrift für Erich Lüddeckens zum 15. Juni 1983*, edited by H.-J. Thissen and K.-Th. Zauzich, pp. 171–87. Würzburg: Gisela Zauzich Verlag.

Rübsam, Winifried

1974   *Götter und Kulte in Faijum während der griechisch-römisch-byzantinischen Zeit*. Bonn: Rudolf Habelt Verlag.

Rupprecht, Hans-Albert

1988   *Sammelbuch griechischer Urkunden aus Ägypten 16 (Nr. 12220–13084)*. Wiesbaden: Otto Harrassowitz.

1993   *Sammelbuch griechischer Urkunden aus Ägypten 18 (Nr. 13085–14068)*. Wiesbaden: Otto Harrassowitz.

Sauneron, Serge

1952   "Le 'Chancelier du dieu' (⸠ ⸡) dans son double role d'embaulmeur et de prêtre d'Abydos." *Bulletin de l'Institut Français d'Archéologie Orientale* 51: 137–71.

1959   "Le Prêtre astronome du temple d'Esna." *Kêmi* 15: 36–41.

Seidl, Erwin

1939   "Die Teilungsschrift." *Mitteilungen des Deutschen Archäologischen Instituts, Abteilung Kairo* 8: 198–200.

1969   "Studien an den Hawara-Urkunden I." *Aegyptus* 49: 43–68.

1974   "Nachgiebiges oder zwingendes Erbrecht in Ägypten." *Studia et Documenta Historiae et Iuris* 40: 99–110.

Shore, A. F.

1980   "Declaration of Tikas, 184 B.C. (P. BM 10789)." *Serapis* 6: 121–24.

1988   "Swapping Property at Asyut in the Persian Period." In *Pyramid Studies and Other Essays Presented to I. E. S. Edwards*, edited by J. Baines, T. G. H. James, A. Leahy, and A. F. Shore, pp. 200–06. London: Egypt Exploration Society.

Shore, A. F. and Smith, H. S.

1960   "A Demotic Embalmers' Agreement (Pap. dem. B.M. 10561)." *Acta Orientalia* 25: 277–94.

Skeat, T. C.

1954   *The Reigns of the Ptolemies*. Münchener Beiträge zur Papyrusforschung und antiken Rechtsgeschichte 39. Munich: C. H. Becks.

1959   "A Receipt for *ENKYKLION*." *Journal of Egyptian Archaeology* 45: 75–78.

Smith, H. S.

1958   "Another Witness-copy Document from the Fayyum." *Journal of Egyptian Archaeology* 44: 86–96.

1980   "The Story of ʿOnchsheshonqy." *Serapis* 6: 133–56.

Smith, H. S. and Tait, W. J.

1983   *Saqqâra Demotic Papyri I (P. Dem. Saq. 1)*. Texts from Excavations 7. London: Egypt Exploration Society.

Smith, Mark

1983   Review of *Papyri from Tebtunis in Egyptian and Greek,* by W. J. Tait. *Journal of Egyptian Archaeology* 69: 199–203.

1987   *The Mortuary Texts of Papyrus BM 10507.* Catalogue of Demotic Papyri in the British Museum 3. London: British Museum Publications.

Spiegelberg, Wilhelm

1904   *Die demotischen Denkmäler I (30601–31166): Die demotischen Inschriften.* Catalogue Général des Antiquités Égyptiennes du Musée du Caire. Leipzig: W. Drugulin.

1928   *Demotica II (20–34).* Sitzungsberichte der Bayerischen Akademie der Wissenschaften, Philosophisch-philologische und historische Klasse, Jahrgang 1928, 2. Abhandlung. Munich: Verlag der Bayerischen Akademie der Wissenschaften.

1929   *Die demotischen Urkunden des Zenon-Archivs.* Leipzig: J. C. Hinrichs.

1932   *Die demotischen Denkmäler III: Demotische Inschriften und Papyri, Fortsetzung: 50023–50165.* Catalogue Général des Antiquités Égyptiennes du Musée du Caire. Berlin: Reichsdruckerei.

Tait, W. J.

1984   "A Demotic List of Temple and Court Occupations: P. Carlsberg 23." In *Grammata Demotika: Festschrift für Erich Lüddeckens zum 15. Juni 1983,* edited by H.-J. Thissen and K.-Th. Zauzich, pp. 211–33. Würzburg: Gisela Zauzich Verlag.

1988   "Rush and Reed: The Pens of Egyptian and Greek Scribes." In *Proceedings of the XVIIIth International Congress of Papyrology, Athens, 25–31 May 1986, Volume 2,* edited by B. G. Mandilaras, pp. 477–81. Athens: Greek Papyrological Society.

Thirion, Michelle

1979   "Notes d'onomastique: Contribution à une révision de Ranke *PN.*" *Revue d'Égyptologie* 31: 81–96.

1982–83   "Notes d'onomastique: Contribution à une révision du Ranke *PN* (troisième série)." *Revue d'Égyptologie* 34: 101–14.

Thissen, Heinz-Josef

1972   "Zu den demotischen Graffiti von Medinet Habu." *Enchoria* 2: 37–54.

1979   "Demotische Graffiti des Paneions im Wadi Hammamat." *Enchoria* 9: 63–92.

1980a   "Chronologie der frühdemotischen Papyri." *Enchoria* 10: 105–25.

1980b   "Ein demotischer Brief aus dem Anubieion." *Serapis* 6: 165–69.

1984a   *Die Lehre des Anchscheschonqi (P. BM 10508).* Papyrologische Texte und Abhandlungen 32. Bonn: Dr. Rudolf Habelt.

1984b   "Der demotische Ammenvertrag aus Tebtynis." In *Grammata Demotika: Festschrift für Erich Lüddeckens zum 15. Juni 1983,* edited by H.-J. Thissen and K.-Th. Zauzich, pp. 235–44. Würzburg: Gisela Zauzich Verlag.

1989   *Die demotischen Graffiti von Medinet Habu.* Demotische Studien 10. Sommerhausen: Gisela Zauzich Verlag.

Thompson, Dorothy J.

1988   *Memphis Under the Ptolemies.* Princeton: Princeton University Press.

1992a   "Literacy and the Administration in Early Ptolemaic Egypt." In *Life in a Multi-Cultural Society,* edited by J. H. Johnson, pp. 323–26. Studies in Ancient Oriental Civilization, no. 51. Chicago: The Oriental Institute.

1992b   "Language and Literacy in Early Hellenistic Egypt." In *Ethnicity in Hellenistic Egypt,* edited by P. Bilde, T. Engberg-Pedersen, L. Hannestad, and J. Zahle, pp. 39–52. Studies in Hellenistic Civilization 3. Aarhus: Aarhus University Press.

Thompson, Sir Herbert

1934   *A Family Archive from Siut.* 2 vols. Oxford: Oxford University Press.

Vandorpe, Katelijn

1995   *Breaking the Seal of Secrecy: Sealing Practices in Greco-Roman and Byzantine Egypt Based on Greek, Demotic and Latin Papyrological Evidence.* Uitgaven vanwege de stichting "Het Leids Papyrologisch Instituut" 18. Leiden: Het Leids Papyrologisch Instituut.

van Minnen, Peter

1992   "P. Hawara 208 Revised." *Zeitschrift für Papyrologie und Epigraphik* 93: 205–08.

Vernus, P.

1976   "Inscriptions de le troisième période intermédiaire (III)." *Bulletin de l'Institut Français d'Archéologie Orientale* 76: 1–15.

Vittmann, Günther

1980   "Ein thebanischer Verpfründungsvertrag aus der Zeit Ptolemaios' III." *Enchoria* 10: 127–39.

1982   "Ein demotischer Ehevertrag aus dem 12. Jahr des Ptolemaios VI." *Enchoria* 11: 77–84.

1986   "Taricheut." In *Lexikon der Ägyptologie, Band 6*, edited by W. Helck and W. Westendorf, cols. 233–36. Wiesbaden: Otto Harrassowitz.

Vleeming, Sven P.

1979   "Some Notes on the Artabe in Pathyris." *Enchoria* 9: 93–100.

1984   "Some Notes on P. IFAO 901 & 902." *Enchoria* 12: 57–62.

1991   *The Gooseherds of Hou (Pap. Hou).* Studia Demotica 3. Leuven: Peeters.

Volten, Aksel

1942   *Demotische Traumdeutung (Pap. Carlsberg XIII und XIV Verso).* Analecta Aegyptiaca 3. Copenhagen: Einar Munksgaard.

Yoyotte, Jean

1972   "Pétoubastis III." *Revue d'Égyptologie* 24: 216–23.

Zauzich, Karl-Theodor

1968   *Die ägyptische Schreibertradition in Aufbau, Sprache und Schrift der demotischen Kaufverträge aus ptolemäischer Zeit.* 2 vols. Ägyptologische Abhandlungen 19. Wiesbaden: Otto Harrassowitz.

1970   "Ein Kaufvertrag aus der Zeit des Nektanebos." *Mitteilungen des Deutschen Archäologischen Instituts, Abteilung Kairo* 25: 223–29.

1971   *Ägyptische Handschriften, Teil 2.* Verzeichnis der orientalischen Handschriften in Deutschland 19, 2. Wiesbaden: Franz Steiner Verlag.

1974   "Die demotischen Dokumente." In *Textes et langages de l'Égypte pharaonique.* Bibliothèque d'Étude 64/3, pp. 93–110. Cairo: Institut Français d'Archéologie Orientale.

1976   "Sesophnois aus Hawara." *Enchoria* 6: 129–30.

1977   "Zwei neue demotische Ortsnamen." *Enchoria* 7: 195–97.

1980   "Ein demotisches Darlehen vom Ende der 30. Dynastie." *Serapis* 6: 241–43.

1985   "Ägyptologische Bemerkungen zu den neuen aramäischen Papyri aus Saqqara." *Enchoria* 13: 115–18.

1988   "Ein rätselhafter Personenname." *Enchoria* 16: 95–99.

Zivie, Alain-Pierre

1984   "Un Chancelier nommé Nehesy." In *Mélanges Adolphe Gutbub*, pp. 245–52. Montpellier: Publication de la Recherche-Université de Montpellier.

INTRODUCTION

The ten Demotic papyri and one Greek papyrus published in this book are in the collection of the Oriental Institute.[1] William F. Edgerton purchased the papyri, still rolled-up, from the dealer Maurice Nahman in Cairo in 1932.[2] These ten rolls and numerous fragments[3] contained a total of ten Demotic contracts and one Greek tax receipt. They belonged to a large family archive from Hawara in the Fayum, portions of which are in the museums of Cairo, Copenhagen, Hamburg, and London.[4] The Chicago papyri are the earliest documents of the archive; the oldest of the Copenhagen lot overlap chronologically with the latest of the Chicago documents.[5] The first of the series, P. O.I. 17481 (= Chicago Hawara Papyrus 1), has already been published by Charles F. Nims (1958: 237–46). I have also included in an appendix to this book the translation of the "Rendell Papyrus" (Rendell and Rendell 1979: 98), which is not in the collection of the Oriental Institute but manifestly belongs to this archive. In addition to their intrinsic interest, several of these documents are masterpieces of calligraphy. The older Hawara scribal hands are distinguished by their clarity and regularity, displaying on occasion a marked

---

1. Hughes (1975: 2–3; 1976: 2–3) published a description of the papyri and they were mentioned by Breasted (1933: 413) shortly after they were purchased.

2. John Larson, Oriental Institute Museum Archivist, discovered correspondence from Edgerton that confirms Nahman as the dealer (letter dated June 14, 1932). For this dealer, see Dawson and Uphill 1972: 213. Nims' (1958: 237) identification of Nicolas Tano as the source seems, therefore, to be an error. The Hawara papyri in the Ashmolean Museum were possibly bought from Tano in 1935 (see Reymond 1973: 1). For this important dealer, see Dawson and Uphill 1972: 284. It could be that the actual sellers were his son Georges or nephew Phocion Jean Tano, since Dawson and Uphill record Nicolas Tano's death as occurring in 1924.

3. Hughes later reconstructed these loose fragments into a single papyrus, Chicago Hawara Papyrus 10.

4. According to Lüddeckens (1978: 221–26), who is editing the Hawara papyri in Copenhagen and Hamburg, the Demotic papyri from Hawara date from 365 B.C. to 67 B.C. The older studies employ a system of designations that has now been superseded; I list here the old and new numbering for the Copenhagen Hawara papyri:

Old	New
P. Carlsberg/Copenhagen 240 (Hawara 1)	34
P. Carlsberg/Copenhagen 241 (Hawara 2)	35
P. Carlsberg/Copenhagen 242 (Hawara 3)	36
P. Carlsberg/Copenhagen 243 (Hawara 4)	37
P. Carlsberg/Copenhagen 244 (Hawara 5)	38
P. Carlsberg/Copenhagen 245 (Hawara 6)	39

Bülow-Jacobsen (1982: 12–16) published three Greek documents pertaining to this archive in the Copenhagen collection. Clarysse (1984: 1345–53, especially pp. 1345–46) discusses the Copenhagen Hawara Greek texts as well as other Greek Hawara papyri.

5. See particularly Chicago Hawara Papyrus 9.

hieratic influence.[6] At the time of writing most of the papyri in the archive stored in other museums are being actively prepared for publication.[7] When all are available, the Hawara archive will certainly be acknowledged as one of the more extensive and important archives surviving from ancient Egypt.[8]

THE SITE AND PAPYRI OF HAWARA

Hawara is located approximately nine kilometers to the southeast of the town of Medinet el-Fayum.[9] It is near the desert edge, north of where the Bahr Yusef branch of the Nile enters the Fayum. Amenemhet III is the pharaoh most closely associated with the Fayum, his pyramid being the outstanding monument of Hawara. Such names as *imn-m-ḥ3.t* and *M3ʿ-Rʿ* in the papyri bear witness to the continued veneration of that pharaoh at the site.[10] During the Ptolemaic period Hawara belonged administratively to the Division of Herakleides in the Arsinoite Nome (see Pestman et al. 1981: 480). The inhabitants themselves generally designate Hawara a "Sobek town" (Chicago Hawara Papyrus 4). A more elaborate description is in Chicago Hawara Papyrus 7, wherein the scribe writes that a house is "in the Sobek town of Hawara, which is on the northern shore of the Canal of Moeris, in the Nome of Arsinoe."[11] The crocodile god Sobek was, of course, the chief deity of the locality, which explains his prominence in the Hawara onomasticon.[12] In the Greek tax-receipt P. O.I. 25260 (= Chicago Hawara Greek Papyrus 7C), which accompanies Chicago Hawara Papyrus 7A–B, the house of the transaction is described as being situated in the Labyrinth.[13] The Chicago Hawara papyri are not very informative about the topography of Hawara, being naturally concerned with the specific dwellings and building plots that form the subject of the transactions. One of the houses is said to border "the temple of Hawara" (Chicago Hawara Papyrus 9). Few other localities apart from Hawara and cemeteries in the neighborhood appear in these documents.[14]

---

6. For remarks on the influence of hieratic on Demotic hands, see Vleeming 1991: 111.

7. In addition to the article by Lüddeckens (1978: 221–26), I cite the following discussions mentioning the Demotic Hawara papyri in the collections of Chicago, Hamburg, and Copenhagen: Erichsen 1958: 320–27; Hughes 1958: 149; Nims 1960: 272–73; Pestman 1961: 160–61; Seidl 1969: 43–68.

8. Recent noteworthy discussions and publications of Demotic archives include Quaegebeur 1979a: 40–48; idem 1979b: 707–29; Pernigotti 1984: 727–32; Pestman et al. 1989; Andrews 1990; Pestman 1992; idem 1993.

9. See Habachi 1977: 1072–74. Reymond (1973: 12–13) also provides a historical sketch of Hawara.

10. On the popularity of the name *M3ʿ-Rʿ* in the Fayum, see Clarysse 1980: 120. For the cult of Amenemhet III, see Riad 1958: 203–06; Crawford 1971: 40; Bresciani 1986: 49–58.

11. The "Canal of Moeris" is perhaps the Bahr Yusef; see Cruz-Uribe 1992: 64.

12. For crocodile cemeteries at Hawara and other Fayum towns, see Crawford 1971: 95; Kessler 1989: 25, 39, n. 18. On the cults of the Fayum in general, see Rübsam 1974.

13. On the Labyrinth, see Obsomer 1992: 221–324.

14. See, e.g., Chicago Hawara Papyrus 4, lines 2–3.

While the site has been productive of antiquities, most notably the well-known mummy portraits, it has not been scientifically excavated since Petrie's time.[15] A number of Greek[16] and Demotic texts[17] are known from Hawara, but as already remarked, many of these documents still await publication. E. A. E. Reymond (1973) has thus far produced the sole volume dedicated to Demotic papyri from Hawara.[18] The twenty-one Hawara Demotic papyri published by her date from 187/186 B.C. to about the middle of the first century B.C.[19] The Ashmolean documents edited by Reymond might not comprise a single archive; no connection with the significantly older Chicago Hawara texts is apparent. Spiegelberg included several Hawara papyri in his catalog of holdings in the Cairo Museum. According to Spiegelberg, the texts numbered 50119–50136 were discovered in the museum still rolled up in a tin box. Upon the box was a note written by G. Lefebvre: "Les papyrus proviennent du Haouàra, à l'ouest de la pyramide-Mars 1911." Most of the papyri are records from the archive of a *ḥtmw-ntr wyt* "god's sealer and embalmer" named *Mꜣꜥ-Rꜥ*, the elder, son of *Nḫt-Sbk*.[20] They also exhibit no obvious relationship to the Chicago Hawara papyri.[21]

OVERVIEW OF THE CHICAGO HAWARA PAPYRI

Very prominent indeed in this corpus are the *sꜥnḫ*-documents or annuity contracts. Chicago Hawara Papyri 1, 2, 3, 6, and 8 are specimens of this genre, wherein Party A, in every case a male, having received a sum of money from Party B, in every case a female, agrees to provide the latter with a stipulated yearly amount of goods and money. These have also been termed

---

15. Petrie (1889) was the first to excavate the site systematically. An interesting description of Petrie's work at Hawara is found in Drower 1985: 133–41. On the Hawara mummy portraits, see Corcoran 1988; 1992; 1995.

16. The Greek texts most relevant for the Chicago Hawara papyri are cited in footnote 4, above. Milne (1913: 378–97) published or reedited a number of texts purchased by Petrie. Barns was responsible for the editions of Greek papyri in Reymond 1973. Cockle (1988: 173) discusses the history and location of some Hawara Greek papyri. For a collection of Greek inscriptions from Hawara, see Bernand 1975: 84–120. Further publications or discussions of Greek Hawara texts are found in Edgar 1938:76–77; Lewis 1972: 64–65; Hagedorn 1976: 165–67; Boswinkel and Pestman 1978: 229–30; Jordan 1988: 245–59, with mention of a Hawara text on p. 247; Hagedorn 1991: 39, n. 5; Hoogendijk and van Minnen 1991: 112–19; van Minnen 1992: 205–08; Hans-Albert Rupprecht 1993: numbers 13219–13245.

17. In addition to the Demotic texts already mentioned, there are the short funerary texts on a coffin that might be from Hawara (Jasnow 1990: 95–96). The Thirtieth Dynasty coffin of Anch-rui of Hawara could preserve the oldest version of the Book of the Fayum (hieroglyphic script); see Beinlich 1991: 65–66. Reymond (1968: 55–77) has also republished a noteworthy document. An interesting mention of Hawara is in Kurth, Thissen, and Weber 1980: 61.

18. See the review by Pierce 1975: 26–28. Zauzich (1976: 129–30; idem 1977: 195–97) discusses several points of interest in these texts. Clarysse (1976: 3–4) offers a revised reading of the name of an athlophoros and publishes (1975: 253–54) corrections to the Greek papyri edited in the Reymond volume. See also Boswinkel and Pestman 1978: 245; Quaegebeur and Rammant-Peeters 1982: 200.

19. Clarysse's (1976: 4) correction results in an earlier dating for one papyrus.

20. See Spiegelberg 1932: 82–97 and the comments of Reymond (1973: 6) concerning the location of the papyri.

21. On the possible relationship of the Cairo texts to the papyri published by Reymond, see Pierce 1975: 26.

marriage settlements, and they do in fact seem to be closely associated with marriage.[22] Such annuities became part of the family inheritance. In the Rendell Papyrus, for example, ꜥnḫ-mr-wr, the elder, settles on his younger brother a share of the sꜥnḫ which came to them through their parents. The amount of capital involved varies, though the amount of yearly support remains remarkably constant over the years:[23]

Papyrus	Capital	Yearly Payment
Chicago Hawara Papyrus 1 (365/364 B.C.)	30 silver (*deben*)	36 (sacks) emmer, 1 silver (*deben*), 2 *kite*
Chicago Hawara Papyrus 2 (331 B.C.)	10 silver (*deben*)	36 (sacks) emmer, 1 silver (*deben*), 2 *kite*
Chicago Hawara Papyrus 3 (311/310 B.C.)	10 silver (*deben*)	36 (sacks) emmer, 1 silver (*deben*), 2 *kite*
Chicago Hawara Papyrus 6 (259 B.C.)	10 silver (*deben*)	36 (sacks) emmer, 1 silver (*deben*), 2 *kite*
Chicago Hawara Papyrus 8 (243 B.C.)	21 silver (*deben*)	36 (sacks) emmer, 1 silver (*deben*), 8 *kite*

The women beneficiaries of these annuities have a significant claim on the property of the men guaranteeing the sꜥnḫ-payments. Those contracts, for example, involving the conveyance of real estate conclude with declarations by one of the sꜥnḫ-parties expressly giving permission or consent for the transaction to take place (e.g., Chicago Hawara Papyrus 5).

The Chicago Hawara papyri well reflect the complicated familial and economic relationships that existed in the Egyptian middle class of the Hellenistic period. These are evidently well-to-do people, who seem to possess a fair amount of property.[24] The desire to keep real estate within the family was very strong, which Nims (1958: 244) suggests was the reason for the consanguineous marriage of Chicago Hawara Papyrus 1. Inevitably, the property shares became diminutive over time. Chicago Hawara Papyrus 5, for example, records the sale of one-eighteenth share of a house.

"Houses," "cells," and "building plots" are the more common forms of real estate transferred in the Hawara papyri. The most detailed document is the Rendell Papyrus, in which the elder brother transfers to his younger sibling a share of a house, lane, bench, and building plots.[25]

Since the transactions concern almost exclusively Hawara embalmers, income from the necropolis is also a natural topic in the texts. It is a portion of his "shares in the necropolis of

---

22. On these documents, see now Johnson 1994: 113–32. The economic and social aspects of marriage in ancient Egypt require further investigation. In addition to the two basic volumes on the subject, namely, Lüddeckens 1960 and Pestman 1961, see also Allam 1981: 116–35; Grunert 1984: 61–69; Eyre 1992: 208–12.

23. On the amounts paid out in such annuities, see Clarysse and Lanciers 1989: 119.

24. For a discussion of the property-holdings of the Egyptian priesthood, see Johnson 1986: 70–84. The words of the great Danish Demoticist Erichsen (1958: 321), who began work on the Hamburg and Copenhagen Hawara papyri, are still worth quoting: "Obwohl sie (scil. the Hawara priests of these archives) nur niedere Priester waren, geht es aus den Urkunden klar hervor, daß sie recht erhebliche Besitztümer an Land und Vieh besassen und gewinnende Sporteln aus ihrer Tätigkeit in den verschiedenen Nekropolen von Hawara und Umgebung bezogen. Aus den Papyri ersehen wir ebenfalls, wie die Familien untereinander ihre Besitztümer veräussert haben; für erbrechtliche Untersuchungen werden sie genügend Stoff liefern."

25. On the towns and houses of the Fayum, see the fine contribution by Maehler (1983: 119–37), noting especially the discussion of the small shares of houses sold that are recorded in Greek papyri. Crawford (1971: 46) also describes typical Fayumic houses in some detail.

Hawara" that a father gives to his son in Chicago Hawara Papyrus 4. The same papyrus mentions other cemeteries as well, of uncertain location. In the Rendell Papyrus a share in the income from tombs and burials in the concession of one of these embalmers is also transferred.

Table 1. Synopsis of the Chicago Hawara Papyri and Rendell Papyrus

Chicago Hawara Papyrus	Museum Number	Date B.C.	Type	Party A	Party B
1	P. O.I. 17481	365/364	Annuity contract	*ꜥnḫ-mr-wr* son of *ꜥnḫ-Ḥp*	*Psṯ* daughter of *ꜥnḫ-Ḥp*
2	P. O.I. 25257	331	Annuity contract	*Pꜣ-tỉ-Wsỉr* son of *ꜥnḫ-Ḥp*	*ꜥnḫ.t* daughter of *ꜥnḫ-mr-wr*
3ᵃ	P. O.I. 25259	311/310	Annuity contract	*ꜥnḫ-mr-wr* son of *Pꜣ-tỉ-nꜣ-ntr.w*	*Nꜣ-nfr-ỉb-Ptḥ* daughter of *Pꜣy-ꜥr-ỉmn*
4ᵇ	P. O.I. 25262	292	Donation	*ꜥnḫ-mr-wr* son of *Pꜣ-tỉ-nꜣ-ntr.w*	*Pꜣ-tỉ-Wsỉr* son of *ꜥnḫ-mr-wr*
5	P. O.I. 25258	285–246	Sale	*ỉmn-m-hꜣ.t* son of *Pꜣ-tỉ-nꜣ-ntr.w*	*ꜥnḫ.t* daughter of *S-n-Wsr.t*
6	P. O.I. 25388	259	Annuity contract	*Pꜣ-tỉ-Wsỉr* son of *ꜥnḫ-mr-wr*	*Ḥr-ꜥnḫ* daughter of *Mꜣꜥ-Rꜥ*
7A	P. O.I. 25255	245	Provisional sale	*Pa-tr (= Pꜣ-tỉ-nꜣ-ntr.w)* son of *ꜥnḫ-mr-wr*	*Sbk-ḥtp* son of *Pa-wꜣ* and *Ḥr-ꜥnḫ*
7B	P. O.I. 25255	245	Mortgage agreement	*Pa-tr (= Pꜣ-tỉ-nꜣ-ntr.w)* son of *ꜥnḫ-mr-wr*	*Sbk-ḥtp* son of *Pa-wꜣ* and *Ḥr-ꜥnḫ*
7Cᶜ	P. O.I. 25260	245	Mortgage-tax receipt	—	—
8	P. O.I. 25256	243	Annuity contract	*Smꜣ-tꜣ.wy* son of *Pꜣ-š-mtre*	*Šty* daughter of *Pꜣ-šwt* and *Ḥr-ꜥnḫ*
9	P. O.I. 25263	239	Provisional sale	*ꜥnḫ-mr-wr* son of *Pꜣ-tỉ-nꜣ-ntr.w*	*Ḥr-ꜥnḫ* daughter of *Mꜣꜥ-Rꜥ*
10ᵈ	P. O.I. 25261	221	Loan repayment	*Mꜣꜥ-Rꜥ* son of *Nḫt-pꜣ-Rꜥ*	*ꜥnḫ-mr-wr* son of *Pa-se*
Rendell Papyrus		232	Donation	*ꜥnḫ-mr-wr* son of *Pꜣ-tỉ-Wsỉr, pꜣ ꜥꜣ*	*ꜥnḫ-mr-wr* son of *Pꜣ-tỉ-Wsỉr, pꜣ ḫm*

ᵃFour witness copies   ᵇFound rolled in Chicago Hawara Papyrus 9

ᶜGreek, found rolled in Chicago Hawara Papyrus 7   ᵈFound in Chicago Hawara Papyrus 2

Most of the people mentioned in the papyri are "god's sealers and embalmers," but other occupations and priestly titles do occur. Among the neighbors of these embalmers, for example, are the "temple sculptor of Sobek-Re" and the "chief tailor of the domain of Sobek" (both in Chicago Hawara Papyrus 5). In the Rendell Papyrus a bearer of the military title *kalasiris* (*gl-šr*) appears as the possessor of a house. A "fisherman of the lake" seems to have married into the family of embalmers (Chicago Hawara Papyrus 8). The scribe of Chicago Hawara Papyrus 1 describes himself as an "astronomer of Sobek," though the precise functions of this title are still unclear. The elaborate witness list of that papyrus contains two other scribal titles, namely, "scribe of the divine book" and "scribe of the domain of Sobek." The most common priestly designation in that witness list is *ḥm-nṯr* "prophet," but a "*fḳt*-priest," "deputy," "*wʿb*-priest," and possibly a "lesonis" also appear. While Sobek is the most prominent deity in the documents, we also find a "prophet of Amun" and a "servant of Neith" (Chicago Hawara Papyri 3 and 5).[26] One of the parties of Chicago Hawara Papyrus 10 is a "choachyte of Pharaoh *Mꜣʿ-Rʿ*," another confirmation of an active cult dedicated to Amenemhet at Hawara.

CHIEF PERSONS MENTIONED IN THE CHICAGO HAWARA PAPYRI

Inasmuch as the Chicago Hawara papyri comprise only a portion of the extant documents, it is impossible to form a complete impression of the nature of the archive. I present a genealogy on the basis of the Chicago papyri, supplemented by the Rendell Papyrus, in table 2. I also indicate the various contractual and *sʿnḫ*-relationships. The key figure in the archive seems to be *Ḥr-ʿnḫ*, who appears in Chicago Hawara Papyri 6–10 as well as in the Rendell Papyrus.[27]

Certain names, such as *ʿnḫ.t* and *ʿnḫ-mr-wr*, occur frequently in these papyri. Particularly when the names of the father and mother are omitted, it is impossible to identify an individual with confidence. It is quite possible, therefore, that names assigned to separate individuals could in fact belong to the same person. Such possibilities and problems are indicated in the footnotes.

NOTE ON DATES

The Demotic scribes seem to have generally employed the Egyptian regnal year system for dating documents. The Julian equivalents have been calculated according to T. C. Skeat (1954). Three documents published here have Greek dockets: Chicago Hawara Papyri 6, 9, and the Rendell Papyrus. In contrast to their Demotic-writing colleagues, the Greek scribes appear to have been accustomed to employ the financial year, which explains the apparent difference in the dates in two texts:

Text	Date
Chicago Hawara Papyrus 6	(Demotic) Year 26; (Greek) Year 27
Rendell Papyrus	(Demotic) Year 15; (Greek) Year 16

A Greek tax-receipt (Chicago Hawara Greek Papyrus 7C) that accompanies Demotic texts (Chicago Hawara Papyrus 7A–B) is dated to year 3, while the Demotic documents are dated to year 2. The scribe of the Demotic documents expressly declares that this year 2 "corresponds to year 3 of the Greeks." In this case, too, it seems that the first date is the Egyptian regnal year and the second is the financial year (see Pestman 1967: 6).

---

26. On the cult of Neith, see the valuable article by Quaegebeur, Clarysse, and van Maele (1985: 217–32, with the discussion of Neith on pp. 222–24).

27. *Ḥr-ʿnḫ* also plays a key role in the three documents published by Bülow-Jacobsen (1982: 12–16).

In one text the Greek and the Demotic scribes both seem to write the same year:

Text	Date
Chicago Hawara Papyrus 9	(Demotic) lost; (Greek) Year 8

Since Chicago Hawara Papyrus 9 was apparently drawn up on the same day as Copenhagen Hawara Papyrus 1 (= P. Carlsberg 34),[28] and that text is dated to year 8, it is probable that "year 8" is to be restored in the Demotic of Chicago Hawara Papyrus 9, the same as year 8 in the Greek docket. However, here the scribes are nevertheless also using different calendars. The apparent congruity is explained by the fact that this text is dated to Tybi 19 (March 9, 239 B.C.), and the financial year only advanced, i.e., became year 9, on the first of Mekheir (March 21, 239 B.C.) (see Pestman 1967: 30–31).

Table 2. Genealogy of Persons Mentioned in the Chicago Hawara Papyri and Rendell Papyrus

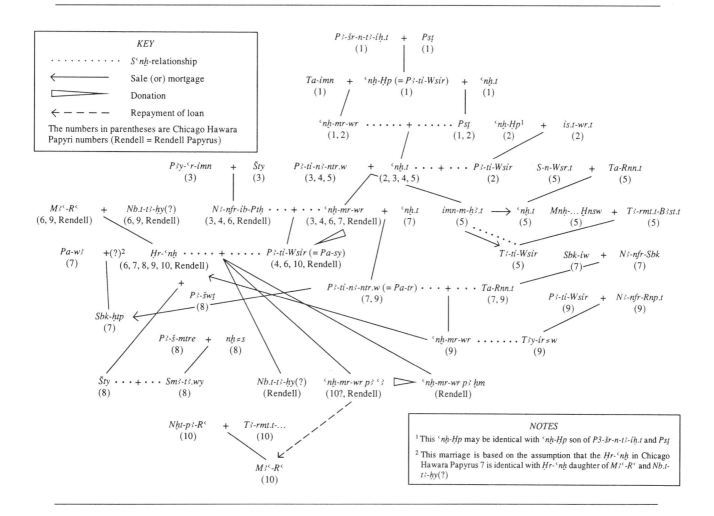

TEXT EDITIONS

CHICAGO HAWARA PAPYRUS 1

Illustrations: Plates 1–7
Museum number: P. O.I. 17481[29]
Length: 230 cm
Height: 37 cm
Physical description: The papyrus comprises twelve separate sheets, each averaging ca. 20 cm.
Type: Annuity contract
Party A: ꜥnḫ-mr-wr, son of ꜥnḫ-Ḥp and Ta-ỉmn
Party B: Psṯ, daughter of ꜥnḫ-Ḥp and ꜥnḫ.t
Date: 365/364 B.C.
Scribe: The astronomer Mꜣꜥ-Rꜥ, son of Ptḥ-nfr

TRANSLITERATION

LINES 1–4

1. ḥꜣ.t-sp 17 ỉbt 2 ꜣḥ.t n Pr-ꜥꜣ ꜥ.w.s. Nḫt-nb≈f[A] ḏ ḥtmw-ntr wyt[B] ꜥnḫ-mr-wr[C] sꜣ ꜥnḫ-Ḥp ḏṯ n≈f Pꜣ-tỉ-Wsỉr mw.t≈f Ta-ỉmn n s-ḥm.t Psṯ[D] sꜣ.t n ḫtmw-ntr wyt ꜥnḫ-Ḥp ḏṯ n≈f Pꜣ-tỉ-Wsỉr mw.t≈s ꜥnḫ.t[E] tỉ≈t mtr ḥꜣ.t≈y n ḥḏ 30 n nꜣ tnỉ.t[F] nt n pr-ḥḏ n Ptḥ[G] n wtḥ[H] r ḥḏ[I] 29 qt 9 2/3 1/6 1/10 1/30 1/60 1/60 r ḥḏ 30 n nꜣ tnỉ.t nt n pr-ḥḏ n Ptḥ n wtḥ ꜥn n nꜣ[J] pꜣy≈t sꜥnḫ[K] mtw nꜣ ḥrṯ.w nt ỉw≈t r ms.ṯ.w n≈y nt nb.t nt mtw≈y ḥnꜥ nꜣ nt ỉw≈y r tỉ.t ḫpr≈w

2. pr[L] ꜣḥ ỉnḥ wrḫ[M] bꜣk bꜣk.t ỉꜣw.wt nb.t qnb.wt nb.t[N] mt nmḥ.w[O] nb n pꜣ tꜣ mtw≈y mtw≈y tỉ.t n≈t bt[P] 36 tꜣ ḥn 40[Q] r ỉt 24 tꜣ ḥn 40 r bt 36 tꜣ ḥn 40 ꜥn ḥḏ 1 qt 2 n nꜣ tnỉ.t nt (n) pr-ḥḏ n Ptḥ n wtḥ r ḥḏ 1 qt 1 2/3 1/6 1/10 1/30 1/60 1/60 r ḥḏ 1 qt 2 n nꜣ tnỉ.t nt (n) pr-ḥḏ n Ptḥ n wtḥ ꜥn n pꜣy≈t ꜥq-ḥbs[R] ḥr rnp.t r pꜣ ꜥ.wy nt ỉw mr(≈t) s mtw≈t nt nh.ṯ r tꜣ wḏꜣ.t[S] n pꜣy≈t ꜥq-ḥbs nt ỉ(w)≈s r ḫpr ꜥ.wy≈y mtw≈y tỉ.t s n≈t nt nb.t nt mtw≈y ḥnꜥ

3. nꜣ nt ỉw≈y r tỉ.t ḫpr≈w n tꜣ ỉwꜣ.t[T] n pꜣy≈t sꜥnḫ nt ḥry bn ỉw≈y rḫ ḏ n≈t šp pꜣy≈t sꜥnḫ nt ḥry pꜣy≈t sw n wḥꜣ≈f ỉw≈y r tỉ.t s n≈t bn ỉw≈y rḫ tỉ.t ꜥnḫ m-sꜣ≈t[U] ḥnꜥ pꜣ mtr n pꜣ sḫ[V] pꜣ bnr n pꜣ ꜥ.wy nt ỉw nꜣ wpṯy.w n-ỉm≈f[W] ỉw ḫtmw-ntr wyt ꜥnḫ-Ḥp ḏṯ n≈f Pꜣ-tỉ-

---

29. As already mentioned, this papyrus was published by Nims (1958: 237–46). Nims did a masterful job of editing the text, and the reader is still advised to refer to the earlier publication. I do hope, however, that the photographs published here do more justice to this impressive papyrus than those of the *editio princeps*.

Wsir sꜣ Pꜣ-šr-n-tꜣ-iḥ.t mw.t≠f Psṯ pꜣy≠f it ḏ[X] *šp pꜣ ḫtmw-ntr wyt ꜥnḫ-mr-wr pꜣy≠y šr
ꜥꜣ mw.t≠f Ta-imn nt ḥry r ti̯.t*

4. *ir≠f n≠t pꜣ sḫ n sꜥnḫ nt ḥry mtw≠f ir n≠t pꜣy≠f hp*[Y] *iw≠f ḏ ꜥn i-ir mt nb.t nt ḥry
ḥꜣ.t≠y mtr.w n-im≠w m-sḫ imy-wnw.t n Sbk*[Z] *Mꜣꜥ-Rꜥ sꜣ Ptḥ-nfr*

WITNESS LIST [30]

Column One

1. *Pꜣ-ti̯-is.t sꜣ ꜥnḫ-mr-wr Ḥr-wḏꜣ sꜣ Pꜣ-sn-ky sꜣ Mꜣꜥ-Rꜥ sꜣ Ḥry.w(?)*[AA]

2. *Mꜣꜥ-Rꜥ sꜣ ḥm-ntr Ḏ-Bꜣst.t-iw≠f-ꜥnḫ*[BB]

3. *ḥm-ntr Ḥtr sꜣ ḥm-ntr Ns-Bꜣst.t*[CC]

4. *ḥm-ntr Sbk-ḥtp sꜣ ḥm-ntr Wn-nfr*

5. *iꜥḥ-ms sꜣ ḥm-ntr Sbk-tꜣy sꜣ ...*[DD]

6. *ir.t≠w-r-r≠w Tꜣy-nḫt-r-r≠w(?) sꜣ ḥm-ntr Ti-n≠y-iꜣw(?)*[EE]

7. *Mꜣꜥ-Rꜥ sꜣ ḥm-ntr Ḏ-Bꜣst.t-iw≠f-ꜥnḫ*[FF]

8. *Ḏ-Bꜣst.t-iw≠f-ꜥnḫ sꜣ iw≠f-iw pꜣ ḥm-ntr imn*[GG]

9. *Sbk-ḥtp sꜣ ḥm-ntr Ḥr-ḥb pꜣ fkṯ*[HH]

10. *Mꜣꜥ-Rꜥ sꜣ ḥm-ntr Sbk-ḥtp*

11. *Sbk-mn sꜣ ḥm-ntr Ḥr-ḥb*

12. *Ḥr-wḏꜣ sꜣ ḥm-ntr Sy-Sbk pꜣ sḫ mḏꜣ.t-ntr*[II]

13. *Sbk-mn sꜣ sḫ pr Sbk sḫ ḫtmw-ntr Sbk ḥm-ntr Ḥr-sy-Sbk*[JJ]

14. *Sbk-ḥtp sꜣ Ḥr-Ḏḥwty*[KK]

15. *Sbk-... ḫ... sꜣ ꜥr...(?)*[LL]

16. *ḥm-ntr Smꜣ-tꜣ.wy-tꜣy≠f-nḫt*[MM] *sꜣ ḥm-ntr Ḥr-wḏꜣ*

17. *Pꜣ-ti̯-Wsir sꜣ Pꜣ-ḥm-ntr-4.nw*[NN]

18. *Wsrkn sꜣ ḥm-ntr Mꜣꜥ-Rꜥ*[OO]

Column Two

19. *itnw Sbk Sbk-ḥtp sꜣ Sy-Sbk pꜣ itnw*[PP]

20. *ḥm-ntr Sy-Sbk sꜣ ḥm-ntr Ti-Bꜣst.t-iꜣw(?) pꜣ wꜥb(?)*[QQ]

21. *ḥm-ntr ꜥnḫ-imn sꜣ ḥm-ntr Ḥr-wḏꜣ*[RR]

22. *ḥm-ntr Ḥr-ḥb sꜣ ḥm-ntr Sy-Sbk*

23. *Ḥr-ḥb sꜣ Wsrkn*[SS]

24. *Wꜣḥ-ib-Rꜥ-mr-N.t sꜣ ꜥnḫ-Ḥp*[TT]

25. *ꜥnḫ-nꜣ-... sꜣ Ti-Bꜣst.t-iꜣw(?) pꜣ mr-šn(?)*[UU]

26. Check mark *Ḥr-wḏꜣ sꜣ Sbk-i-ir-ti̯-s(?) sꜣ Pꜣ-ti̯-Wsir*[VV]

---

30. For the stroke over the witness list, see now Pestman 1992: 225–32.

27. Check mark *Ḥr-Ḏḥwty s3 Pa-Ptḥ*

28. *iy-m-ḥtp s3 ḥm-ntr Sbk-iw*^{WW}

29. *Sbk-Ḥ°py*^{XX} *s3 ḥm-ntr ir.t-Ḥr-r-r≠w*

30. *Sbk-ḥtp s3 Sy-Sbk*

31. *Ḏ-B3st.t-iw≠f-°nḫ(?) s3 ḥm-ntr °nḫ-Ḫnsw*^{YY}

32. *Sy-Sbk s3 ḥm-ntr Ḥr-sy-Sbk s3 M3°-R°(?)*^{ZZ}

33. *Wn-nfr s3 Ḥr-Ḏḥwty*

34. *°nḫ-m3°-R° s3 Ḥr-Ḏḥwty*^{AAA}

35. *fkṯ... ḥm-ntr Ḥr-wḏ3 s3 ḥm-ntr Ḥr-ḫb*^{BBB}

36. *Ḏ-B3st.t-iw≠f-°nḫ s3 ḥm-ntr °3-imn s3 Ḥr-ḫb*^{CCC}

TRANSLATION

1. Year 17, second month of the season *akhet*, of Pharaoh l.p.h. Nektanebo (I). The god's sealer and embalmer *°nḫ-mr-wr*, son of *°nḫ-Ḥp*, called *P3-ti-Wsir*, whose mother is *Ta-imn*, has declared to the woman *Psṯ*, daughter of the god's sealer and embalmer *°nḫ-Ḥp*, called *P3-ti-Wsir*, whose mother is *°nḫ.t*: "You have caused my heart to agree to the 30 silver (*deben*) (weighed) by the pieces which are in the Treasury of Ptah, of refined (silver), being 29 silver (*deben*) and 9, 2/3, 1/6, 1/10, 1/30, 1/60, 1/60 *kite* of silver, being again 30 silver (*deben*) (weighed) by the pieces which are in the Treasury of Ptah, of refined (silver), as your annuity. There belong to the children whom you will bear to me everything which I possess and that which I shall acquire,

2. house, field, courtyard, building plot, male servant, female servant, every animal, every title deed and every free thing in the world which I possess. I am to give to you 36 (sacks) emmer (by the measure of) 40-*hin*, being 24 (sacks) barley (by the measure of) 40-*hin*, being again 36 (sacks) emmer (by the measure of) 40-*hin* and 1 silver (*deben*) (and) 2 *kite* of silver (weighed) by the pieces which are in the Treasury of Ptah, of refined (silver), being 1 silver (*deben*) and 1 *kite*, 2/3, 1/6, 1/10, 1/30, 1/60, 1/60 *kite* of silver, being again 1 silver (*deben*) 9 (and) 2 *kite* of silver (weighed) by the pieces which are in the Treasury of Ptah, of refined (silver), for your subsistence each year at whatever house you desire. You are the one authorized with regard to the arrears of your subsistence which shall be to my debit, and I am to give it to you. Everything which I possess and

3. that which I shall acquire is the pledge of your aforesaid annuity. I shall not be able to say to you, 'Take your aforesaid annuity,' (but on) whatever day you desire it, I will give it to you. I shall not be able to require an oath from you nor (from) the witness to the document except in the house in which the judges are." Whereas the god's sealer and embalmer *°nḫ-Ḥp*, who is called *P3-ti-Wsir*, son of *P3-šr-n-t3-iḥ.t*, whose mother is *Psṯ*, his father, says: "Receive the aforesaid god's sealer and embalmer *°nḫ-mr-wr*, my eldest son, whose mother is *Ta-imn*,

4. that he may execute the aforesaid document of annuity for you and that he may fulfill its
    obligations for you." He says also: "Do everything aforesaid; my heart is satisfied there-
    with." The astronomer of Sobek, *Mȝꜥ-Rꜥ*, son of *Ptḥ-nfr*, has written.

COMMENTARY

A The date is equivalent to December 22, 365–January 20, 364 B.C. For other documents from
the Thirtieth Dynasty, see, for example, Zauzich 1970: 223–29; idem 1980: 241–43; and, in
general, Thissen 1980: 118–20. See also note C below.

  Documents lacking specific dates seem to have been considered legally valid from the first
day of the month named; see H. Smith 1958: 94; Vittmann 1980: 134.

  An alternative translation of the *n* here as "under" is employed by several scholars; see,
for example, Andrews 1990: 24.

B The basic articles on the title *ḫtmw-ntr*, which was a standard designation for an undertaker in
the Memphite area, are still Sauneron 1952: 137–71 and Pestman 1963: 8–23. See further
Botti 1969: 74–75; de Cenival 1972: 12; Johnson 1986: 79; Vittmann 1986: 233–36; Devauchelle 1987:146–47, 152–53. The precise transliteration and translation of the title have
posed problems; see the comments of D. Thompson (1988: 156–57). The compound has frequently been transliterated as *sdȝwty-ntr* (see *Glossar*, p. 693), but for the reading *ḫtmw*,
which is now generally accepted, see Franke 1984: 112–14. On the meanings of *ḫtm*, see the
remarks of Mueller (1975: 222–26). *ḫtm* "seal" occurs as a component of other titles as well;
e.g., *sẖ ḫtm* "scribe of the seal" (El-Amir 1959: 1, 5); *sẖ ḫtm* and *sẖ ḫtm-ntr* (Janssen 1968:
169); *sẖ ḫtm-ntr* (Spiegelberg 1904: 30)[31]; *mr-ḫtm* "overseer of sealing" (Zauzich 1971: 69;
Yoyotte 1972: 218–20; Tait 1984: 223; Zivie 1984: 246).

  wyt "embalmer" (*Glossar*, p. 80) is always found in association with *ḫtmw-ntr* in these
documents; for a discussion of this term, see Devauchelle 1987: 153.

C For *ꜥnḫ-mr-wr*, see *Demot. Nb.*, p. 101. In the Tura and Masarah graffiti dated to the Thirtieth
Dynasty there also occurs an *ꜥnḫ-mr-wr*, son of *Pȝ-tỉ-Wsỉr*. Devauchelle (1983: 175–76) quite
reasonably suggests that he could well be identical with the man in this Chicago papyrus. On
the name *ꜥnḫ-mr-wr*, see further Clarysse 1980: 116–17; Quack 1991: 91–100.

D For the name *Psṯ*, see *Demot. Nb.*, p. 482; this name is also attested in the Hamburg Hawara
papyri. She is the half-sister of *ꜥnḫ-mr-wr*.

E For the name *ꜥnḫ.t*, see *Demot. Nb.*, p. 105. Nims had read *ꜥnḫ-ỉs.t*, but he also considered the
possibility of transliterating merely *ꜥnḫ.t*.

F Instead of *tnỉ.t* (*Glossar*, p. 638), read perhaps *tỉ.t* (*Glossar*, p. 606); see Nims 1958: 240–41.

G On this common formula in general and "Treasury of Ptah" in particular, see Vleeming 1991:
87–89.

H On the phrase *n wtḫ*, see Vleeming 1991: 89. An early example of *ḥd wtḫ*, probably to be
dated to about the eighth century B.C., is found in Edwards 1971: 124.

---

31. Compare also the Theban title *sẖ sdȝ.t-ntr n ỉmn* "scribe of the god's seal of Amun" (Andrews 1990: 18).

^I For a discussion of the various meanings of *ḥḏ*, see Devauchelle 1986: 157–58.

^J For the translation of *n* as old *m* "as," and not as dative "for," see Pestman 1961: 106–07, n. 8.

^K For a detailed discussion of *sꜤnḫ*, variously rendered as "annuity" or "endowment," see Johnson 1995: 113–32, and specifically p. 113, n. 2, for the problems of translation. See also Meeks 1979: 648; Vleeming 1991: 78.

^L For useful remarks on this clause and sequence of items, see Pestman 1961: 120–21; Vleeming 1991:173–74.

^M For *wrḫ*, see Andrews 1961: 20, n. 26; Pestman 1981: 83; Husson 1983: 293–99.

^N For *qnb.t* "title deed," see Vleeming 1991: 91.

^O The literature on *nmḥ* and *rmt-nmḥ* is considerable: see Mattha and Hughes 1975: 70; H. Smith 1980: 144, n. z; Thissen 1989: 39–40; Felber 1991: 27–36. On the plural writing of *nmḥ.w*, see Malinine 1953: 68.

^P On the varied writings of *it* and *bt*, see Vleeming 1979: 93–96.

^Q On this difficult formula, Vleeming (1991: 183) most recently suggests "(by) the (oipe) of 40-*hin*"; see also Cruz-Uribe 1990: 55–68.

^R Hughes (Mattha and Hughes 1975: 93) renders *Ꜥq-ḥbs* as "subsistence." Ritner (1984: 175) also discusses the compound.

^S For this clause, see Pestman 1961: 147; Pierce 1972: 151–58; Mattha and Hughes 1975: 92–93.

^T Nims observed that the signs for *ḥm.t* "wife" seem to have been incorporated into *iwy.t* "pledge"; Lüddeckens (1960: 142) interpreted the group as *iwꜣ.t ḥm.t* "Ehefrauenpfand" in his edition of this papyrus. For another curious writing of *iwy.t*, see Pestman 1977: vol. 1, p. 43. Pestman (1961: 115–17; 1968: 108–10) provides the most extensive analysis of this term. See also the remarks of Pierce (1972: 110–15, 125).

^U For a discussion of the legal nuances of *m-sꜣ*, see Pestman 1977: vol. 2, p. 18.

^V Nims (1958: 242) interpreted the phrase "the witness to/of the document" to refer to the scribe who wrote the text, who could be called in to testify regarding the genuineness of the document; compare *mtr-sḫ* the "witness-scribe" (Malinine 1953: 41, n. 19; Vleeming 1991: 212).

^W On the phrase "the house in which the judges are," see Allam 1991: 117–18.

^X On the subject of declarations by a third party in these documents, see Johnson 1995: 123–24. Nims (1958: 244) believed that "The assent made by the father at the end of the document is not a permission to marry but the acknowledgment of the son as the eldest and an heir, allowing him to pledge, according to the clauses of the document, the property which he would inherit on his father's death." A different view is held by Pestman (1961: 159, n. 3, and see also pp. 128–33).

^Y For an early example of *ḥp.w* "the legal obligations" of a document, see Malinine 1953: 94, n. 16. Nims (1948: 243–60) still provides the most comprehensive treatment of this complex word; additional useful remarks are found in Kaplony-Heckel 1963: 175; Menu 1972: 127;

Ray 1976: 92–93; Pestman 1977: vol. 2, p. 57 n. jj; Vleeming 1984: 60, n. ee; Porten 1992: 262.

Z For the reading *m-sḫ*, see Vleeming 1992: 212.

On the title *imy-wnw.t*, rendered as "Astronom" in *Glossar*, p. 30, see Sauneron 1959: 36–41; Malinine 1974: 49; Vittmann 1980: 135. The title seems to be found in connection with other deities as well; in one of the surety documents published by de Cenival (1973: 224) there appears, for example, a *imy-wnw.t*(?) *n Ḥry-š≠f* "astronomer(?) of Herishef."

AA For the name *P₃-sn-ky*, see *Demot. Nb.*, p. 217. However, this particular example is listed as "Fragliches" in *Demot. Nb.*, p. 510.

The writing of *M₃ꜥ-Rꜥ* found here and in verso, lines 2, 7, 10, 18, and 32, are also queried in *Demot. Nb.*, p. 610.

Nims hesitantly read the last name as *Ḥry.w*, but this is very uncertain; compare the examples in *Demot. Nb.*, pp. 746–48. On this name, see the remarks of Ray 1977: 101. The last element could be *is.t*, and perhaps *P₃-ti-is.t*(?) is a more attractive interpretation, as proposed by *Demot. Nb.*, p. 526. It is possible that the last groups are actually titles and not names at all.

BB Oddly enough, this witness seems to appear again in line 7 of this column. On the personal names of the form *Ḏ-Deity-iw≠f/s-ꜥnḫ*, see Quaegebeur 1973: 105.

CC Instead of *Ḥtr* as Nims, read perhaps *Ir.t≠w-r-r≠w*; see *Demot. Nb.*, p. 70.

Ns-B₃st.t is not common; see *Demot. Nb.*, p. 662. On the cult of Bastet in the Fayum, see de Cenival 1985: 105. One might also suggest *Ti-B₃st.t.-i₃w*(?) for the father's name, comparing column 2, line 20.

DD An alternative to *Sbk-t₃y* is *Sbk-nḥḥ*, but both seem to be unattested. The final group was not read by Nims and remains a puzzle. The last sign could be ᴧ.

EE *ir.t≠w-r-r≠w*, not transliterated by Nims, is a possibility. For the following names, Nims proposed *T₃y-nḫt-r-r≠w*, which is very uncertain, and *Ti-n≠y-...* .

FF As already mentioned, this witness seems to be identical to that in line 2 of this column.

GG The reading *iw≠f-iw* is not secure; see *Demot. Nb.*, p. 82; read perhaps *s₃ ḥm-ntr... p₃ ḥm-ntr imn*.

HH On the priestly title *fkṭ* "the bald one" (*Glossar*, p. 145), see Sauneron 1952: 165; Vernus 1976: 9.

II For the "scribe of the divine book," see Volten 1942: 18–19; Bakry 1968: 15–25; Derchain 1978: 59–61; Boswinkel and Pestman 1982: 123, n. 1; Devauchelle 1983: 124; Zauzich 1985: 116.

JJ The combination of *sḫ* and *ḫtmw-ntr* is not otherwise found in these texts. Instead of *ḥm-ntr Ḥr-sy-Sbk*, read perhaps *ḥm-ntr imn Sy-Sbk*. For *Ḥr-sy-Sbk*, see *Demot. Nb.*, p. 862 (under "Fragliches").

KK For *Ḥr-Ḏḥwty*, see *Demot. Nb.*, p. 841.

LL The *ḥ* seems very probable, but a satisfactory reading escapes me. So, too, *ꜥr* (or *ꜥl*) is quite possible, but I cannot resolve the remaining signs. Nims read *Sbk-... s₃....* .

MM For the reading, see *Demot. Nb.*, p. 926. Nims transliterated *Smɜ-tɜ.wy*.

NN *Pɜ-ḥm-ntr-4.nw* is not otherwise attested, but similarly formed names are not uncommon; see *Demot. Nb.*, pp. 505–06 (under "Fragliches").

OO Nims proposed *it-ntr Trkm* with hesitation. I owe the attractive reading *Wsrkn* "Osorkon" to Rolf Wassermann; for other examples, see *Demot. Nb., p.* 129.

   For remarks on *it-ntr* and other priestly titles, see Vleeming 1991: 53.

PP On the title *itnw* "deputy" (*Glossar*, p. 48), see Thissen 1972: 45.

QQ Nims read the last name as *Ns-Bɜst.t-iɜw-...* , and *Ns* is certainly possible. I suggest the above on the basis of the name *Tɜ-Bɜst.t-iɜw.t* "Bastet gebe Alter(?)," which is not found in *Demot. Nb.*, but is attested in Ranke et al. 1935–77: vol. 1, p. 396/16. On names of this construction, see Thirion 1979: 86–87; 1982–83: 109.

   pɜ wʿb at the end of the line seems plausible.

RR For *ʿnḫ-imn*, *Demot. Nb.*, p. 109, cites a single questionable example; perhaps read *ʿnḫ-Ḥp* (*Demot. Nb.*, pp. 103, 110).

SS Nims read *Trkⱶmⱶ*; see note OO.

TT The first name is not read by Nims; another example is in *Demot. Nb.*, p. 113. *ʿnḫ-Ḥp* is not absolutely certain.

UU *Demot. Nb.*, p. 532, proposes *Pɜ-ti-nfr-tm-...(?)* at the end of the line. Nims read *ʿnḫ-... sɜ Ti-n≠y-...* .

   The concluding group closely resembles *šn*; compare *Glossar*, p. 512.

VV For the check marks before this name and the one in the next line, see Andrews 1990: 24, n. 35.

WW For *Sbk-iw*, see *Demot. Nb.*, p. 915.

XX Nims transcribed *Sbk-m-ḥb*. On the reading of this name, see Clarysse 1987: 21.

YY So Nims, but the reading of the first name seems uncertain to me. For *ʿnḫ-Ḥnsw*, see *Demot. Nb.*, p. 104.

ZZ The editors of the *Demot. Nb.* have accepted Nims' reading of *Ḥr-sy-Sbk*, about which he seems to have harbored some reservations; see *Demot. Nb.*, p. 835. *sɜ Mɜʿ-Rʿ* at the end of the line is very dubious, however, and perhaps *pɜ wʿb* is a better transliteration.

AAA For *ʿnḫ-mɜʿ-Rʿ*, see *Demot. Nb.*, p. 101.

BBB The unread title is perhaps *imy-ibt* "monatlich diensttuender Priester" (*Glossar*, p. 27).

CCC *ʿɜ-imn* is not in *Demot. Nb.* Read perhaps *ʿnḫ-imn*; see Lüddeckens 1985: 77.

CHICAGO HAWARA PAPYRUS 2

Illustrations: Plates 8–13
Museum number: P. O.I. 25257
Maximum length: 116.5 cm
Maximum height: 35.0 cm
Physical description: The papyrus roll is composed of eight separate sheets, each ca. 15.0 cm in width. The rightmost portion is much damaged and was restored by Hughes.
Type: Annuity contract
Party A: *Pȝ-tỉ-Wsỉr*, son of *ʿnḫ-Ḥp* and *ỉs.t-wr.t*
Party B: *ʿnḫ.t*, daughter of *ʿnḫ-mr-wr* and *Psṱ*
Date: October 10–November 8, 331 B.C.
Scribe: *Mȝ ʿ-Rʿ*, son of *Ḏ-Ḫnsw-ỉw≠f-ʿnḫ*

TRANSLITERATION

LINES 1–4

1. *ḥȝ.t-sp 1.t ỉbt 4 šmm n P[r-]ʿȝ ʿ.[w.]s. ȝlygsnṱrs* **A** *ḏ ḥtmw-nṯr wyt Pȝ-tỉ-Wsỉr sȝ ʿnḫ-Ḥp mw.t≠f ỉs.t-wr(.t) n s-ḥm.t ʿnḫ.t sȝ.t n ḥtmw-nṯr wyt ʿnḫ-mr-wr mw.t≠s Psṱ* **B** *tỉ≠t mtry ḥȝ.t≠y n ḥḏ 10 n nȝ tnỉ.wt nt n pr-ḥḏ n Ptḥ n wtḥ r ḥḏ 9 qt 9 5/6 1/10 1/30 1/60 1/60 r ḥḏ 10 (n) nȝ tnỉ.wt nt n pr-ḥḏ n Ptḥ n wtḥ ʿn*

2. *n pȝ⌐y⌐≠t s ʿnḫ mtw nȝ ḥrṱ.w nt [ỉw≠t r] ms.ṱ.w n≠y nt nb nk nb* **C** *nt mtw≠y ḥnʿ nȝw nt ỉw≠y r tỉ.t ḫpr≠w n pr ȝḥ ỉnḥ wrḥ bȝk bȝk.t ỉḥ.t ʿȝ tp-n-ỉȝw.t nb.t ỉȝw.t nb qnb.t nb mt (n) rmt-nmḥ.w nb n pȝ tȝ mtw≠y mtw≠y tỉ.t n≠t bt 36 n tȝ hn 40 r ỉt 24 n tȝ hn 40 r bt 36 (n) tȝ hn 40 ʿn ḥḏ 1 qt 2 n nȝ tnỉ.wt nt n pr-ḥḏ n Ptḥ n wtḥ r ḥḏ 1 qt 1 5/6 1/10 1/30 1/60 1/60*

3. *r ḥḏ 1 qt ⌐2⌐ n nȝ tni.wt nt n p[r-ḥḏ n Ptḥ n wt]ḥ ʿn n nȝ pȝy≠t ʿq-ḥbs ḥr rnp.t r pȝ ʿ.wy nt mr≠t s mtw≠t tȝ nt nḥe.ṱ r tȝ wḏȝy n pȝy≠t ʿq-ḥbs nt ỉw≠s r ḫpr r ʿ.wy≠y mtw≠y tỉ.t s n≠t nt nb nk nb nt mtw≠y ḥnʿ nȝw nt ỉw≠y r tỉ.t ḫpr≠w n(?) pr ȝḥ ỉnḥ wrḥ bȝk bȝk.t ỉḥ.t ʿȝ tp-n-ỉȝw.t nb ỉȝw.t nb qnb.t nb mt n rmt-nmḥ.w nb n pȝ tȝ* **D** *mtw≠y*

4. *st ḫ[pr] n ỉw[.t n pȝy≠t s ʿnḫ] nt ḥry bn ỉw≠y rḫ ḏ n≠t ⌐š⌐p pȝy≠t s ʿnḫ nt ḥry pȝy≠t sw n wḥȝ≠f ỉw≠y r tỉ.t s [n≠t n-ỉ]m≠f bn ỉw≠y rḫ tỉ.t ʿnḫ m-sȝ≠t ḥnʿ pȝ m[tre n] pȝ sḫ nt ḥry* **E** *pȝ bnr n pȝ ʿ.wy nt ỉw nȝ wpṱy.w n-ỉm≠f m-sḫ Mȝʿ-Rʿ sȝ Ḏ-Ḫnsw-ỉw≠f-ʿnḫ*

WITNESS LIST

Column One

1. ... *sȝ*... *-mn* **F**

2. *Pȝ-tỉ-Ḥr-pȝ-šr-ỉs.t sȝ Ḏ-Bȝst.t-ỉw≠f-ʿnḫ*

3. Check mark *Sy-Sbk sȝ ỉmn-m-ḥȝ.t*

4. Check mark *ʿ-Ḥr* **G** *sȝ Sy-Sbk*

5. *P3-tỉ-Wsỉr s3 ḥm-ntr Sbk-p3-ym* **H**

6. Check mark *Sbk-ḥtp s3 P3-tỉ-Sbk-ḥtp*

7. Check mark *Ḥp-mn*(?) *s3 ḥm-ntr Sbk-ḥtp*

8. Check mark *Ḥr-wḏ3 s3 ꜥnḫ-Ḥp*

9. *P3y=f-ỉwỉw s3 P3-ḥtr*

10. Check mark *ꜥnḫ-⸢nb.t⸣-ḥ.t* **I** *s3 M3ꜥ-Rꜥ*

11. *Ḥr-wḏ3 s3 Pa-tr.t*(?)**J**

12. Check mark *ḥm-ntr P3-tỉ-ỉs.t s3 Sbk-ḥtp*

13. Check mark *Ḥr-wḏ3 s3 Sbk-ỉw s3 P3-tỉ-Wsỉr*

14. *ỉy-m-ḥtp* (*s3*) *Ḏ-B3st.t-ỉw≥f-ꜥnḫ*

15. *Ḥr-wḏ3 s3 Ḥr*

16. Check mark *Sbk-ḥtp s3 P3-tỉ-Wsỉr*

Column Two

17. *Ḥm-ntr-3.nw* **K** *s3 ỉmn-m-ḥ3.t*

18. *ỉmn-m-ḥ3.t s3 Ḥr-wḏ3*

19. Check mark *Ḥr-wḏ3 s3 Ḏ-B3st.t-ỉw≥f-ꜥnḫ*

20. *ỉmn-m-ḥ3.t s3 M3ꜥ-Rꜥ s3 Ḏ-B3st.t-ỉw≥f-ꜥnḫ*

21. *Sbk-… s3 M3ꜥ-Rꜥ…*

22. *P3-tỉ-Sbk*(?) …

23. …

24. …

TRANSLATION

1. Year 1, fourth month of the season *shemu* of Ph[ar]aoh l.[p.]h. Alexander. The god's sealer and embalmer *P3-tỉ-Wsỉr,* son of *ꜥnḫ-Ḥp,* whose mother is *ỉs.t-wr*(*.t*), has declared to the woman *ꜥnḫ.t,* daughter of the god's sealer and embalmer *ꜥnḫ-mr-wr,* whose mother is *Psṯ*: "You have caused my heart to agree to the 10 silver (*deben*) (weighed) by the pieces which are in the Treasury of Ptah, of refined (silver), being 9 silver (*deben*) and *kite* 9, 5/6, 1/10, 1/30, 1/60, 1/60 being 10 silver (*deben*) (weighed by) the pieces which are in the Treasury of Ptah, of refined (silver), again,

2. as your annuity. There belong to the children whom [you will be]ar to me everything of all property which I possess and that which I shall acquire in house, field, courtyard, building plot, male servant, female servant, cow, ass, every animal, every office, every title deed, and every matter of a freeman whatsoever of mine. And I shall give to you 36 (sacks) emmer (by the measure of) 40-*hin*, being 24 (sacks) barley (by the measure of) 40-*hin*, being 36 (sacks) emmer (by the measure of) 40-*hin* again and 1 silver (*deben*) and 2 *kite* (weighed) by the pieces which are in the Treasury of Ptah, of refined (silver), being 1 silver (*deben*) and 1, 5/6, 1/10, 1/30, 1/60, 1/60 *kite,*

3. being 1 silver (*deben*) and 2 *kite* (weighed) by the pieces which are in the Tre[asury of Ptah, of refine]d (silver), again for your subsistence each year at whatever house you desire. You are the one authorized with regard to the arrears of your subsistence which will be to my debit, and I am to give it to you. As for everything of all property that I possess and that which I shall acquire in house, field, courtyard, building plot, male servant, female servant, cow, ass, every animal, every office, every title deed, and every matter of a free-man whatsoever of mine,

4. they become a pledge [for your annuity] aforesaid. I shall not be able to say to you "Take your aforesaid annuity," but on [what]ever day you desire it, I will give it [to you]. I shall not be able to require an oath from you [nor from the witne]ss to the aforesaid document except in the house in which the judges are." Written by *Mȝᶜ-Rᶜ*, son of *Ḏ-Ḥnsw-iw≥f-ᶜnḫ*.

COMMENTARY [32]

A The date is equivalent to October 10–November 8, 331 B.C. Note the writing *šmm* in place of the standard *šmw*, an orthography found also in Chicago Hawara Papyri 6, 7, 8, and the Rendell Papyrus. The scribe clearly distinguished between "r" and "l" in the writing of Alexander. On the differentiation between these letters, see Clarysse and van der Veken 1983: 142, the earliest example cited therein is from P. Louvre 2424, dated to year 19 of Ptolemy II (= 267 B.C.; Steve Vinson, pers. comm.).

B *ᶜnḫ.t* is the daughter of the couple whose annuity contract is preserved in Chicago Hawara Papyrus 1, drawn up in 365/364 B.C. For *is.t-wr.t*, see *Demot. Nb.*, 76–77; the name also appears in the Copenhagen Hawara papyri.

C Erichsen (1950: 276) observes that the older, early Demotic form of the phrase is *nt nb (n) nk* and that the later formulation is *nt nb nk nb*. See also the remarks of Pestman (1977: vol. 2, pp. 97–98).

D The scribe has here written *tȝ* in the typical Demotic fashion, in contrast to the strongly hieratic orthography in line 2.

E A parallel for "the witness to the document" is in Chicago Hawara Papyrus 1, line 3.

F Perhaps [*Pȝ*]-*sn-ky sȝ ḥm-ntr… Ḥr-mn*.

G This might be an abbreviated writing of *ᶜ(nḫ)-Ḥr* or *ᶜ(w)-Ḥr*, but I find no such spelling in *Demot. Nb*.

H I have no parallel for the name *Sbk-pȝ-ym*, but the reading is plausible.

I The reading is not certain. Also possible is *ᶜnḫ-nȝ-wn.w* or *ᶜnḫ-tȝ.ḥ.t*.

J Or read perhaps *i*[*mn*]-*m-ḥȝ.t*.

K For similarly formed personal names, see *Demot. Nb.*, pp. 505–06.

---

32. A number of standard phrases and words already discussed in the commentary to Chicago Hawara Papyrus 1 naturally reoccur in several of the following papyri. I have thought it unnecessary to add a cross-reference in each instance but have included a *Selective Index of Words and Phrases Discussed in the Commentaries*.

CHICAGO HAWARA PAPYRUS 3

Illustrations: Plates 14–19

Museum number: P. O.I. 25259

Maximum length: 142 cm

Maximum height: 35 cm

Physical description: The roll is made up of ten individual papyrus sheets, each ca. 14 cm in width. A 4 cm papyrus strip is on the right end and a 5 cm papyrus strip is on the left end.

Description: Annuity contract with four witness copies[33]

Party A: ^{c}nh-mr-wr, son of $P3$-ti-$n3$-$ntr.w$ and $^{c}nh.t$

Party B: $N3$-nfr-mn-ib-Pth ($= N3$-nfr-ib-Pth), daughter of $P3y$-^{c}r-imn and $Šty$

Date: December 9, 311–January 7, 310 B.C.

Scribe: Sy-Sbk, son of iy-m-htp

TRANSLITERATION

LINES 1–4

1. $h3.t$-sp 7^{34} ibt 2 $3h.t$ n Pr-$^{c}3$ $3rgs3ntrs$ $s3$ $3rgs3ntrs$^{35A} d $htmw$-ntr wt^{36} ^{c}nh-mr-wr $s3$ $P3$-ti-$n3$-$ntr.w$^{37} $mw.t$≠f $^{c}nh.t$ n s-$hm.t$ $N3$-nfr-mn-ib-Pth^{38} $s3.t$ n $htmw$-ntr wty^{39} $P3y$-^{c}r-imn $mw.t$≠s $Šty$^{B} ti≠t $mtre$ $h3.t$($≠y$) n hd 10 n $n3$ $tni.wt$ n pr-hd Pth^{40} wth^{C}

2. r hd 9 qt 9^{41} $5/6$ $1/10$ $1/30$ $1/60$ $1/60$ r hd 10 n^{42} $n3$ $tni.wt$ n pr-hd^{43} Pth wth ^{c}n n $p3y$≠t $s^{c}nh$ mtw≠t^{44} $n3$ $hrt.w$ nt iw≠t r^{45} $ms.t$≠w n≠y nt nb nt mtw≠y hn^{c} $n3$ nt iw≠y r $ti.t$^{D}

---

33. On witness copy documents, see H. Smith 1958: 87; Zauzich 1968: 247, n. 40. According to H. Smith, the latest such text dates to 213 B.C. Andrews (1990: 16–22, P. BM 10026; 265–264 B.C.) recently published a fine example.

34. Witness copies 1–4: $7.t$.

35. Witness copy 4: $3rgs$[nt]rs $s3$ $3rgsntrs$ (N.B. no beginning of cartouche).

36. Witness copies 1, 2, 4: wyt; witness copy 3: wty.

37. Witness copy 1: [$s3$ $P3$-ti-$n3$-nt]$r.w$.

38. Witness copy 4: $N3$-nfr-ib-Pth.

39. Witness copy 2: wyt.

40. Witness copies 1 and 3: n hd 10 $n3$ $tni.wt$ nt (n) pr-hd; witness copy 2: $n3$ $tni.wt$ nt n pr-hd; witness copy 4: hd 10 n $n3$ $tni.wt$ nt (n) pr-hd.

41. Witness copy 4: r hd 9 hd qt 9.

42. Witness copy 1: n omitted.

43. Witness copy 2: $n3$ $tni.wt$ nt n pr-hd; witness copy 3: $n3$ $tni.wt$ nt (n) pr-hd; witness copy 4: hd 10 n $n3$ $tni.wt$ nt (n) pr-hd.

44. Witness copy 1: mtw.

45. Witness copy 2: mtw $n3$ $hrt.w$ [nt] i-ir≠t; witness copy 3: nt i-ir≠t r; witness copy 4: mtw($≠t$) $n3$ $hrt.w$ nt i-ir($≠t$).

ḫpr≠w pr ꜣḥ⁴⁶ ỉnḥ wrḥ bꜣk bꜣk.t ỉḥ.t ꜥꜣ tp-ỉꜣw.t nb ỉꜣw.t⁴⁷ nb⁴⁸ sḫ nb mt rmt-nmḥ⁴⁹ nb n pꜣ tꜣ mtw≠y mtw(≠t) st⁵⁰ mtw≠y tỉ.t n≠t bt 36 n tꜣ 40

3. *r ỉt 24 n tꜣ 40 r bt 36 n tꜣ 40 ꜥn ḥḏ 1 qt 2 n nꜣ tnỉ.wt n pr-ḥḏ Ptḥ⁵¹ wtḥ r ḥḏ 1 qt 1 5/6 1/10 1/30 1/60 1/60 r ḥḏ 1 qt 2 n nꜣ tnỉ.wt n pr-ḥḏ Ptḥ⁵² wtḥ ꜥn n pꜣy≠t ꜥq-ḥbs ḥr rnp.t r pꜣ ꜥ.wy nt ỉw mr(≠t) s⁵³ mtw≠t tꜣ nt nhe.ṯ⁵⁴ r tꜣ wḏꜣ n pꜣy≠t ꜥq-ḥbs nt ỉ(w)≠s (r) ḫpr (r-)ꜥ.wy≠y⁵⁵ mtw≠y tỉ.ts n≠t nt nb nt mtw≠y⁵⁶ ḥnꜥ nꜣ nt ỉw≠y r tỉ.t ḫpr≠w n ỉwꜣ.t⁵⁷ n pꜣy≠t sꜥnḫ nt ḥry nꜣw bn ỉw≠y⁵⁸*

4. *rḫ ḏ n≠t šp pꜣy≠t sꜥnḫ⁵⁹ pꜣy≠t sw n wḫꜣ≠f ỉw≠y r tỉ.ts n≠t n-ỉm≠f ỉw≠w^E tỉ.t ꜥnḫ m-sꜣ≠t r ỉr≠f n≠y ỉ-ỉr≠t (r) ỉr≠f⁶⁰ n≠y n⁶¹ pꜣ ꜥ.wy nt ỉw nꜣ wpwty.w⁶² n-ỉm≠f sḫ Sy-Sbk sꜣ ỉy-m-ḥtp*

TEXTUAL VARIANTS IN WITNESS COPIES

Witness Copy 1

1. *ḥm N.t^F Sbk-ḥtp sꜣ Ḥr-wḏꜣ ỉw≠f (n) mtr n ḥꜣ.t-sp 7.t* (etc.) *n ḏ ỉ-ỉr...*

4. At the end of the line: *sḫ≠y nꜣw* "I have written this."

Witness Copy 2

ꜥnḫ-smꜣ-tꜣ.wy sꜣ ỉmn-m-ḥꜣ.t^G ỉw≠f n mtre n ḥꜣ.t-sp 7.t (etc.) *n ḏ ỉ-ỉr*

4. At the end of the line: *sḫ≠y nꜣy* "I have written this."

Witness Copy 3

Pꜣ-tỉ-Ḥr-pꜣ-šr-ỉs.t sꜣ Pꜣ-Rꜥ-nt-rq(?)^H ỉw≠f n mtr n ḥꜣ.t-sp 7.t (etc.) *n ḏ ỉ-ỉr*

5. At the end of the line: *sḫ≠y nꜣy* "I have written this."

---

46. Witness copy 4: note the writing of *ꜣḥ*.
47. Witness copy 4: note the writing of *ỉꜣw.t*.
48. Witness copy 1: *ỉꜣw[.t n]b*.
49. Witness copy 2: *mt rmt nmḥ.w*; witness copy 4: *qnb.t mt rmt nmḥ*.
50. Witness copy 1: *mtw≠y st*; witness copies 3 and 4: *mtw≠t st*.
51. Witness copy 1: *n Ptḥ*; witness copy 3: *n nꜣ tnỉ.wt nt (n) pr-ḥḏ Ptḥ*; witness copy 4: ⌈*n nꜣ tnỉ.wt nt (n) pr.ḥḏ*⌉ *n Ptḥ*.
52. Witness copy 1: *n Ptḥ*; witness copy 3: *nt (n) pr-ḥḏ Ptḥ*; witness copy 4: *nt (n) pr-ḥḏ n Ptḥ*.
53. Witness copy 1: *nt [ỉw m]r(≠t) st*; witness copies 2 and 4: *nt ỉw mr≠t s*; witness copy 3: *r pꜣy ꜥ.wy nt mr(≠t) s*.
54. Witness copies 2 and 4: *mtw≠t nt nḥ.ṯ*.
55. Witness copy 2: *nt ỉ(w)≠s r ḫpr r-ꜥ.wy≠y*; witness copy 3: *ḫpr r-[ꜥ.wy≠y]*.
56. Witness copy 4: *nt nb nk nb nt mtw≠y*.
57. Witness copy 1: *n tꜣ ỉwy.t*; witness copy 3: *ḫpr≠w (n) tꜣ ỉwy.t*.
58. Witness copy 4: *n pꜣy≠t sꜥnḫ bn-ỉw≠y*.
59. Witness copy 4: *pꜣy≠t sꜥnḫ nt ḥry*.
60. Witness copies 1 and 3: *ỉ-ỉr≠t r ỉr≠f*.
61. Witness copy 2: *r*.
62. Witness copy 1: *wpṱy.w*; witness copy 3: [*wpṱ*].*w*.

Witness Copy 4

> *Dḥwty-iw sꜣ Pꜣ-ti-nꜣ-ntr.w* [1] *iw=f* (*n*) *mtr n ḥꜣ.t-sp 7.t* (etc.) *n ḏ i-ir*

7. At the end of the line: *sẖ=y nꜣy* "I have written this."

TRANSLATION

1. Year 7, second month of the season *akhet*, of Pharaoh Alexander (IV), son of Alexander (the Great). The god's sealer and embalmer *ꜥnḫ-mr-wr*, son of *Pꜣ-ti-nꜣ-ntr.w*, whose mother is *ꜥnḫ.t*, has declared to the woman *Nꜣ-nfr-mn-ib-Ptḥ*, daughter of the god's sealer and embalmer *Pꜣy-ꜥr-imn*, whose mother is *Šty*: "You have caused (my) heart to agree to the 10 silver (*deben*) (weighed) by the pieces in the Treasury of Ptah, (of) refined (silver),

2. being 9 silver (*deben*) 9, 5/6, 1/10, 1/30, 1/60, 1/60 *kite*, being 10 silver (*deben*) (weighed) by the pieces in the Treasury of Ptah, (of) refined (silver), again, as your annuity. There belong to you and the children whom you will bear to me everything which I possess and that which I shall acquire (in) house, field, courtyard, building plot, male servant, female servant, cow, ass, every animal, every office, every document, every matter of a freeman in the world belonging to me. To you do they belong. I am to give to you 36 (sacks) emmer (by the measure of) 40-*hin*,

3. being 24 (sacks) barley (by the measure of) 40-*hin*, being 36 (sacks) emmer (by the measure of) 40-*hin* again, and 1 silver (*deben*) and 2 *kite* (weighed) by the pieces in the Treasury of Ptah, (of) refined (silver), being 1 silver (*deben*) and 1, 5/6, 1/10, 1/30, 1/60, 1/60, *kite*, being 1 silver (*deben*) and 2 *kite* (weighed) by the pieces in the Treasury of Ptah, (of) refined (silver), again, for your subsistence each year at whatever house you desire. You are the one authorized with regard to the arrears of your subsistence which shall be to my debit, and I am to give it to you. Everything which I possess and that which I shall acquire are the pledge of your aforesaid annuity. I shall not

4. be able to say to you, 'Take your annuity,' but on whatever day you desire it, I will give it to you. If an oath is required of you to be taken for me, it is in the house in which the judges are that you are to take it for me." Written by *Sy-Sbk*, son of *iy-m-ḥtp*.

Beginning of Witness Copy 1   "Servant of Neith, *Sbk-ḥtp*, son of *Ḥr-wḏꜣ*, being a witness in year 7 etc. to the statement made …"

Beginning of Witness Copy 2   "*ꜥnḫ-smꜣ-tꜣ.wy*, son of *imn-m-ḥꜣt*, being a witness in year 7 etc. to the statement made …"

Beginning of Witness Copy 3   "*Pꜣ-ti-Ḥr-pꜣ-šr-is.t*, son of *Pꜣ-Rꜥ-nt-rq*(?), being a witness in year 7 etc. to the statement made …"

Beginning of Witness Copy 4   "*Dḥwty-iw*, son of *Pꜣ-ti-nꜣ-ntr.w*, being a witness in year 7 etc. to the statement made …"

COMMENTARY

A The date is equivalent to December 9, 311 B.C.–January 7, 310 B.C.

B Party A in this text, *ʿnḫ-mr-wr*, is the son of *ʿnḫ.t* (Party B) in Chicago Hawara Papyrus 2. *P3-tí-Wsìr*, Party A in Chicago Hawara Papyrus 2, could then have been her first husband, *P3-tí-n3-ntr.w*, her second.

For *P3-tí-n3-ntr.w*, see *Demot. Nb.*, p. 316. Other examples of the name *P3-tí-n3-ntr.w* are found in Devauchelle 1983: 258; Andrews 1988: p. 195; eadem 1990: 54.

The woman (Party B) is to be identified with *N3-nfr-íb-Ptḥ* in Chicago Hawara Papyrus 4/1. However, in this text the name is clearly spelled *N3-nfr-mn-íb-Ptḥ*, except in witness copy 4, line 2, where *N3-nfr-íb-Ptḥ* is written. It is not found in *Demot. Nb.*

P3y-ʿr-ìmn is also not in *Demot. Nb.*, but a name of similar construction, *T3* (= *Ta*)-*ʿr-Ḥpy*, is attested in Ranke et al. 1935–77: vol. 1, p. 359/1.

C *wtḥ* is written in an abbreviated fashion.

D *r tí.t* is ligatured.

E *ìw≠w* in witness copy 4 has a supralinear stroke (witness copy 4, line 7).

F On the title *ḥm N.t* "servant of Neith," see Spiegelberg 1928: 29–30[63]; de Meulenaere 1977: 251, n. 1; Devauchelle 1983: 171. For another servant of Neith in Hawara, see Daressy 1914: 73–82. The title occurs again in Chicago Hawara Papyrus 5, line 3. See also Quaegebeur 1984: 167.

G For *ʿnḫ-sm3-t3.wy*, see *Demot. Nb.*, p. 105.

Instead of *ìmn-m-ḫ3.t*, read perhaps *ìmn-ḥtp*.

H *P3-Rʿ-nt-rq* is very uncertain.

I On the problems of reading the name of this witness, see Clarysse 1987: 20. He might be a brother of *ʿnḫ-mr-wr*, son of *P3-tí-n3-ntr.w*, Party A in this text.

---

63. The title occurs on a mummy ticket, bought in Medinet el-Fayum, which Spiegelberg understandably wished to date to the Saite period on the basis of the hieratic form of the script and the names (*Ḏ-B3st.t-ìw≠f-ʿnḫ* and *Mn-ì-ìr-tì-s*). However, in view of the hieratic appearance of these Hawara scripts and the fact that such names also appear in the Hawara papyri, a date in the fourth century for the mummy ticket seems perfectly plausible.

CHICAGO HAWARA PAPYRUS 4

Illustrations: Plates 20–24

Museum number: P. O.I. 25262

Maximum length: 108.0 cm

Maximum height: 36.5 cm

Physical description: The roll is composed of eight papyrus sheets, averaging 13.0 cm in width. The papyrus, light brown in color, is in virtually perfect condition. This papyrus was rolled inside of Chicago Hawara Papyrus 9, dated to March 9, 239 B.C.

Type: Donation document drawn up for a father on behalf of his son

Party A: *ꜥnḫ-mr-wr*, son of *P₃-ti-n₃-ntr.w* and *ꜥnḫ.t*

Party B: *P₃-ti-Wsir*, son of *ꜥnḫ-mr-wr* and *N₃-nfr-ib-Ptḥ*

Date: March 4–April 2, 292 B.C.

Scribe: *Nḫt-Ḥr*(?), son of *P₃-ti-Ḥr*

TRANSLITERATION

LINES 1–5

1. *ḥ₃.t-sp 13 ibt 1 pr.t n Pr-ꜥ₃ Ptlwmys* **A** *ḏ ḫtmw-ntr wyt ꜥnḫ-mr-wr s₃ P₃-ti-n₃-ntr.w mw.t≈f ꜥnḫ.t n ḫtmw-ntr wyt P₃-ti-Wsir s₃ ꜥnḫ-mr-wr mw.t≈f N₃-nfr-ib-Ptḥ* **B** *p₃y≈y šr* **C** *ti≈y n≈k p₃ 2/3 (n) t₃y≈y tni.t (n) n₃y≈y ꜥ.wy.w* **D** *nt qt iw≈w grg (n) sy sb₃ p₃y≈w wn* **E** *n₃y≈y tni.wt n(?) p₃y ꜥ.wy nt (n) ḥ.t-ntr Sbk*

2. *nt ir mḥ-ntr* **F** *21 n rs r mḥt iw≈f ir mḥ-ntr 22 (n) imnt (r) i₃bt* **G** *ḥnꜥ p₃ 2/3 n p₃y≈y ꜥ.wy nt (n) tmi Sbk* **H** *Ḥ.t-wr.t nt ir mḥ-ntr 18 n rs r mḥt iw≈f ir mḥ-ntr 19 (n) imnt (r) i₃bt* **I** *ḥnꜥ p₃ 2/3 (n) n₃ ꜥ.wy.w nt iw≈y r (sic) mtw≈y ḥnꜥ t₃ pš.t (n) n₃ ꜥ.wy.w nt iw≈y (r) ti.t ḫpr≈w t p₃ hrw r-ḥry n₃ tni.wt pš.w (n) n₃y≈y tni.wt (n) t₃ ḫ₃s.t (n) Ḥ.t-wr.t ḥnꜥ t₃ ḫ₃s.t P₃-bw-n-ym* **J** *ḥnꜥ t₃ tni.t pš (n) n₃ tni.wt*

3. *r-ti≈w n≈y (n) t₃ tni.t (n) P₃-ti-n₃-ntr.w p₃y≈y it (n) t₃ ḫ₃s.t (n) Ḥ.t-wr.t ḥnꜥ t₃ ḫ₃s.t W₃ḥ-r-qr(?)* **K** *ḥnꜥ t₃ pš (n) t₃ tni.t r-in≈y r-ḏb₃ ḥḏ i-ir ḫtmw-ntr wyt P₃y-N.t-wr(.t)* **L** *s₃ Wn-nfr ḥnꜥ t₃ pš (n) t₃ tni.t (n) Pa-g₃y s₃ P₃-ti-imn ḥnꜥ t₃ pš (n) n₃ tni.wt nt iw≈y r ti.t ḫpr≈w ḥr t₃ ḫ₃s.t ḥnꜥ t₃ pš (n) nt nb nk nb nt iw≈y r ti.t ḫpr≈w t p₃ hrw r-ḥry mtw≈k st t p₃ hrw r-ḥry bn iw rḫ*

4. *rmt nb (n) p₃ t₃ ir sḫy n n₃ tni.wt nt ḥry bnr≈k t p₃ hrw r-ḥry mtw≈k st ḥnꜥ p₃y≈w hp p₃ šr (n) p₃ t₃ nt mtw≈y nt iw≈f r iy r-r≈k r-ḏb₃ n₃ tni.wt nt iw p₃y≈w wn r (sic) sḫ r-ḥry t p₃ hrw r-ḥry iw≈f r ti.t n≈k ḥḏ 100 n sttr r sttr 500 r ḥḏ 100 (n) sttr ꜥn wꜥ hrw ḥn hrw 10 (n) iy r-r≈k r-ḏb₃.t≈w nt iw≈f r ir≈f n ḥtr iwty mn* **M** *iw≈k m-s₃≈f r tm sḫ* **N** *r-r≈k n-im≈w ꜥn*

5. *mtw≈k p₃ 2/3 (n) n₃y≈y b₃k.w ḥwt ḥnꜥ p₃ 2/3 (n) n₃y≈y b₃k.w(t) s-ḥm.wt nt mtw≈y t p₃ hrw r-ḥry m-sḫ Nḫt-Ḥr(?)* **O** *s₃ P₃-ti-Ḥr*

23

RIGHT MARGIN

 ᶜnḫ-mr-wr sꜣ Pꜣ-tỉ-Wsỉr(?) *pꜣ* ᶜꜣ **P**

WITNESS LIST

1. *Ḥr-ḫb* (*sꜣ*) *ḥm-ntr Ḥr-Dḥwty*
2. *ỉᶜḥ-ỉ-ỉr-tỉ-s sꜣ Ḥr-wḏꜣ*
3. *Pꜣy-Ḥr-sꜣ-ỉs.t*^Q *sꜣ Wn-nfr*
4. *ỉy-m-ḥtp sꜣ Sbk-ḥtp*
5. *Ḥr-ḫb sꜣ Wn-nfr*
6. *Mꜣᶜ-Rᶜ*(?) (*sꜣ*) *Pꜣ-tỉ≠w* **R**
7. *Wn-nfr sꜣ Ḥr-Dḥwty*(?)^S
8. *Sbk-Ḥᶜpy sꜣ Pꜣ-tỉ-Rnn.t* **T**
9. *Smꜣ-tꜣ.wy sꜣ ỉnp* **U**
10. ... *sꜣ Hgr*(?)^V
11. *Pa-N.t-wr(.t)* **W** *sꜣ Wn-nfr*
12. *Sbk-ḥtp sꜣ Pꜣ-tỉ-pꜣ-Rᶜ*(?)

TRANSLATION

1. Year 13, first month of the season *peret*, of Pharaoh Ptolemy. The god's sealer and em-balmer *ᶜnḫ-mr-wr*, son of *Pꜣ-tỉ-nꜣ-ntr.w*, whose mother is *ᶜnḫ.t*, has declared to the god's sealer and embalmer *Pꜣ-tỉ-Wsỉr*, son of *ᶜnḫ-mr-wr*, whose mother is *Nꜣ-nfr-ỉb-Ptḥ*: "My son, I have given to you the two-thirds (of) my share of my hous[es] which are built (and) provided (with) beam and door. Their specification: my shares of (?) this house which is (in) the temple of Sobek (precinct),

2. which measures 21 divine cubits from south to north and measures 22 divine cubits (from) west (to) east; also, the two-thirds of my house which is in the Sobek town, Hawara, which measures 18 divine cubits from south to north and 19 divine cubits (from) west (to) east; also, the two-thirds of the houses which are mine(?); and the half of the houses which I shall acquire from today onward: the halves of my shares in the necropolis of Hawara and in the necropolis of *Pꜣ-bw-n-ym*; also the half of the shares

3. which were given to me from the share of *Pꜣ-tỉ-nꜣ-ntr.w*, my father, in the necropolis of Hawara and the necropolis of *Wꜣḥ-r-qr*(?); and the half of the share which I bought from the god's sealer and embalmer *Pꜣy-N.t-wr(.t)*, son of *Wn-nfr*; and the half of the share of *Pa-gꜣy*, son of *Pꜣ-tỉ-ỉmn*, and the half of the shares which I shall acquire in the necropolis and the half of all and everything which I shall acquire from today onward. They are yours from today onward. No one in the world shall

4. be able to exercise control over the aforesaid shares except you from today onward. They are yours and the legal right to them. As for any son of mine at all who will come against you regarding the shares, of which the specifications are written above, from today on-ward, he must give to you 100 silver (*deben*) in *staters*, being 500 *staters*, being 100 silver

(*deben*) in *staters* again within ten days of his coming against you regarding them, of necessity and without delay, while you will still have claim on him not to hinder you with regard to them.

5. Yours are the two-thirds of my male servants and the two-thirds of my female servants which belong to me from today onward." Written by *Nḫt-Ḥr*(?) son of *P3-ti-Ḥr*.

RIGHT MARGIN

  ʿnḫ-mr-wr, son of *P3-ti-Wsir*(?), the elder.

COMMENTARY

A The date is equivalent to March 4–April 2, 292 B.C. in the reign of Ptolemy I Soter.

B *ʿnḫ-mr-wr* and *N3-nfr-ib-Ptḥ* concluded an annuity contract in 311/310 B.C. (= Chicago Hawara Papyrus 3). On the name *N3-nfr-ib-Ptḥ*, see note B to Chicago Hawara Papyrus 3.

C This document is a donation from father and son; for which, see Seidl 1939: 198–200, who prefers the designation "*Teilungsschrift*"; Zauzich 1974: 102. In such documents Party A often states explicitly the relationship obtaining with Party B; in this text *ʿnḫ-mr-wr* addresses *P3-ti-Wsir* as "my son." Two fine examples of this type of text have recently been published by Andrews (1990: 48–50, 89–92).

D Here *ʿ.wy.w* seems to mean "houses"; on the possible distinction between *ʿ.wy* "house" and *ʿ.wy.w* "localities," see Vleeming 1991: 36–37; see also Glanville 1939: xxxi, n. i.

E See Pestman 1987: 63–64 for a discussion of the various meanings of *wn* "specification, list."

F Lüddeckens (1968: 19–20) provides a useful treatment of *mḥ-ntr*, including remarks on the different writings of this word in the Hawara texts. See further Parker 1972: 11; Andrews 1990: 47, n. 5.

G In neither case are the boundaries or neighbors of the houses delineated.

H On the compound *tmi Sbk* "Sobek town," see de Cenival 1984: 32–33.

I The second house is probably identical with the house of Chicago Hawara Papyrus 7A.

J I have not found this place-name elsewhere. The reading is not secure; for a discussion of *bw* and its cognates, see Clarysse and Winnicki 1989: 58–59.

K This reading is extremely uncertain; perhaps *nt ḥr r-r≠s* is better.

L I owe the decipherment of this personal name, which is not in *Demot. Nb.*, to Christina Di Cerbo. *wr.t* is damaged, but compare the same word in *Ḥ.t-wr.t* of line 2. This individual is also a witness to the document, having signed his name on line 11 of the verso of the papyrus.

M Pierce (1972: 133–43) gives the most detailed analysis of the phrase *n ḥtr iwty mn*.

N For *sḫ* "to hinder, obstruct" (*Glossar*, pp. 451–52), see Jasnow 1982: 21–22.

O Or read *r-sḫ*. *Nḫt-Ḥr* is possible, though *Ḥr* lacks the supralinear stroke; see *Demot. Nb.*, p. 654.

P The reading seems probable enough, but it is difficult to determine the meaning of the signature to the right of the main text. This papyrus was found rolled up within Chicago Hawara Papyrus 9, dated to March 9, 239 B.C. While in that papyrus no person of this name appears, there is an important figure in the archive during the same time period, namely, ʿnḫ-mr-wr pꜣ ʿꜣ sꜣ Pꜣ-tỉ-Wsỉr, Party A in the Rendell Papyrus of 232 B.C. It is possible, therefore, that this personage signed his name to the earlier papyrus.

Q Compare *Pa-Ḥr-sꜣ-ỉs.t* (*Demot. Nb.*, p. 403).

R *Mꜣʿ-Rʿ* is very doubtful; read perhaps *Sn.w*. For *Pꜣ-tỉ≠w* (*Demot. Nb.*, p. 296), see especially Thissen 1980: 166.

S *Ḥr-Ḏḥwty* is problematic; read possibly *Pꜣ-mr-ꜣḥ*.

T On the reading of the first name, see note XX for Chicago Hawara Papyrus 1. For *Pꜣ-tỉ-Rnn.t*, see *Demot. Nb.*, p. 321.

U *ỉnp* is very uncertain; the name is not in *Demot. Nb.*

V *mr* might be an element of the first name, but the transliteration of the entire line is dubious.

W See note L.

———————————

CHICAGO HAWARA PAPYRUS 5

Illustrations: Plates 25–29
Museum number: P. O.I. 25258
Maximum length: 114.5 cm
Maximum height: 40.0 cm
Physical description: Light brown in color. The roll is composed of seven papyrus sheets, averaging ca. 17.0 cm in width. The rightmost portion of the papyrus is damaged.[64]
Type: Sale document for one-eighteenth share of a house. The names of seven witnesses are inscribed to the left of the main text.
Party A: *ỉmn-m-ḥ₃.t*, son of *P₃-tỉ-n₃-ntr.w* and *ʿnḥ.t*
Party B: *ʿnḥ.t*, daughter of *S-n-wsr.t* and *Ta-Rnn.t*
Date: Regnal year is lost; the papyrus dates to reign of Ptolemy II Philadelphos (285–246 B.C.).
Scribe: *Prl*, son of *M₃ʿ-Rʿ*

TRANSLITERATION

LINES 1–10

1. [*ḥ₃.t-sp... ỉbt... n Pr-ʿ₃*] *ʿ.w.s.* ⌜*Pṭlwmys*⌝ *s₃ Pṭlwmys* **A** *ḏ ḥtmw-ntr wyt ỉmn-m-ḥ₃.t s₃ P₃-tỉ-n₃-ntr.w mw.t≠f ʿnḥ.t n s-ḥm.t ʿnḥ.t s₃.t n ḥtmw-ntr wyt S-n-Wsr(.t) mw.t≠s Ta-Rnn.t* **B** *tỉ≠t mtre ḥ₃.t≠y n p₃ ḥḏ n t₃y≠y tnỉ.t 1/18 n p₃y ʿ.wy*

2. [*nt qt ỉw≠f grg*] *n sy sb₃ nt ỉr mḥ-ntr 25 n rs r mḥt ỉw≠f ỉr mḥ-ntr 24 n ỉmnt (r) ỉ₃bt* **C** *ḥr p₃y≠f m₃ʿ rs ḥry ḥry* **D** *nt n ḥ.t-ntr Sbk-Rʿ* **E** *n₃ hyn.w n p₃y ʿ.wy nt ḥry rs p₃ ʿ.wy n ḥm-s-ʿnḫ* **F** *n ḥ.t-ntr n ḥ.t-ntr Sbk-Rʿ P₃-tỉ-ỉn-ḥr.t* **G** [*s₃*] *Nb-wʿb* **H** *r-tỉ≠w r-ḏb₃ ḥḏ ḥnʿ n₃ ʿ.wy.w*

3. *n šwt* **I** *n* [*... ʿn*]*ḥ-mr-wr s₃ Ṭ-Ḥp-n-ỉm≠w nt ḥr n₃y≠f ḥrṭ.w ỉw p₃ ḥr ỉwt≠w mḥt n₃ ʿ.wy.w n ḥm N.t* **J** *Ḥr-wḏ₃ s₃ Wn-nfr nt ḥr n₃y≠f ḥrṭ.w ḥnʿ ḥm N.t M₃ʿ-Rʿ s₃ P₃y≠f-ỉwỉw* **K** *nt ḥr n₃y≠f ḥrṭ.w hn n≠w ỉmnt n₃ ʿ.wy.w n ʿ-n-ỉr-ḥbs.w* **L** *(n) pr Sbk ỉy-m-ḥtp s₃ P₃-tỉ-Ḥr-p₃-šr-ỉs.t hn n≠w*

4. *ỉ₃bt n*[*₃ ʿ.wy.w n*] *ʿ-n-ỉr-ḥbs.w (n) pr Sbk Ḥm-n₃y≠f-šms.w* **M** *s₃ P₃-tỉ-Ḥr-p₃-šr-ỉs.t hn n≠w mtw≠t p₃ 1/18 n p₃y ʿ.wy nt ḥry ḥr p₃y≠f m₃ʿ rs ḥry* ⌜*ḥry*⌝ *nt ỉw n₃y≠f ḥy.w n₃y≠f hyn.w šḫ r-ḥry ṭ p₃ hrw r-ḥry bn* **N** *ỉw rḫ rmt nb n p₃ t₃ ỉnk n mỉ.t ỉr sḫry* **O** *n-ỉm≠f*

5. *bnr≠t* [*ṭ*] *p₃ hrw r-ḥry p₃ nt ỉw≠f ỉy r-ḥr≠t r-ḏb₃.ṭ≠f ỉw≠y r tỉ.t wy≠f r-ḥr≠t* **P** *ỉw≠y tm tỉ.t wy≠f r-ḥr≠t ỉw≠y r tỉ.t wy≠f r-ḥr≠t mtw≠y tỉ.t wʿb≠f n≠t r qnb.t nb.t mt nb n p₃ t₃* **Q** *mtw≠t šḫ nb r-ỉr≠w r-r≠w ḥnʿ šḫ nb r-ỉr≠w n p₃y≠y ỉt t₃y≠y mw.t r-r≠w ḥnʿ šḫ nb r-ỉr≠w n≠y r-r≠w*

---

64. A few minor misalignments due to shifts in the papyrus fragments are visible in the photograph; e.g., *s-ḥm.t* in line 1 (middle), and in the phrase *nt šm n rs* in line 7. Since the reading and sense are clear, it was thought best not to unglass and remount the papyrus.

6. ḥn[ʿ sḫ nb] nt ỉw≠y mȝʿ.k n-ỉm≠f n rn≠w **R** [mtw≠t s]t ḥnʿ pȝy≠w ḥp mtw≠t pȝ nt ỉw≠y
   mȝʿ.k n-ỉm≠f n rn≠w pȝ ʿnḫ pȝ ʿḥʿ-rṯ **S** nt ỉw≠w r tỉ.t s m-sȝ≠t r tỉ.t ỉr≠y s n rn≠w ỉw≠y
   r ỉr≠f mtw≠t šm r-ḥry ḥry tbn **T** n pr ḥr pȝ trt **U** n pȝy ʿ.wy nt ḥry mtw≠t pr r-ḫn

7. bnr [n tȝ] ḫy[t pȝ] **V** rȝ ʿȝ n [pȝy] ʿ.wy [nt] ḥry **W** ḥnʿ pȝy≠f myt pr nt šm n rs r pȝ ḫr
   mtw[≠t] ỉr n(?) ḥy nb n-ỉm≠f ỉrm nȝy[≠t] rmt nȝy≠t nk.w r-ḫ tȝy≠t tnỉ.t 1/18 nt ḥry ṯ pȝ
   ḥrw r-ḥry šʿ ḏ.t ỉw **X** s-ḥm.t Tȝ-tỉ-Wsỉr sȝ.t n Mnḫ-…-Ḫnsw **Y**

8. mw.t≠s Tȝ-rmt.t-Bȝst.t ḏ sḫ ỉ-ỉry mt nb nt ḥry ḥȝ.t≠y mtre.w n-ỉm≠w ỉw≠y m-sȝ ḫtmw-ntr
   wyt ỉmn-m-ḥȝt sȝ Pȝ-tỉ-nȝ-ntr.w mw.t≠f ʿnḫ[.t] nt ḥry n pȝ ḥp n pȝ sḫ n sʿnḫ ḥnʿ pȝ ḥp
   n pȝ sḫ **Z** n ḏbȝ-ḥḏ ỉw mḥ sḫ 2 [r-]ỉr≠f n≠y r ỉr n≠y pȝy≠w **AA** ḥp tw≠y wy.k

9. r **BB** s-ḥm.t ʿnḫ.t sȝ.t n ḫtmw-ntr wyt S-n-Wsr(.t) mw.t≠s Ta-Rnn.t nt ḥry n pȝ 1/18 n pȝy
   ʿ.wy nt ḥry ḥr pȝy≠f mȝʿ rs ḥry ḥry nt ỉw nȝy≠f ḥy.w nȝy≠f ḥyn.w sḫ r-ḥry mn mtw≠y nt
   nb mt nb n pȝ tȝ ỉ-ỉr n≠s n rn≠f n ṯ pȝ ḥrw r-ḥry ỉ(w)≠s

10. ḏ ʿn sḫ ỉ-ỉry mt nb nt ḥry ḥȝ.t≠y mtre.w n-ỉm≠w m-sḫ Prl sȝ Mȝʿ-Rʿ **CC**

WITNESS LIST AT UPPER LEFT END OF PAPYRUS

1. Nḫt-Sbk(?)…-Rnn.t(?) **DD**
2. Sṯȝ-ỉr.t-bn sȝ Ḫyrk(?) **EE**
3. … … **FF**
4. Ḏ-ḥr(?) sȝ Pȝ-tỉ-Sbk-ḥtp **GG**
5. Ḏ-… Mȝʿ-Rʿ-sȝ-Sbk(?) **HH**
6. … **II**
7. Mȝʿ-Rʿ(?) … -tȝ.wy(?) **JJ**

TRANSLATION

1. [Year… , month … of Pharaoh] l.p.h. ⌜Ptolemy,⌝ son of Ptolemy. The god's sealer and embalmer ỉmn-m-ḥȝ.t, son of Pȝ-tỉ-nȝ-ntr.w, whose mother is ʿnḫ.t, has declared to the woman
   ʿnḫ.t, daughter of the god's sealer and embalmer S-n-Wsr(.t), whose mother is Ta-Rnn.t:
   "You have caused my heart to agree to the money for my one-eighteenth share of this
   house

2. [which is built (and) provided] with beam and door, which measures 25 divine cubits from
   south to north, measuring 24 divine cubits from west (to) east upon its southern part, below
   and above, which (is) in the Temple of Sobek-Re. The neighbors of this aforesaid house
   are: south, the house of the temple sculptor of the temple of Sobek-Re Pȝ-tỉ-ỉn-ḥr.t, [son
   of] Nb-wʿb, which has been sold together with the houses

3. of the merchant … [… ʿn]ḫ-mr-wr, son of Ṯ-Ḥp-n-ỉm≠w, which belongs to his children, the
   street being between them; north, the houses of the servant of Neith, Ḥr-wḏȝ, son of Wn-
   nfr, which belong to his children together with the servant of Neith, Mȝʿ-Rʿ, son of Pȝy≠f-
   ỉwỉw, which belong to his children, adjoin them (sic); west, the houses of the chief tailor of
   the domain of Sobek ỉy-m-ḥtp, son of Pȝ-tỉ-Ḥr-pȝ-šr-ỉs.t, adjoin them;

4. east, th[e houses of] the chief tailor of the domain of Sobek *Ḥm-nȝy≠f-šms.w*, son of *Pȝ-tí-Ḥr-pȝ-šr-ís.t*, adjoin them. Yours is [the] one-eighteenth of this aforesaid house upon its southern part below and ⌈above⌉, the measurements and neighbors of which are written above, from this day onward. No one in the world, myself included, shall be able to exercise control over it

5. except you [from] today onward. As for him who might come against you concerning it, I will make him withdraw from you. If I do not make him withdraw from you, I will make him withdraw from [you] and I will clear it for you of any title deed or anything in the world. To you belong every document that was (ever) drawn up regarding them (*sic*) and every document that was (ever) drawn up for my father or my mother regarding them (*sic*) and every document which was (ever) drawn up for me regarding them (*sic*)

6. a[nd every document] by which I am entitled to it. Th[ey belong to you] together with the legal right conferred by them. To you belongs that by which I am entitled to it. The oath or the court proof that might be required of you in order to cause that I perform it concerning them, I shall perform it. You may go up (to) and down (from) the roof(?) on the stairway of this aforesaid house and you may go in

7. and out [of the] fore[hall, (by means of) the] main doorway of [this afore]said house and its house-path(?) which goes from the south to the street and [you] may make any alteration on it with [your] (work-)men and your materials in proportion to your aforesaid one-eighteenth share from today onward forever." Whereas the woman *Tȝ-tí-Wsír*, daughter of *Mnḫ-...-Ḫnsw*,

8. whose mother is *Tȝ-rmt.t-Bȝst.t*, says: "Write! Do everything aforesaid. I am agreed thereto, I having a claim on the aforesaid god's sealer and embalmer *ímn-m-ḥȝ.t*, son of *Pȝ-tí-nȝ-ntr.w*, whose mother is *ꜥnḫ[.t]*, through the legal right(s) of the document of annuity and the right(s) of the document of payment, making two documents in all, [which] he drew up for me, to execute for me the legal obligations conferred by them. I relinquish

9. to the aforesaid woman *ꜥnḫ.t*, daughter of the god's sealer and embalmer *S-n-Wsr(.t)*, whose mother is *Ta-Rnn.t*, the one-eighteenth of this aforesaid house upon its southern part, below and above, the measurements (and) the neighbors of which are written above. I do not have anything at all in the world against her in respect to it from today onward." She

10. says again: "Write! 'Do everything aforementioned. I am agreed thereto.'" Written by *Prl*, son of *Mȝꜥ-Rꜥ*.

COMMENTARY

A The papyrus dates to the reign of Ptolemy II Philadelphos (285–246 B.C.), but the regnal year is lost.

B Party A in this text is the brother of Party A (*ꜥnḫ-mr-wr*) in Chicago Hawara Papyrus 4.

C See figure 1 for a plan of the house.

D For the translation of *mȝ*ᶜ as "part, region," see M. Smith 1983: 199. "Below and above" seems to mean ground floor and above. The phrase also occurs in Chicago Hawara Papyri 7A, line 3; 9, lines 3 ("above and below"), 5; Rendell Papyrus, line 3.

E The property is within the temple precinct; for a discussion of private ownership of temple land, see Pestman 1969: 148; idem 1977: vol. 2, p. 106, n. 6.

   For the syncretistic deity Sobek-Re (*Glossar*, p. 423), see Bonnet 1952: 757.

F For the title *ḥm-s*ᶜ*nḫ* "sculptor," see *Glossar*, p. 303.

G For the name *Pȝ-ti-in-ḥr.t*, see *Demot. Nb.*, p. 286.

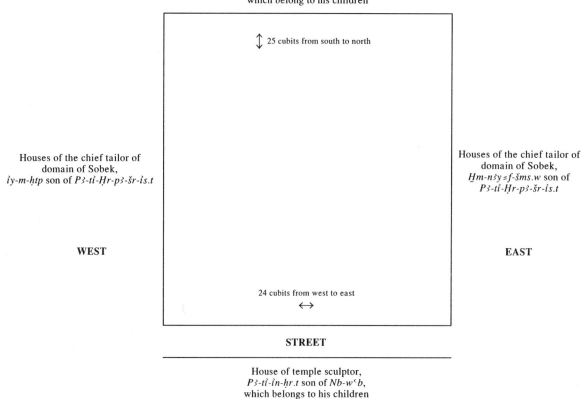

Figure 1. House Plan from Chicago Hawara Papyrus 5

H *Nb-w*ᶜ*b* is not in *Demot. Nb.*

I For the title *šwt* "merchant," see Hughes 1956: 80–88; another example is in Andrews 1990: 31 (line 8).

J For the title *ḥm N.t* "servant of Neith," see note F to Chicago Hawara Papyrus 3.

K *Demot. Nb.*, p. 568, has only one queried Demotic example of the name, but this reading in the Chicago Hawara text is secure.

ᴸ The title is not in *Glossar*.

ᴹ The name does not appear to be otherwise attested.

ᴺ The writing of *bn* is unusual.

ᴼ *sḥry* is written for the more common Demotic *sḥy* (*Glossar*, pp. 452–53).

ᴾ On this clause, see Pestman 1977: vol. 2, p. 16.

ꟴ On the legal nuances of *wˁb*, see Pestman 1984: 37.

ᴿ On the phrase, see Pestman 1977: vol. 2, p. 87, n. aa; Boswinkel and Pestman 1978: 47–48.

ˢ On *ˁḥˁ-rt* "court proof," see Mattha and Hughes 1975: 91; Pestman et al. 1985: 120, 132.

ᵀ In Demotic *tbn* seems to occur most often as part of a compound preposition *ḥr tbn* "near," which has been taken to be a possible variant of *ḥr twn*; see Thissen 1984: 131; de Cenival 1988: 76. In this context, however, *tbn* certainly means "roof, top" (*Glossar*, p. 624); see also Parker 1972a: 52.

ᵁ For *trt* "stair-case," see *Glossar*, p. 649; additional examples of the word are in Andrews 1990: 17, line 3; 66, line 2; see especially p. 67, note 8.

ⱽ For *hyꜣ.t/ḥyt* "forehall, porch, entrance hall" (*Glossar*, p. 377), see Pestman 1977: vol. 2, pp. 85–86, n. l; H. Smith and Tait 1983: 12–13.

ᵂ Perhaps understand *n* "through" before *pꜣ rꜣ ˁꜣ*, rendering "and you may go in and out [of the] foreha[ll (through) the] main doorway of [this afore]said house … ."

ˣ See note X to Chicago Hawara Papyrus 1 on such third party declarations. It is possible that *imn-m-ḥꜣ.t* and *Tꜣ-ti-Wsir* are married, but this is not certain. The annuity contract and document of sale mentioned by *Tꜣ-ti-Wsir* are not preserved in this archive. The house share might have been part of the security for a loan made by *Tꜣ-ti-Wsir* to *imn-m-ḥꜣ.t*, much as *ˁnḫ-mr-wr* had entered into an annuity arrangement with *Ḥr-ˁnḫ* and prepared for her a document of sale for one-third share of a house, as recorded in Chicago Hawara Papyrus 9, Copenhagen Hawara Papyrus 1 (= P. Carlsberg 34), and Copenhagen Hawara Papyrus 3 (= P. Carlsberg 36); see the discussion at Chicago Hawara Papyrus 9, note C, below.

ʸ *Mnḫ-…-Ḥnsw* is not in *Demot. Nb.*

ᶻ On the phrase *pꜣ ḥp n pꜣ sḫ*, see note Y to Chicago Hawara Papyrus 1.

ᴬᴬ The writing of *pꜣy⸗w* is unusual.

ᴮᴮ *Tꜣ-ti-Wsir* declares that she has no claim on *ˁnḫ.t* with regard to the one-eighteenth share of the house.

ᶜᶜ *Prl* is not in *Demot. Nb.* The son of this man is perhaps the scribe of Chicago Hawara Papyrus 6.

ᴰᴰ For *Nḫt-Sbk*, see *Demot. Nb.*, p. 657. *Rnn.t* is quite uncertain.

ᴱᴱ The reading of the entire line is dubious.

FF I can make nothing of these traces apart from the probable divine determinative at the end of the line.

GG For *Pꜣ-ti̯-Sbk-ḥtp*, see *Demot. Nb.*, p. 341.

HH For *MꜣꜤ-RꜤ-sꜣ-Sbk*, see *Demot. Nb.*, pp. 582–83.

II Read possibly *Sbk-gr sꜣ Ḥr*.

JJ Read perhaps rather *Mw.t* or *MꜣꜤ-RꜤ* at the end of the line.

CHICAGO HAWARA PAPYRUS 6

Illustrations: Plates 30–37
Museum number: P. O.I. 25388
Maximum length: 161.0 cm
Maximum height: 45.0 cm
Physical description: The roll, light brown in color, is composed of ten individual sheets of papyrus, averaging 16.5 cm in width. While the inscribed portions are excellently preserved, both ends have suffered damage.
Type: Annuity contract. A Greek docket is appended to the Demotic text.
Party A: *Pꜣ-tỉ-Wsỉr*, son of *ꜥnḫ-mr-wr* and *Nꜣ-nfr-ỉb-Ptḥ*
Party B: *Ḥr-ꜥnḫ*, daughter of *Mꜣꜥ-Rꜥ* and *Nb.t-tꜣ-ḥy*(?)
Date: August 23–September 10, 259 B.C. during the reign of Ptolemy II Philadelphos according to the Demotic date; the Greek docket is dated to September 10, 259 B.C.
Scribe: *Ḏ-Ḫnsw-ỉw≠f-ꜥnḫ*, son of *Prl* and (below Greek docket) *Pꜣ-tỉ-Wsỉr*, son of *ỉy-m-ḥtp*

TRANSLITERATION

LINES 1–4

1. *ḥꜣ.t-sp 26 ỉbt 3 šmm n Pr-ꜥꜣ Pṯlwmys sꜣ Pṯlwmys ỉrm pꜣy≠f šr Ptlwmys* **A** *wꜥb n ꜣlgsꜣntrs ỉrm nꜣ nṯr.w sn.w sn.w* (sic) *Mꜣts sꜣ Lmpn ỉw Mꜣṯlꜣ sꜣ.t n ꜣntrwgtws fy tn nb m-bꜣḥ ꜣrsynꜣ tꜣ mr-sn* **B** *ḏ ḥtmw-nṯr wyt Pꜣ-tỉ-Wsỉr sꜣ ꜥnḫ-mr-wr mw.t≠f Nꜣ-nfr-ỉb-Ptḥ*

2. *n s-ḥm.t Ḥr-ꜥnḫ sꜣ.t n ḥtmw-nṯr wyt Mꜣꜥ-Rꜥ mw.t≠s Nb.t-tꜣ-ḥy*(?)**C** *tỉ≠t mtre ḥꜣ.t≠y n ḥḏ 10 n nꜣ tnỉ.wt nt n pr-ḥḏ n Ptḥ n wtḫ r ḥḏ 9 qt 9 5/6 1/10 1/30 1/60 1/60 r ḥḏ 10 n nꜣ tnỉ.wt nt n pr-ḥḏ n Ptḥ n wtḫ ꜥn n pꜣy≠t sꜥnḫ mtw nꜣ ḥrṯ.w nt ỉ-ỉr≠t r ms.ṯ≠w n≠y nt nb nk nb nt mtw≠y ḥnꜥ nꜣ nt ỉw≠y r tỉ.t ḫpr≠w n*(?) *pr ꜣḥ ỉnḥ wrḥ bꜣk bꜣk.t ỉḥ ꜥꜣ tp-(n)-ỉꜣw.t nb ỉꜣw.t nb sḫ nb qnb.t nb*

3. *mt rmt-nmḥ.w nb n pꜣ tꜣ mtw≠y mtw≠y tỉ.t n≠t bt 36 n tꜣ hn 40 r ỉt 24 n tꜣ hn 40 r bt 36 n tꜣ hn 40 ꜥn ḥḏ 1 qt 2 n n nꜣ tnỉ.wt nt n pr-ḥḏ n Ptḥ n wtḫ r ḥḏ 1 qt 1 5/6 1/10 1/30 1/60 1/60 r ḥḏ 1 qt 2 n nꜣ tnỉ.wt nt n pr-ḥḏ n Ptḥ n wtḫ ꜥn n pꜣy≠t ꜥq-ḥbs ḥr rnp.t r pꜣ ꜥ.wy nt ỉw mr≠t s mtw≠t tꜣ nt nḥte r tꜣ wḏꜣ n pꜣy≠t ꜥq-ḥbs nt ỉ(w)≠s r ḫpr r-ꜥ.wy≠y mtw≠y tỉ.t s n≠t nt nb nk nb nt mtw≠y ḥnꜥ nꜣ nt ỉw≠y r tỉ.t ḫpr≠w tꜣ ỉwꜣ.t n pꜣy≠t sꜥnḫ*

4. *nt ḥry ỉw*(?) *bn ỉw≠y rḫ ḏ n≠t šp pꜣy≠t sꜥnḫ nt ḥry pꜣy≠t sw n wḥꜣ≠f ỉw≠y r tỉ.t s n≠t n-ỉm≠f ỉw≠w tỉ.t ꜥnḫ m-sꜣ≠t r ỉr≠f n≠y ỉ-ỉr≠t r ỉr≠f n≠y n pꜣ ꜥ.wy nt ỉw nꜣ wpṯy.w n-ỉm≠f m-sḫ Ḏ-Ḫnsw-ỉw≠f-ꜥnḫ sꜣ Prl* **D**

GREEK DOCKET

1. (Ἔτους) κζ Ἐπεὶφ ιθ πέπτωκεν εἰς κιβωτ[ὸν] ἐν Κροκοδίλων πόλει
2. τῆς Λίμνης δι᾽Ανδραγάθου τοῦ π[αρὰ] Φιλίνου.

3. (Ἔτους) κζ Ἐπεὶπ ιθ καὶ διὰ Κυρπίδ[ο]υ τοῦ ἐξειληφότος

4. καὶ διὰ Σωσιπάτρου τοῦ παρὰ Πολέμωνος.

BELOW GREEK DOCKET

r-sḫ Pȝ-tî-Wsîr sȝ îy-m-ḥtp **E**

WITNESS LIST

1. îy-m-ḥtp sȝ ꜥnḫ-smȝ-tȝ.wy **F**
2. Pȝ-tî-Sbk sȝ Ḥr-sȝ-îs.t(?) **G**
3. Pȝ-... sȝ Sy-Sbk(?) **H**
4. Ḥr-ḫb sȝ Sbk-ḥtp(?)
5. ... Ḏḥwty-î-îr-tî-s(?) **I**
6. ... **J**
7. Nḫt-... **K**
8. Sbk-... Ḏḥwty-...(?) **L**
9. Ḥr-sȝ-îs.t sȝ ... **M**
10. Sbk-... Wn-nfr(?) **N**
11. ... **O**
12. Pȝ-ḫȝꜥ⸗s ... **P**
13. ... sȝ Pȝ-rl **Q**
14. ... **R**
15. Pȝ-gwr(?) sȝ Twt(?) **S**
16. îmn-pȝ-ym sȝ Sbk-ḥtp **T**

SIGNATURE ON VERSO

[...]ḫ sȝ Mȝꜥ-Rꜥ(?) **U**

TRANSLATION

1. Year 26, third month of the season *shemu*, of Pharaoh Ptolemy, son of Ptolemy and his son, Ptolemy, the priest of Alexander and of the gods Adelphoi Adelphoi (*sic*) being Medeios, son of Lampon, while Matela, daughter of Androkades, is Kanephoros before Arsinoe Philadelphos. The god's sealer and embalmer *Pȝ-tî-Wsîr*, son of *ꜥnḫ-mr-wr*, whose mother is *Nȝ-nfr-îb-Ptḥ*, has declared

2. to the woman *Ḥr-ꜥnḫ*, daughter of the god's sealer and embalmer *Mȝꜥ-Rꜥ*, whose mother is *Nb.t-tȝ-ḥy*(?): "You have caused my heart to agree to the 10 silver (*deben*) (weighed) by the pieces which are in the Treasury of Ptah, of refined (silver), being 9 silver (*deben*) and 9, 5/6, 1/10, 1/30, 1/60, and 1/60 *kite*, being 10 silver (*deben*) (weighed) by the pieces which are in the Treasury of Ptah, of refined (silver), again, as your annuity. There belong to the children whom you will bear to me all of everything which I possess and that which I

shall acquire in(?) house, field, courtyard, building plot, male servant, female servant, cow, ass, every animal, every office, every document, every title deed, and

3. every matter of a freeman in the world belonging to me, and I shall give to you 36 (sacks) emmer (by the measure of) 40-*hin*, being 24 (sacks) barley (by the measure of) 40-*hin*, being 36 (sacks) emmer (by the measure of) 40-*hin* again and 1 silver (*deben*), 2 *kite* (weighed) by the pieces which are in the Treasury of Ptah, of refined (silver), being 1 silver (*deben*), 1 and 5/6, 1/10, 1/30, 1/60, and 1/60 *kite*, being 1 silver (*deben*) and 2 *kite* (weighed) by the pieces which are in the Treasury of Ptah, of refined (silver), again, for your subsistence each year at whatever house you desire. You are the one authorized with regard to the arrears of your subsistence which shall be to my debit, and I am to give it to you. All of everything that I possess and that which I shall acquire is the pledge of your annuity

4. aforesaid. I shall not be able to say to you: 'Take your aforesaid annuity,' but on whatever day you desire it, I will give it to you. If an oath is required of you to be taken for me, it is in the house in which the judges are that you are to take it for me." Written by *Ḏ-Ḥnsw-iw=f-ʿnḫ*, son of *Prl*.

GREEK DOCKET

First Hand   (Year) 27, Epeiph 19, it (sc. the agreement) has been deposited in the (official) chest at Crocodilopolis of the Lake District by Andragathos, the agent of Philinos.

Second Hand   (Year) 27, Epeip (*sic*) 19, and by Kuprides, the tax-farmer(?), and by Sosipatros, the agent of Polemon.

BELOW GREEK DOCKET

Written by *Pȝ-ti-Wsir*, son of *iy-m-ḥtp*

COMMENTARY ON THE DEMOTIC TEXT

A The date of the Demotic text is equivalent to August 23–September 10, 259 B.C. during the reign of Ptolemy II Philadelphos. According to the date of the Greek docket, the document was registered on September 10, 259 B.C.; compare Pestman 1967: 21.

B The priest of Alexander and the deified Ptolemies is Μήδειος, son of Λάμπων, while the Kanephoros of Arsinoe Philadelphos is Μάτελα (or Μήταλα), daughter of Ἀναδροκάδης (or Ἀνδρωκάδης); see Clarysse and van der Veken 1983: 6–7, who, in fact, cite this text in note 32. On the basis of the certain *Lmpn* in the Demotic, the reading Λάμπων is supported by this papyrus, as opposed to the alternative Λαάγων also mentioned by Clarysse and van der Veken.

C *Pȝ-ti-Wsir* is clearly the husband of *Ḥr-ʿnḫ*. The latter first appears here but is prominent in the remainder of the documents published in this volume.

I have adopted the queried reading of *Demot. Nb.*, p. 700, *Nb.t-tȝ-ḥy*(?), for the mother of *Ḥr-ʿnḫ*. It could be an unetymological writing of *Nb.t-ḥ.t* (Old Coptic Νεβθω), but this deity hardly seems to occur in personal names; see Zauzich 1988: 96–97. A very doubtful example is in Chicago Hawara Papyrus 2, verso column 1, line 10.

D *Prl* is perhaps the scribe of Chicago Hawara Papyrus 5.

E Or *m-sḫ*. This individual does not seem to be attested elsewhere in these texts. *Pꜣ-tꜣ-Wsir* might have been the Egyptian scribe responsible for the writing of the second Greek docket; see the commentary on the docket.

F For *ꜥnḫ-smꜣ-tꜣ.wy*, see *Demot. Nb.*, p. 105.

G *Ḥr* is very crudely written in the name *Ḥr-sꜣ-is.t*.

H Perhaps read the first name as *Pꜣ-wp.ṯ*(?); see *Demot. Nb.*, p. 494.

I *Ḏḥwty* is uncertain, but the name does seem to end in *i-ir-ti-s*.

J Perhaps … *sꜣ it-ntr Pꜣ-tꜣ-Wsir*.

K *Ḥr-wr* might be a component of the father's name.

L Possibly *Ḏḥwty-mꜣꜥ* or *Ḏḥwty-iw*(?).

M The father's name might end with *Ḥr*.

N *Wn-nfr*(?) might be preceded by *sꜣ*, though *pꜣ* is also possible.

O Perhaps *Pꜣ-tꜣ≠w sꜣ Ḥr-ḫb*.

P For *Pꜣ-ḫꜣꜥ≠s*, see *Demot. Nb.*, p. 207.

Q For *Pꜣ-rl*, see *Pꜣ-rr* (*Demot. Nb.*, p. 198).

R The first name is perhaps *Pa-pꜣ-ḫr*, comparing *Pa-pꜣ-ḫr* (*Demot. Nb.*, p. 366).

S The reading of this line is very doubtful.

T For *imn-pꜣ-ym*, see *Demot. Nb.*, p. 63.

U The first name is possibly […]-*ꜥnḫ*. The individual seems to be otherwise unattested in these documents.

COMMENTARY ON THE GREEK DOCKET[65]

GENERAL REMARKS

The docket, written below the far right of the Demotic text, is in two parts. The first two lines were written in a tiny, very fine hand. Two lines were then added by a second writer, using a rush pen, suited to the writing of Demotic, not the reed pen generally used for writing Greek; on this phenomenon in the third century B.C. Fayum, see Tait 1988: 477–81; Clarysse 1993: 186–201; D. Thompson 1992b: 39–52, and specifically p. 47; eadem 1992a: 324, each time referring to the documents in Harrauer 1987. This would be one of several signs that this writer was an

---

65. According to Pierce (1972: 179), "Greek dockets are found appended to Demotic instruments beginning with the reign of Ptolemy II Philadelphos." On this subject, see also Pestman 1985a: 17–23.

Egyptian attempting to write Greek.[66] Note, additionally, the spelling of Epeiph with two *pi*s and the failure to provide a cross-bar for *theta* in the numeral 19 (and the absence of a superstroke over the numeral). For early archival dockets such as this and the dockets in Chicago Hawara Papyrus 9 and the Rendell Papyrus (translated in the *Appendix*), see Pierce 1972: 180–83. The deciphered names in the Chicago Hawara dockets resemble those in the Zenon archives, but the absence of sufficient detail precludes confident prosopographical identifications.

COMMENTS ON LINES

1 (3). Year 27 (of Ptolemy II Philadelphos). On the assumption that the Greek scribe reckoned according to the financial year, Epeiph 19 corresponds to September 10, 259.[67] As subject of the verb of deposit, understand τὸ συνάλλαγμα "the agreement (sc. in writing)"; compare Pierce 1972: 180–83.

2. τῆς Λίμνης "the Lake District" is the designation of the Fayum before its renaming as the Arsinoite Nome; see Grenfell and Hunt 1907: 350; Calderini and Daris 1978: 202 s.v.

3. Κυρπίδ[ο]υ (read Κυπρίδου) is tentatively suggested by Willy Clarysse; it looks far from impossible.

ἐξειληφότος is the participle often applied to tax farmers; see Preisigke 1925: 447, s.v. ἐκλαμβάνω.

4. Πολέμωνος was read by Willy Clarysse.

---

66. This might in fact explain the otherwise puzzling signature directly below the Greek docket, namely, "Written by *Pꜣ-ti-Wsir*, son of *iy-m-ḥtp*."

67. See *A Note on Dates,* p. 6, above.

CHICAGO HAWARA PAPYRUS 7A–B

Illustrations: Plates 38–41
Museum number: P. O.I. 25255
Maximum length: 136 cm
Maximum height: 35 cm
Physical description: The roll is made up of seven sheets of papyrus, averaging 20 cm in width
Type: Text 7A is a provisional sale for one-third share of house; text 7B is a mortgage agreement for this same one-third of a house. Associated with these documents is Chicago Hawara Greek Papyrus 7C, a tax receipt found rolled up within Chicago Hawara Papyrus 7.
Party A: *Pa-tr* (= *P3-ti-n3-ntr.w*), son of *ʿnḫ-mr-wr* and *ʿnḫ.t*
Party B: *Sbk-ḥtp*, son of *Pa-w3* and *Ḥr-ʿnḫ*
Date: July 21, 245 B.C.
Scribe: Astronomer of Sobek, *Sṯ3=w-t3-wty*, son of *P3-ti-Wsir*

TRANSLITERATION OF CHICAGO HAWARA PAPYRUS 7A

LINES 1–10

1. *ḥ3.t-sp 2.t ibt 2 šmm ⌈sw⌉ 2 Pr-ʿ3 Pṯlwmys ʿnḫ ḏ.t s3 Pṯlwmys irm 3rsn3 n3 ntr.w sn.w nt ir ḥ3.t-sp 3.t n n3 Wynn.w* **A** *wʿb n 3lgs3ntrs irm n3 ntr.w sn.w 3rkylws s3 ṯym3 iw 3rsyn3 s3.t n Pwlmwqrts fy tn nb*

2. *m-b3ḥ 3rsn3 t3 mr-sn* **B** *ḏ ḥtmw-ntr wyt Pa-tr s3 ʿnḫ-mr-wr mw.t=f ʿnḫ.t n ḥtmw-ntr wyt Sbk-ḥtp s3 Pa-w3 mw.t=f Ḥr-ʿnḫ* **C** *ti=k mtry ḥ3.t=y n p3 ḥḏ n t3y=y tni.t 1/3 n p3y ʿ.wy nt qt iw=f grg n sy sb3 nt ir mḥ-ntr 18 n rs r mḥt iw=f ir mḥ-ntr*

3. *19 n imnt r i3bt* **D** *ḥr p3y=f m3ʿ rs ḥry ḥry* **E** *nt n tmi Sbk Ḥ.t-wr.t nt ḥr p3 ʿt mḥṯ n t3 ḥny Mr-wr ḫn p3 tš 3rsn3* **F** *n3 hyn.w n p3y ʿ.wy r-ti=y n=k p3y=f 1/3 r-ḏb3 ḥḏ nt ḥry rs p3 ʿ.wy n ḥtmw-ntr wyt Sbk-ḥtp s3 Pa-sy iw p3 ḥr*

4. *iwt=w mḥt p3 ʿ.wy n s-ḥm.t T3-ḫn3* **G** *s3.t n ḥtmw-ntr wyt ʿnḫ-mr-wr ḥn n=f imnt p3 inḥ n ḥtmw-ntr wyt M3ʿ-Rʿ s3 P3-šr-(n)-t3-iḥ.t nt ḥr n3y=f ḥrṯ.w ḥn n=f i3bt p3y=y ʿ.wy ḥn n=f mtw=k p3 1/3 n p3y ʿ.wy nt ḥry ḥr p3y=f m3ʿ rs ḥry ḥry ḥn ʿ p3 1/3 n t3y=y nsy.t* **H**

5. *nt ir n=f imnt* **I** *nt ḥry nt iw n3y=w ḥy.w n3y=w hyn.w sḫ r-ḥry ṯ p3 hrw (r)-ḥry bn iw rḫ rmt nb n p3 t3 ink m-mi.t ir sḫy n-im=w bnr=k n ṯ p3 hrw (r)-ḥry p3 nt iw=f r iy r-r=k r-ḏb3.ṯ=w iw=y r ti.t wy=f r-r=k iw=y tm ti.t wy=f r-r=k iw=y r ti.t wy=f r-r=k mtw=y ti.t wʿb=w n=k*

6. *r qnb.t nb mt nb n p3 t3 mtw=k sḫ nb r-ir=w r-r=w ḥn ʿ sḫ nb r-ir=w n p3y=y it t3y=y mw.t r-r=w ḥn ʿ sḫ nb r-ir=w n=y r-r=w ḥn ʿ sḫ nb nt iw=y m3ʿ.k n-im=w n rn=w* **J** *mtw=k st ḥn ʿ p3y=w ḥp mtw=k p3 nt iw=y m3ʿ.k n-im=f n rn=w p3 ʿnḫ p3 ʿḥʿ-rt nt iw=w (r) ti.t s m-s3=k r ti.t ir=y s n rn=w iw=y*

7. *r ir≠f mtw≠k šm r-ḥry ḫry tbn n pr ḥr p3 trt n p3y ʿ.wy nt ḥry mtw≠k pr r-ḫn bnr n t3*
   ḫytᴷ p3 r3 ʿ3 n3 r3.w n pr n p3y ʿ.wy p3y inḥ nt ḥry mtw≠k ir ḥy nb ḫn≠w irm n3y≠k
   rmt.w n3y≠k nk.r-ḫ t3y≠k tni.t 1/3 nt ḥry ṯ p3 hrw r-ḥry ʿn

8. *[i]wᴸ s-ḥm.tᴹ Ta-Rnn.t s3.t n ḥtmw-ntr wyt Sbk-iw mw.t≠s N3-nfr-Sbkᴺ ḏ šḫ i-iryᴼ mt*
   nb nt ḥry ḫ3.t≠y mtre.w n-im≠w i-ir≠y ir p3y ʿš nt ḥry iw≠y m-s3 ḥtmw-ntr wyt Pa-tr s3
   ʿnḫ-mr-wr mw.t≠f ʿnḫ.t nt ḥry n p3 ḥp n p3 šḫ (n) sʿnḫ r-ir≠f n≠y mtw≠f ir n≠y

9. *[p3y]≠f ḥp iw≠y wy.ṯ r ḥtmw-ntr wyt Sbk-ḥtp s3 Pa-w3 nt ḥry n p3 1/3 n p3y ʿ.wy nt ḥry*
   ḫnʿ p3 1/3 n t3 nsy.(t) ḥr p3y≠w m3ʿ rs ḫry ḥry nt iw n3y≠w ḥy.w n3y≠w hyn.w šḫ r-ḥry
   mn mtw≠y mt nb n p3 t3 i-ir n≠k n rn≠w ṯ p3 hrw r-ḥry ʿn m-šḫ imy-wnw.t n Sbk

10. *Sṯ3≠w-t3-wty s3 P3-ti-Wsirᴾ*

TRANSLATION OF CHICAGO HAWARA PAPYRUS 7A

1. Year 2, second month of the season *shemu*, ⌈day⌉ 2 of Pharaoh Ptolemy, who lives forever, son of Ptolemy and Arsinoe, the gods Adelphoi, which is year three of the Greeks, the priest of Alexander and the gods Adelphoi being Archelaos, son of Damas, while Arsinoe, daughter of Polemokrates, is the Kanephoros

2. before Arsinoe Philadelphos. The god's sealer and embalmer *Pa-tr*, son of *ʿnḫ-mr-wr*, whose mother is *ʿnḫ.t*, has declared to the god's sealer and embalmer *Sbk-ḥtp*, son of *Pa-w3*, whose mother is *Ḥr-ʿnḫ*: "You have caused my heart to agree to the money for my one-third share of this house which is built, it being provided with beam and door, which measures 18 god's cubits from south to north and measures

3. 19 god's cubits from west to east, upon its southern part, below and above, which is in the Sobek town of Hawara, which is on the northern shore of the Canal of Moeris, in the Nome of Arsinoe. The neighbors of this house, of which I have sold to you its aforesaid one-third, are: south, the house of the god's sealer and embalmer *Sbk-ḥtp*, son of *Pa-sy*, the street being

4. between them; north, the house of the woman *T3-ḥn3*, daughter of the god's sealer and embalmer *ʿnḫ-mr-wr*, adjoins it; west, the courtyard of the god's sealer and embalmer *M3ʿ-Rʿ*, son of *P3-šr-(n)-t3-iḥ.t*, which is in the possession of his children, adjoins it; east, my house adjoins it. Yours is the one-third of this aforesaid house upon its southern part, below and above, together with the aforesaid one-third of my bench,

5. which is on its western (side), the measurements and neighbors of which are written above, from today onward. No one in the world, myself included, shall be able to exercise control over them except you from today onward. As for him who might come against you regarding them, I will make him withdraw from you. If I do not make him withdraw from you, I will make him withdraw from you, and I will clear them for you

6. of any title deed or anything in the world. To you belongs every document that was (ever) drawn up regarding them, and every document that was (ever) drawn up for my father and my mother concerning them, and every document that was (ever) drawn up for me regarding them and every document by which I am entitled to them. They are yours together with the legal rights conferred by them. To you belongs that by which I am entitled through

them. Any oath or court proof that might be required of you in order to cause that I execute it concerning them, I

7. shall perform it. You may go up (to) and down (from) the roof on the stairway of this aforesaid house and you may go in and out of the forehall and the main doorway, and of the exits of this house and this aforesaid courtyard. You may make any alterations on them with your (work-)men and your materials in proportion to your aforesaid one-third share from today onward also."

8. [Wh]ereas the woman *Ta-Rnn.t*, daughter of the god's sealer and embalmer *Sbk-iw*, whose mother is *N3-nfr-Sbk*, says: "Write! Do everything above. I am agreed thereto. It is because I have claim on the aforesaid god's sealer and embalmer *Pa-tr*, son of *'nh-mr-wr*, whose mother is *'nh.t*, for the legal rights conferred by the document of annuity which he made for me that I give this consent above, and he shall execute for me

9. the legal obligations conferred by it, but I cede claim on the aforesaid god's sealer and embalmer, *Sbk-htp*, son of *Pa-w3*, for the aforesaid one-third of this house and the one-third of the bench upon their southern part, below and above, the measurements and neighbors of which are written above. I do not have anything in the world against you in regard to them from today onward also." Written by the astronomer of Sobek,

10. *St3=w-t3-wty*, son of *P3-ti-Wsir*.

COMMENTARY ON CHICAGO HAWARA PAPYRUS 7A

A The date is equivalent to July 21, 245 B.C. during the reign of Ptolemy III Euergetes I. This agrees also with the date of the Chicago Hawara Greek Papyrus 7C.

The phrase "which is year three of the Greeks" refers to the financial year; see Pestman 1967: 6.

B For the priest of Alexander and the deified Ptolemies, and the Kanephoros of Arsinoe Philadelphos, see Clarysse and van der Veken 1983: 10–11 (no. 46).

'nh d.t is written in a cartouche.

C Neither *Pa-tr* (Party A) nor *Sbk-htp* (Party B) has hitherto appeared in these papyri. The mother of *Sbk-htp*, namely, *Hr-'nh*, is Party B in the annuity contract (Chicago Hawara Papyrus 6), dated to 259 B.C. However, Party A in the annuity contract is *P3-ti-Wsir*; in this document she is described as the wife of *Pa-w3*.

Pa-tr is not found in *Demot. Nb.*, but the reading of the name is assured by Πατῆρις in Chicago Hawara Greek Papyrus 7C, line 9. The same one-third share of the house is mortgaged by a man named *'nh-mr-wr*, son of *P3-ti-n3-ntr.w* and *Ta-Rnn.t* in Chicago Hawara Papyrus 9, dated to March 9, 239 B.C.[68] Since *Pa-tr* is also married to a woman named *Ta-Rnn.t* (Chicago Hawara Papyrus 7B, line 23) and since he is the son of a man named *'nh-mr-wr*, it is probable that *Pa-tr* is a variant form of *P3-ti-n3-ntr.w*. It is hardly possible that he is identical with the *P3-ti-n3-ntr.w* who appears in Chicago Hawara Papyri 3 (311/310 B.C.), 4 (292 B.C.), and 5 (ca. 285–246 B.C.). However, it could well be the case that he is the grandson of that *P3-*

---

68. The measurements and boundaries for the house in Chicago Hawara Papyrus 9 differ slightly from those given in this papyrus.

tỉ-nꜣ-ntr.w. This is rendered more probable, because *Pꜣ-tỉ-nꜣ-ntr.w* had a son called *ꜥnḫ-mr-wr*, who appears in Chicago Hawara Papyrus 3 (311/310 B.C.), 4 (292 B.C.), and 6 (259 B.C.). I would suggest, then, that this *ꜥnḫ-mr-wr* is the father of the *Pa-tr* (= *Pꜣ-tỉ-nꜣ-ntr.w*) of this text. It is more difficult to identify the mother of *Pa-tr*. This *ꜥnḫ-mr-wr* is known to have been married to *Nꜣ-nfr-ỉb-Ptḥ* (e.g., Chicago Hawara Papyrus 3), and we must therefore assume that *ꜥnḫ.t* is a later (or earlier) wife of this man.

Chicago Hawara Papyrus 7B and Chicago Hawara Greek Papyrus 7C make it clear that the sale document 7A is in fact part of a mortgage transaction, i.e., the one-third share is the security for a loan. On Egyptian mortgages and provisional sales, see Pierce 1972: 119–32; Pestman 1983: 296–302.

D This is probably identical with the second house described in Chicago Hawara Papyrus 4. See figure 2 for the plan of the house.

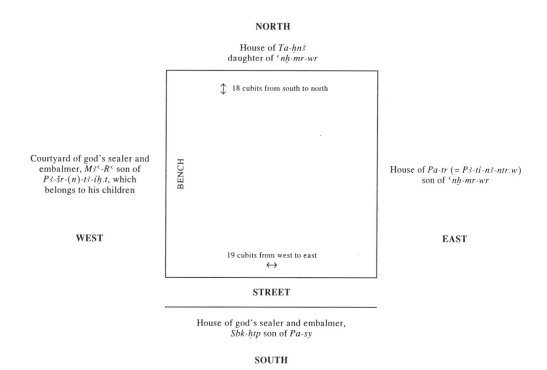

NORTH

House of *Ta-ḫnꜣ*
daughter of *ꜥnḫ-mr-wr*

↕ 18 cubits from south to north

Courtyard of god's sealer and embalmer, *Mꜣꜥ-Rꜥ* son of *Pꜣ-šr-(n)-tꜣ-ỉḥ.t*, which belongs to his children

BENCH

House of *Pa-tr* (= *Pꜣ-tỉ-nꜣ-ntr.w*) son of *ꜥnḫ-mr-wr*

WEST

EAST

19 cubits from west to east
↔

STREET

House of god's sealer and embalmer, *Sbk-ḥtp* son of *Pa-sy*

SOUTH

Figure 2. House Plan from Chicago Hawara Papyrus 7A

E The same phrase appears in Chicago Hawara Papyrus 5, line 2, and Rendell Papyrus, line 3.

F This is the most extended description of a house location in the Chicago Hawara papyri. For the phrase "north shore of the Canal of Moeris," see Reymond 1973: 13–14; Cruz-Uribe 1992: 63–66; Beinlich 1991: 79–80; de Cenival 1968: 48.

For an extensive discussion of *tš* "nome," see Vleeming 1991: 37–40.

G On the name *Tꜣ-ḫnꜣ*, see Hughes 1980: 63.

H On *nsy.t* "bench, mastaba" (*Glossar*, p. 228), see Husson 1983: 237. In line 9 the determinative is clearly the house sign. A "bench" (*nsy.t*) also appears in the Rendell Papyrus, lines 3 and 7.

I Contrast the markedly hieratic writing of *ỉmnt* in line 4 with the characteristically Demotic spelling here.

J The man-with-hand-to-mouth determinative is very strangely written in *rn≠w*; compare the more regular writing later in the same line. One is tempted to read *rn nꜣ.w*.

K Note the very prominent *t* in *ḥyt*.

L A trace of the reed leaf is preserved after the break.

M The writing of *s-ḥm.t* is also in the hieratic fashion.

N *Ta-Rnn.t* is the wife of *Pa-tr*, if the identification of *Pa-tr* with *Pꜣ-tỉ-nꜣ-ntr.w* is correct. She has a claim on his property due to an annuity contract that he had drawn up for her. That text is not preserved among the Chicago papyri.

For *Nꜣ-nfr-Sbk*, see *Demot. Nb.*, p. 619.

O Nims (1968: 96) discusses the clause beginning with *ỉ-ỉry*.

P The same scribe wrote Chicago Hawara Papyri 7B and 8 (243 B.C.).

TRANSLITERATION OF CHICAGO HAWARA PAPYRUS 7B

LINES 1–28

1. *n* **A** *ḥꜣ.t-sp 2.t nt ỉr ḥꜣ.t-sp 3.t [ỉbt 2] šmm sw 2 Pr-ꜥꜣ Pṯlwmys*

2. *ꜥnḫ ḏ.t sꜣ [P]ṯlwmys ỉrm ꜣrsnꜣ*

3. *nꜣ ntr.w sn.w nꜣ [ḥn].w* **B** *r-ỉr ḥtmw-ntr wyt Pa-tr sꜣ*

4. *ꜥnḫ-mr-wr ỉrm [mỉ-nn?]* **C** *Sbk-ḥtp sꜣ Pa-wꜣ ỉw Pa-tr sꜣ*

5. *ꜥnḫ-mr-wr nt ḥry ḏ n Sbk-ḥtp sꜣ Pa-wꜣ nt ḥry wn*

6. *wꜥ sḫ (n) ḏbꜣ-ḥḏ wꜥ sḫ (n) wy r pꜣ 1/3 n wꜥ ꜥ.wy wꜥ.t*

7. *nsy(.t) n Ḥ.t-wr.t ỉw mḥ sḫ 2 tỉ≠y st r-ḏr.t≠k*

8. *ḥr ḥn* **D** *ḏ tỉ≠k n≠y ḥḏ 1 qt 6 n sttr.t sttr 8*

9. *r ḥḏ 1 qt 6 ꜥn st n ḥw r-ḥr≠y tn ḏbꜥ.t 1/2 1/4 m-sꜣ*

10. *wꜥ.t sttr ḥr ỉbt nt ỉr ḏbꜥ.t 6 ḥr ỉbt ṯ ḥꜣ.t-sp 2.t nt ỉr ḥꜣ.t-sp 3.t*

11. *ỉbt 2 šmm šꜥ pꜣ mḥ n rnp.t 2.t r ỉbt 24 1/3* **E** *r*

12. *rnp.t 2.t ꜥn ḥr ỉr pꜣy≠w ḥw n nꜣ sw.w nt ḥry*

13. *ḥḏ 1 qt 2 n ḥmt tn ḏbꜥ.t 24 r wꜥ.t sttr* **F** *ỉw mḥ*

14. *pꜣ ḏꜣḏꜣ ỉrm pꜣ ḥw ḥḏ 2 qt 8* **G** *pꜣy≠w wn*

15. *pꜣ ḏꜣḏꜣ ḥḏ sp-2* **H** *ḥḏ 1 qt 6 tꜣ ms.t* **I** *ḥḏ 1 qt 2 ỉw mḥ*

16. *ḥḏ 2 qt 8 [ỉ]w≠f ḫpr ỉw bn-(p)≠y tỉ.t n≠k pꜣy ḥḏ 2 qt 8*

17. *nt ḥry šꜥ pꜣ [m]ḥ n tꜣ rnp.t 2.t nt ḥry mn mtw≠y*

18. *mt nb (n) p3 t3 r-ir n=k n rn n3 sḫ.w nt ḥry ḥn[ʿ] p3y=w*

19. *ḥp iw=f ḫpr r ti̯=y n=k p3y ḥd 2 qt 8 nt ḥry*

20. *šʿ p3 mḥ n n3 sw.w nt ḥry iw=k r ti̯.t n=y* **J** *n3 sḫ.w nt ḥry ḥnʿ p3y=w*

21. *ḥp iw=w ḏ n p3 s 2 sḫ i-iry mt nb nt ḥry*

22. *ḥ3.t=n mtr.w n-im=w mn qrf* **K** *(n) ḥn mtw=n <iw Pa-tr nt ḥry ḏ>* **L**

23. *my n3 sḫ.w nt ḥry n s-ḥm.t Ta-Rnn.t t3y=y ḥm.t* **M**

24. *n p3 hrw n ti̯.t n=k n3 ḥḏ(.w) nt iw=y (r) ir=f iw=f ḏ ʿn*

25. *p3 ḥḏ nt iw=y r ti̯.t s n=k irm t3y=f ms.t ḥn n3 ḥḏ(.w)*

26. *nt ḥry (n) ḥ3.t p3y sw-hrw nt ḥry iw=w r šp=w n-ḏr.ṯ=y*

27. *mtw=w ti̯.t ṯ[=w st] ḥn n3 ḥḏ(.w) nt ḥry ʿn m-sḫ*

28. *Sṯ3=w-[t3]-wty s3 P3-ti̯-Wsir* **N**

TRANSLATION OF CHICAGO HAWARA PAPYRUS 7B

1. In(?) year 2, which is year 3, [second month] of the season *shemu*, day 2, of Pharaoh Ptolemy,

2. who lives forever, son of [P]tolemy and Arsinoe,

3. the gods Adelphoi. The [agreement]s which the god's sealer and embalmer *Pa-tr*, son of

4. *ʿnḫ-mr-wr*, made with [the like-titled(?)] *Sbk-ḥtp*, son of *Pa-w3*, *Pa-tr*, son of

5. *ʿnḫ-mr-wr*, aforesaid, saying to *Sbk-ḥtp*, son of *Pa-w3*, aforesaid: "There are

6. a document of payment and a document of cession for the one-third of a house and a

7. bench in Hawara, so as to make two documents. I have put them in your hand

8. upon agreement because you have given to me 1 silver (*deben*) and 6 *kite*, in *staters*, 8 *staters*,

9. being 1 silver (*deben*) and 6 *kite* again. They increase my debit at the rate of 3/4 *obols* for

10. each *stater* per month, which makes 6 *obols* per month, beginning with year 2, which is year 3,

11. the second month of the season *shemu*, until the completion of two years, being 24 and 1/3 months, being

12. two years again. There increase amounts in the aforesaid period

13. to 1 silver (*deben*) and 2 *kite*, in copper at the rate of 24 *obols* to 1 *stater*, making in all,

14. the principal and interest, 2 silver (*deben*) and 8 *kite*. The details thereof:

15. the principal in real silver, 1 silver (*deben*) and 6 *kite*; the interest, 1 silver (*deben*) and 2 *kite*, making in all

16. 2 silver (*deben*) and 8 *kite*. [I]f it happens that I have not given to you these 2 silver (*deben*) and 8 *kite*

17. aforesaid by the end of the two years aforesaid, I have no

18. claim in the world against you with respect to the aforesaid documents and the

19. legal rights which they convey. If, however, it happens that I have given to you these 2 silver (*deben*) and 8 *kite* aforesaid

20. by the end of the period aforesaid, you shall give back to me the aforesaid documents and the

21. legal rights which they convey." Whereas they say, the two parties: "Write! Do everything above.

22. We are agreed thereto. There is no subterfuge in any agreement of ours." <Whereas *Pa-tr*, aforesaid, says:>

23. "Give the aforesaid documents to the woman *Ta-Rnn.t*, my wife,

24. on the day on which I shall give the money to you." Whereas he says also:

25. "The money which I shall give back to you with its interest out of the money

26. aforesaid before this aforesaid date, it will be accepted from me

27. and one will cause that [it be] deducted from the aforesaid (total sum of) money also." Written by

28. *Sṯꜣ=w-[tꜣ]-wty*, son of *Pꜣ-ti-Wsir*.

COMMENTARY ON CHICAGO HAWARA PAPYRUS 7B

A For the possible reading *n ḥꜣ.t-sp*, see Pestman 1980: 22. Year 3 refers to the financial year.

B On *ḥn* "agreement" (*Glossar*, p. 276), see Hughes 1980: 65–66, who quotes this text (and particularly discusses the phrase *ḥr ḥn* in line 8); Shore 1980: 121–23; Chauveau 1991: 107.

C A short writing of *mi-nn* (*Glossar*, p. 152) fills the space admirably. On this compound, see now Vleeming 1991: 251.

D The lender himself receives custody of the two documents confirming possession of the one-third share of the house. They are to be given back to the borrower upon repayment of the loan. There is no mention of a third party, the *ꜥrbt* "trustee" who often takes custody of documents; for which, see Shore 1980: 121. Interestingly enough, *Pa-tr* specifies in line 23 of this text that the documents are to be given to his wife, *Ta-Rnn.t*, upon repayment of the debt.

E I.e., twelve months plus the ten epagomenal days. The original loan is 1 silver (*deben*) and 6 *kite*. The amount is consistent with contemporary mortgages. In 237 B.C. a house in Thebes, for example, was mortgaged for 1 silver (*deben*) and 5 *kite* for a year; see El-Amir 1959: second part, p. 36. The average cost of a house in the third century B.C. is approximately 200 silver drachmas.[69] In the accompanying Greek document (Chicago Hawara Greek Papyrus 7C), the one-third share of the house was apparently assessed as 20 drachmas, implying a total cost of 60 drachmas; see the note to line 10 of that text. According to the Demotic documents, how-

69. See Reekmans 1948: 15–43, who mentions the average cost of a house on p. 24. On the difficult subject of currency, see now the important article of Clarysse and Lanciers 1989: 117–32.

ever, the original loan is 8 *staters* = 1 silver (*deben*) and 6 *kite* = 32 silver drachmas, while the final payment, including interest, is 2 (*deben*) and 8 *kite* = 56 silver drachmas.

F For the conversion formula, see Boswinkel and Pestman 1982: 89, n. w; Vittmann 1982: 81.

G The rate of interest is therefore 37.5% per year. This is high but does not seem to be impossible in Ptolemaic Egypt.[70]

H For the phrase *ḥḏ sp-2*, see Pestman 1972: 33–36.

I On *ms.t* "interest" (*Glossar*, p. 178), see Boswinkel and Pestman 1982: 134.

J *r tỉ.t n⸗y* is written above the line.

K For *qrf* "deceit" (*Glossar*, p. 544), see de Cenival 1985a: 204. Compare the use of *glꜥ / gyl* "deceit, lie" (*Glossar*, p. 588), discussed by de Cenival 1978: 3.

L This supplement seems to be necessary.

M As already remarked, in Chicago Hawara Papyrus 9 (dated March 9, 239 B.C.), which deals with the same one-third share of a house, *ꜥnḫ-mr-wr* (Party A) is described as the son of *Pꜣ-tỉ-nꜣ-ntr.w* and *Ta-Rnn.t*. This argues strongly in favor of the identification of *Pa-tr* with *Pꜣ-tỉ-nꜣ-ntr.w*.

N The same scribe wrote Chicago Hawara Papyri 7A and 8 (243 B.C.).

---

70. See Gagos, Koenen, and McNellen 1992: 187, n. 29 (a loan with 30% interest in 250/249 B.C.). For a discussion of pre-Ptolemaic rates of interest, see Vleeming 1991: 161. I thank Janet Johnson for discussing this passage with me.

CHICAGO HAWARA GREEK PAPYRUS 7C

Illustrations: Plates 42–44

Museum number: P. O.I. 25260

Maximum width: 8.2 cm

Maximum height: 19.3 cm

Physical description: The papyrus was found rolled up within Chicago Hawara Papyrus 7 (P. O.I. 25255). The writing is against the fibers. This is a double document, with a *scriptura interior*.[71] Two clay seals were still preserved; leftmost 2.6 cm from left edge; rightmost 2.2 cm from right edge; 2.2 cm between the two seals. The papyrus is well preserved; there is one insignificant worm hole between lines 7 and 8 of the *scriptura exterior*, and a larger and more serious hole that has removed some of the writing in the second half of line 10. The edges of the papyrus are relatively well preserved, but the top edge is roughly cut. A vertical space of 2.0 cm separates the writing of the inner and outer texts.

Type: Receipt for 2% tax paid by *Sbk-ḥtp*, son of *Pa-wꜣ*, on conditional transfer of one-third of a house by *Pa-tr*, son of *ꜥnḫ-mr-wr*

Date: July 21, 245 B.C. during the reign of Ptolemy III Euergetes I

GREEK TEXT

Scriptura Interior

1. (Ἔτους) γ Παῦνι β̄ Σοχώτης

2.   χα(λκοῦ) (διωβέλιον) ⌐(ἡμιωβέλιον),⌐ (τέταρτον).

Scriptura Exterior

3. (Ἔτους) γ Παῦνι β̄ ὁμολογεῖ Περίστρα-

4. τος διαγεγραφέναι ἐπὶ τῆς Πύ-

5. θωνος τρ(απέζης) τῆς ἐγ Κροκοδίλων

6. πό(λει) βασιλεῖ Σοχώτης Παυῆτος

7. τέλος (τρίτου) μέρους οἰκίας τῆς

8. ἐν τῶι Λαβυρύνθωι ἧς ἐπέ-

9. θηκεν αὐτῶι Πατῆρις Ἀχομ-

10. μνεύιος (δραχμῶν) κ̄ χαλ(κοῦ) (διωβέλιον) (ἡμιωβέλιον) ἀλλα(γὴ) (τέταρτον).

Critical Apparatus

5. τρ(απέζης): **Ͳ** pap., ἐν 6 πό(λει): ⬯ pap., Σοχώτην

7. (τρίτου): **𐌏** pap., 8 ἦν 10 (δραχμῶν): **⊢** pap.

---

71. For Demotic double documents, see de Cenival 1968: 37; idem 1975: 56; Pestman 1968: 100–11; idem 1980: 9–10; Andrews 1990: 57–59. See also Vandorpe 1995: 8–9, 43.

TRANSLATION

SCRIPTURA INTERIOR

> (Year) 3, Payni 2, Sochotes, in br(onze) 2 1/2 obols, 1/4 obol.

SCRIPTURA EXTERIOR

> (Year) 3, Payni 2. Peristratos agrees that Sochotes, son of Paues, has paid to the King at the b(ank) of Python in Crocodilopo(lis) the tax on a third part of a house in the Labyrinth that Pateris, son of Achommneuis, has made over to him, on (a price of) 20 (drachmas) a tax of 2 1/2 bronze obols, (on which there is an) agio of 1/4 obol.

COMMENTARY

GENERAL REMARKS

This small document was found "tightly rolled, tied and sealed" inside of 7A–B (Hughes 1975: 3). It officially acknowledges the payment of sales tax on the house property mortgaged in 7B, at the rate of 2% (see Pierce 1972: 114[72] and note to line 10 below). The outer text was first transcribed from a photograph by the late Sir Eric Turner in 1963; Turner's transcription was improved in the same year by Mr. T. C. Skeat. The inner text, itself tied up and sealed twice, was unrolled in the winter of 1993. In April 1994, photographs were shown to Willy Clarysse and Peter van Minnen, who advanced helpful suggestions about trouble spots in the text. The solution to lines 2 and 10 presented here was later developed by Clarysse. The format of this document is similar to many of the texts published by Pestman (1980: e.g., no. 1 and pl. 1). The chief difference is the copious amount of blank papyrus (9.5 cm at the left edge, 10.0 cm at the right) below the Greek text, perhaps reserved for a Demotic version of the acknowledgment that was never written.

COMMENTS ON LINES

1 (and 3).   Year 3 (of Ptolemy III Euergetes I), Payni 2 = July 21, 245 B.C. See above, 7A, note A.

2.   This line from the inner text gives only the barest essentials: the tax of 2 1/2 obols and the agio of 1/4 obol. For fuller details, see the note to line 10 below.

3–4.   Though it appears neither in Preisigke 1922 nor in Foraboschi 1967, the name Peristratos, proposed by Skeat, looks correct.[73]

4–5.   Python (Mooren and Swinnen 1975: 95; Peremans and van't Dack 1977: 118–19, no. 1271), who appears frequently in the Zenon papyri, was royal banker. He seems to have been first active at Athribis in the Delta, and subsequently from ca. 255 to 237 B.C. at Crocodilopolis. For a full discussion, see Bogaert 1987: 35–75, especially pp. 37–62.

---

72. Compare also the receipt published in Skeat 1959: 75–78. On the ἐγκύκλιον, see also Boswinkel and Pestman 1978: 214–22.

73. The name *Prsrts* (*Demot. Nb.*, p. 470, without Greek equivalent) appears once in a Demotic Zenon text. That text is dated to 243/242 B.C.; see Spiegelberg 1929: 18–19.

7. After τέλος understand ἐπιθήκης (cf. ἐπέθηκεν in lines 8–9) or ὑποθήκης. Compare P. Carlsberg 46–48 in Bülow-Jacobsen 1982: 12–16.

8. References to the Labyrinth are collected in Calderini and Daris 1978: 176.

10. By these figures, worked out by Willy Clarysse, the house in question was worth 60 drachmas; one-third part of it was worth 20 drachmas.[74] The transfer tax for the one-third house share, amounting to 2 1/2 obols, is the expected 2% (in purely mathematical terms, just a shade more than 2%). The agio, 1/4 obol, is the expected 10% of the tax.

---

74. But see note E to Chicago Hawara Papyrus 7B.

CHICAGO HAWARA PAPYRUS 8

Illustrations: Plates 45–48
Museum number: P. O.I. 25256
Maximum length: 177 cm
Maximum height: 38 cm
Physical description: The papyrus roll, composed of ten sheets, is of light brown color. Each sheet measures ca. 19 cm.
Type: Annuity contract. There is no witness list.
Party A: *Smꜣ-tꜣ.wy*, son of *Pꜣ-š-mtre* and *ꜥnḫ≠s*
Party B: *Šty*, daughter of *Pꜣ-šwṱ* and *Ḥr-ꜥnḫ*
Date: July 20–August 18, 243 B.C.
Scribe: Astronomer of Sobek, *Sṱꜣ≠w-tꜣ-wty*, son of *Pꜣ-tì-Wsìr*

TRANSLITERATION

LINES 1–6

1. *ḥꜣ.t-sp 4.t ìbt 2 šmm n Pr-ꜥꜣ Pṱlwmys ꜥnḫ ḏ.t sꜣ Pṱlwmys ìrm ꜣrsynꜣ nꜣ ntr.w sn.w*[A] *wꜥb n ꜣlgsꜣntrs ìrm nꜣ ntr.w sn.w ꜣrystwbwlws sꜣ ꜣntytwtws ìw Ymnꜣ sꜣ.t n Hprbsꜣ fy tn nb*

2. *m-bꜣḥ ꜣrsynꜣ tꜣ mr-sn*[B] *ḏ why (n) tꜣ mre bꜣk (n) Sbk*[C] *Smꜣ-tꜣ.wy sꜣ Pꜣ-š-mtre mw.t≠f ꜥnḫ≠s n s-ḥm.t Šty sꜣ.t n Pꜣ-šwṱ mw.t≠s Ḥr-ꜥnḫ*[D] *tì≠t mtre ḥꜣ.t≠y n ḥḏ 21 n nꜣ tnì.wt n pr-ḥḏ Ptḥ wtḥ ìr ḥḏ 20 qt 9 5/6 1/10 1/30 1/60 1/60 ìr ḥḏ 21 n nꜣ tnì.wt n*

3. *pr-ḥḏ Ptḥ wtḥ ꜥn n pꜣy≠t sꜥnḫ mtw nꜣ ḥrṱ.w nt ìw≠t r ìr ms.ṱ≠w n≠y tꜣ pš(.t) n nt nb nk nb nt mtw≠y ḥnꜥ tꜣ pš(.t) n nt nb nk nb nt ìw≠y r tì.t ḫpr≠w tꜣ pš(.t) n pr ꜣḥ ìnḥ wrḥ bꜣk bꜣk.t ìḥ.t ꜥꜣ tp-n-ìꜣw.t nb ìꜣw.t nb sḫ nb qnb.t nb mt rmt-nmḥ nb n pꜣ tꜣ mtw≠y*

4. *pꜣy≠t šr ꜥꜣ pꜣy≠y šr ꜥꜣ pꜣy*[E] *ḥn nꜣ ḥrṱ.w nt ìw≠t r ìr ms.ṱ≠w n≠y pꜣ nb n tꜣ pš(.t) n nt nb nk nb nt mtw≠y ḥnꜥ tꜣ pš(.t) n nt nb nk nb nt ìw≠y r tì.t ḫpr≠w pꜣy mtw≠y tì.t n≠t bt 36 n tꜣ ḥn 40 r ìt 24 n tꜣ ḥn 40 r bt 36 n tꜣ ḥn 40 ꜥn ḥḏ 1 qt 8 n nꜣ tnì.wt n pr-ḥḏ Ptḥ wtḥ ìr ḥḏ 1 qt 7 5/6 1/10 1/30 1/60 1/60 ìr ḥḏ 1 qt 8 n nꜣ tnì.wt n*

5. *pr-ḥḏ Ptḥ wtḥ ꜥn n pꜣy≠t ꜥq-ḥbs ḥr rnp.t r pꜣ ꜥ.wy nt ìw mr≠t s mtw≠t tꜣ nt nḥe.ṱ r tꜣ wḏꜣ(.t) n pꜣy≠t ꜥq-ḥbs nt ì(w)≠s r ḫpr (r-)ꜥ.wy≠y mtw≠y tì.t s n≠t tꜣ pš(.t) n nt nb nk nb nt mtw≠y ḥnꜥ tꜣ pš(.t) n nt nb nk nb nt ìw≠y r tì.t ḫpr≠w n tꜣ ìwꜣ(.t) n pꜣy≠t sꜥnḫ nt ḥry bn ìw≠y rḫ ḏ n≠t*

6. *šp pꜣy≠t sꜥnḫ pꜣy≠t sw n wḥꜣ≠f ìw≠y r tì.t s n≠t n-ìm≠f ìw≠w tì.t ꜥnḫ m-sꜣ≠t r ìr≠f n≠y ì-ìr≠t r ìr≠f n≠y n pꜣ ꜥ.wy nt ìw nꜣ wpṱ.w n-ìm≠f r/m-sḫ ìmy-wnw.t n Sbk Sṱꜣ≠w-tꜣ-wty sꜣ Pꜣ-tì-Wsìr*[F]

TRANSLATION

1. Year 4, second month of the season *shemu*, of Pharaoh Ptolemy, who lives forever, son of Ptolemy and Arsinoe, the gods Adelphoi, the priest of Alexander and of the gods Adelphoi being Aristoboulos, son of Antidotos, while Iamneia, daughter of Hyperbassas, is the Kanephoros

2. before Arsinoe Philadelphos. The fisherman of the lake, servant (of) Sobek, *Smȝ-tȝ.wy*, son of *Pȝ-š-mtre*, whose mother is *ˁnḫ≠s*, has declared to the woman *Šty*, daughter of *Pȝ-šwṯ*, whose mother is *Ḥr-ˁnḫ*: "You have caused my heart to agree to the 21 silver (*deben*) (weighed) by the pieces in the Treasury of Ptah, (of) refined (silver), being 20 silver (*deben*) and 9, 5/6, 1/10, 1/30, 1/60, and 1/60 *kite*, being 21 silver (*deben*) (weighed) by the pieces in the

3. Treasury of Ptah, (of) refined (silver) again, as your annuity. There belong to the children whom you will bear to me the half of everything of any property that I possess and the half of everything of any property that I shall acquire: the half of house, field, courtyard, building plot, male servant, female servant, cow, ass, every animal, every office, every document, every title deed, every matter of a freeman in the world whatsoever of mine.

4. Your eldest son is my eldest son among the children whom you will bear to me. He is the owner of half of everything of all property that I possess and half of everything of all property that I shall acquire. And I shall give you 36 (sacks) emmer (by the measure of) 40-*hin*, being 24 (sacks) barley (by the measure of) 40-*hin*, being 36 (sacks) emmer (by the measure of) 40-*hin* again and 1 silver (*deben*) and 8 *kite* (weighed) by the pieces in the Treasury of Ptah, (of) refined (silver), being 1 silver (*deben*) and 7, 5/6, 1/10, 1/30, 1/60, and 1/60 *kite*, being 1 silver (*deben*) and 8 *kite* (weighed) by the pieces in the

5. Treasury of Ptah, (of) refined (silver), again, for your subsistence each year at whatever house you desire. You are the one authorized with regard to the arrears of your subsistence which shall be to my debit, and I am to give it to you. Half of everything of all property that I possess and half of everything of all property that I shall acquire is the pledge for your aforesaid annuity. I shall not be able to say to you:

6. 'Take your aforesaid annuity,' but on whatever day you desire it, I will give it to you. If an oath is required of you to be taken for me, it is at the house in which the judges are that you shall take it." Written by the astronomer of Sobek, *Sṯȝ≠w-tȝ-wty*, son of *Pȝ-tì-Wsìr*.

COMMENTARY

A The date is equivalent to July 20–August 18, 243 B.C. during the reign of Ptolemy III Euergetes I.

B For the eponymous priests, see Clarysse and van der Veken 1983: 10–11 (no. 48). The name of the father of the priest of Alexander and the deified Ptolemies is there given as Diodotos, whereas in this text the scribe has clearly written *ȝntytwtws* (Antidotos).

C This is the only Chicago Hawara papyrus in which a *ḥtmw-ntr* does not occur. A "fisherman and servant of Wepwawet" appears in H. Thompson 1934: vol. 1, p. 60. For the compound *bȝk* "servant" followed by deity, see also Johnson 1986: 72; Reymond 1984: 22–23.

D *Ḥr-ꜥnḫ* seems to be the link between this text and the others in the archive. It is probable, at any rate, that the mother of Party B is to be identified with the *Ḥr-ꜥnḫ* who has already appeared in Chicago Hawara Papyrus 6 (259 B.C.) and Chicago Hawara Papyrus 7 (245 B.C.). If so, she seems to have been married at least three times because in Chicago Hawara Papyrus 6 she is married to *Pꜣ-tỉ-Wsỉr*, in Chicago Hawara Papyrus 7 to *Pa-wꜣ*, and here she is the wife of *Pꜣ-šwṭ*.

For *ꜥnḫ≠s*, see *Demot. Nb.*, p. 104.

For *Pꜣ-šwṭ*, see *Demot. Nb.*, p. 511 (queried example).

E On the role of the eldest son, see Pestman 1981: 307; Mattha and Hughes 1975: 123; Seidl 1974: 99–110; Vittmann 1982: 82.

F The same scribe wrote Chicago Hawara Papyrus 7A–B (245 B.C.).

CHICAGO HAWARA PAPYRUS 9

Illustrations: Plates 49–55

Museum number: P. O.I. 25263

Maximum length: 107.0 cm

Maximum height: 33.5 cm

Physical description: The roll, of a light brown color, is composed of six sheets of papyrus, averaging ca. 19.0 cm in width. The rightmost portion of the papyrus is destroyed.

Type: Provisional sale document for one-third share of house and cell. There is a Greek docket.

Party A: ꜥnḫ-mr-wr, son of Pꜣ-tỉ-nꜣ-ntr.w and Ta-Rnn.t

Party B: Ḥr-ꜥnḫ, daughter of Mꜣꜥ-Rꜥ and Nb.t-tꜣ-ḥy(?)

Date: March 9, 239 B.C. under the reign of Ptolemy III Euergetes I (on the basis of the Greek docket)

Scribe: Pa-nꜣ(?), son of Pꜣ-tỉ-Ḥr-pꜣ-šr-(n)-ỉs.t

TRANSLITERATION

LINES 1–9

1. [ḥꜣ.t-sp 8 ỉbt 1 pr.t n Pr-ꜥꜣ] Ptlwmys ꜥnḫ ḏ.t sꜣ Ptlwmys ỉrm ꜣrsn (tꜣ) mr-sn nꜣ ntr.w sn.w**A** wꜥb (n) ꜣrgsꜣntrws ỉrm nꜣ ntr.w sn.w nꜣ ntr.w mnḫ.w Nwmstws sꜣ Prwn ỉw Glwtrtꜣ tꜣ šr.t Gtsgls fy tn nb m-bꜣḥ ꜣrsn tꜣ mr-sn **B**

2. [ḏ ḫtmw-ntr wyt ꜥn]ḫ-mr-[wr] sꜣ Pꜣ-tỉ-nꜣ-ntr.w mw.t≠f Ta-Rnn.t n s-ḥm.t Ḥr-ꜥnḫ sꜣ.t n ḫtmw-ntr wyt Mꜣꜥ-Rꜥ mw.t≠s Nb.t-tꜣ-ḥy(?)**C** tỉ≠t mtre ḥꜣ.t≠y n pꜣ ḥḏ n tꜣy≠y tnỉ.t 1/3 n pꜣy ꜥ.wy nt qt ỉw≠f grg n sy sbꜣ nt ỉr mḥ-ntr 19 n rs r mḫt ỉw≠f ỉr mḥ-ntr 18 n ỉmnt (r) ỉꜣbt

3. [ḥnꜥ tꜣy≠y tnỉ.t 1/3] tꜣy≠y ry.t ḥry ḥry nt ỉr mḫt.t n pꜣy≠y ꜥ.wy mꜣy nt ỉr mḥ-ntr 20 n rs r mḫt ỉ(w)≠s ỉr mḥ-ntr 5 n ỉmnt r ỉꜣbt**D** nꜣ hyn.w n pꜣy ꜥ.wy nt ḥry rs pꜣ ꜥ.wy n ḫtmw-ntr wyt Sbk-ḥtp sꜣ Pa-sy**E** r pꜣ ḫr ỉwt≠w mḫt pꜣ ꜥ.wy n ḫtmw-ntr wyt

4. [Sbk-ḥtp sꜣ ꜥnḫ-mr-wr**F**] hn n≠w ỉmnt nꜣ ꜥ.wy.w n ḫtmw-ntr wyt Mꜣꜥ-Rꜥ sꜣ Pꜣ-šr-n-tꜣ-ỉḫ.t nt ḥr nꜣy≠f ḫrṭ.w r pꜣ ḫr ỉwt≠w ỉꜣbt pꜣy≠y ꜥ.wy hn n≠w nꜣ hyn.w n tꜣ ry.t rs pꜣy≠y ꜥ.wy hn n≠s mḫt pꜣ ꜥ.wy n ḫtmw-ntr wyt Mꜣꜥ-Rꜥ sꜣ Pḫy**G** hn n≠w ỉmnt nꜣy≠t wrḫ.w hn n≠w

5. [ỉꜣbt pꜣ sbt(?)] n ḥ.t-ntr n Ḥ.t-wr.t r pꜣ myt ꜥꜣ ỉwt≠w mtw≠t pꜣ 1/3 n pꜣy ꜥ.wy ḥr pꜣy≠f mꜣꜥ rs ḥry ḥry ḥnꜥ tꜣ ry.t nt (ỉw) nꜣy≠w ḫy.w nꜣy≠w hyn.w sḫ r-ḥry n ṯ pꜣ hrw r-ḥry mn mtw≠y mt nb nt nb(?)**H** n pꜣ tꜣ ỉ-ỉr n≠t n rn≠w n ṯ pꜣ hrw r-ḥry bn ỉw rḫ rmt nb n pꜣ tꜣ ỉnk m-mỉ.t r ỉr sḫy n-ỉm≠w n bnr≠t n ṯ pꜣ hrw r-ḥry

6. [pꜣ nt ỉw≠f r ỉy r-ḥr]≠t r-ḏbꜣ.ṱ≠w [ỉw]≠y r [tỉ.t] wy≠f r-ḥr≠t ỉw≠y tm tỉ.t wy≠f r-ḥr≠t ỉw≠y r tỉ.t wy≠f r-ḥr≠t mtw≠y tỉ.t wꜥb≠w n≠t r qnb.t nb mt nb n pꜣ tꜣ mtw≠t sḫ nb r-ỉr≠w r-r≠w ḥnꜥ sḫ nb r-ỉr≠w n pꜣy≠y ỉt tꜣy≠y mw.t r-r≠w ḥnꜥ sḫ nb r-ỉr≠w nꜣy r-r≠w

52

ḥnꜥ sẖ nb nt iw≠y mꜣꜥ.k n-im≠w n rn≠w mtw≠t s ḥnꜥ pꜣy≠w ḥp mtw≠t pꜣ nt iw≠y mꜣꜥ.k
n-im≠w n rn≠w (sic) pꜣ ꜥnḫ pꜣ ꜥḥꜥ-rṱ

7. *[nt iw≠w] r tỉ.t s m-sꜣ≠t r tỉ.t ir≠y s n rn≠w iw≠y r ir≠f mtw≠t šm r-ḥry ḥry r tbn*[I] *ḥr*
pꜣ trt n pꜣy ꜥ.wy nt ḥry mtw≠t pr r-ẖn r bnr n tꜣ ḫyt pꜣ rꜣ ꜥꜣ nꜣ rꜣ.w n pr n pꜣy ꜥ.wy nt
ḥry[J] *mtw≠t r ir n(?) ḥy nb n-im≠f r-ḫ tꜣy≠t tnỉ.t 1/3 n ṱ pꜣ hrw r-ḥry šꜥ ḏ.t iw*[K] *s-ḥm.t*
Tꜣy-ỉr≠w sꜣ.t n ḥtmw-ntr wyt Pꜣ-tỉ-Wsỉr mw.t≠s

8. *[Nꜣ-nfr-]rnp.t*[L] *ḏ sẖ i-ỉry mt nb [nt ḥry] ḥꜣ.t≠y mtre.w n-im≠w iw≠s ḏ ꜥn i-ỉr≠y ir pꜣ ꜥš*
nt ḥry iw≠y m-sꜣ ḥtmw-ntr wyt ꜥnḫ-mr-wr sꜣ Pꜣ-tỉ-nꜣ-ntr.w mw.t≠f Ta-Rnn.t nt ḥry n pꜣ
ḥp n sẖ nb r-ir≠f n≠y mtw≠f ir n≠y pꜣy≠w ḥp mtw≠y ir pꜣ ḥp n pꜣy ꜥš nt ḥry tw≠y wy.k
r s-ḥm.t Ḥr-ꜥnḫ sꜣ.t n ḥtmw-ntr wyt Mꜣꜥ-Rꜥ mw.t≠s Nb.t-tꜣ-ḥy(?) n pꜣ 1/3 n pꜣy ꜥ.wy

9. *[ḥnꜥ pꜣ 1/3 n tꜣy] ry.t nt nꜣy≠w ḫy.w nꜣy≠w hyn.w sẖ r-ḥry n ṱ pꜣ hrw r-ḥry mn mtw≠y*
mt nb nt nb n pꜣ tꜣ i-ỉr n≠t n rn≠w n ṱ pꜣ hrw r-ḥry r-sẖ Pa-nꜣ(?)[M] *sꜣ Pꜣ-tỉ-Ḥr-pꜣ-šr-*
(n)-ỉs.t

WITNESS LIST

1. ... [...] *(sꜣ) Pꜣ-tỉ-Mn(?)*[N]
2. *Pa-sy(?) sꜣ Ḥr-sꜣ-ỉs.t*[O]
3. *Pa-ỉmn sꜣ Sy-Sbk*
4. *Sbk-ḥtp (sꜣ) Mꜣꜥ-Rꜥ pꜣ ḥm*
5. *Mꜣꜥ-Rꜥ sꜣ Ḥr-sꜣ-ỉs.t*
6. *Ḥr sꜣ Mꜣꜥ-Rꜥ*
7. *Pꜣ-ỉgš sꜣ Ḥr*[P]
8. *Ḥr sꜣ Ḥr-sꜣ-ỉs.t pꜣ ḥm*
9. *Pꜣ-tỉ-Ḥr (sꜣ) ỉy-m-ḥtp*
10. *Pꜣ-nfr-ḥr sꜣ ...*[Q]
11. *Sbk-Ḥp sꜣ...*[R]
12. *Pꜣ-tỉ-... sꜣ Nḫt-nb≠f*[S]
13. *ꜥnḫ-mr-wr...*[T]
14. *ꜥnḫ-Ḥp (sꜣ) Mꜣꜥ-Rꜥ*
15. *Pꜣ-... sꜣ ỉy-m-ḥtp*
16. *Mꜣꜥ-Rꜥ sꜣ Ḥr-wḏꜣ*

GREEK DOCKETS

1. Ἔτους η Τῦβι ιθ̄ πέπτωκεν εἰς κιβωτὸν ἐν Κροκοδίλων
2. πόλει τοῦ Ἀρσινοίτου διὰ Ἐπιφανοῦς τοῦ παρὰ Ῥοδοκλέους.
3.   (Ἔτους) η Τῦβι ιθ̄ πέπτωκεν ε[ἰ]ς κιβωτὸν
4.   παρόντος Διονυσίου τοῦ πα[ρ]ὰ Βοηθοῦ.

TRANSLATION

1. [Year 8, first month of the season *peret*, of Pharaoh] Ptolemy, who lives forever, son of Ptolemy and Arsinoe Philadelphos, the gods Adelphoi, the priest of Alexander and the gods Adelphoi and the gods Euergetai being Onomastos, son of Pyron, while Arche(s)trate, the daughter of Ktesikles, is the Kanephoros before Arsinoe Philadelphos.

2. [The god's sealer and embalmer ʿn]ḫ-mr-[wr], son of *Pȝ-tỉ-nȝ-ntr.w*, whose mother is *Ta-Rnn.t*, [has declared] to the woman *Ḥr-ʿnḫ*, daughter of the god's sealer and embalmer *Mȝʿ-Rʿ*, whose mother is *Nb.t-tȝ-ḥy*(?): "You have caused my heart to agree to the money for my one-third share of this house which is built, it being provided with beam and door, which measures 19 god's cubits from south to north and 18 god's cubits from west to east

3. [and my one-third share] of my cell, above and below, which is on the north of my new home, which measures 20 god's cubits from south to north and which measures 5 god's cubits from west to east. The neighbors of this aforesaid house are: south, the house of the god's sealer and embalmer *Sbk-ḥtp*, son of *Pa-sy*, the street being between them; north, the house of the god's sealer and embalmer

4. [*Sbk-ḥtp*, son of *ʿnḫ-mr-wr*] adjoins them; west, the houses of the god's sealer and embalmer, *Mȝʿ-Rʿ*, son of *Pȝ-šr-n-tȝ-ỉḥ.t*, which are in the possession of his children, the street being between them; east, my house adjoins them. The neighbors of the cell are: south, my house adjoins it; north, the house of the god's sealer and embalmer *Mȝʿ-Rʿ*, son of *Pḫy*, adjoins them; west, your building plots adjoin them;

5. [east, the wall(?)] of the temple of Hawara, the big path being between them. Yours is one-third of this house on its southern part, below and above, together with the cell, the measurements and neighbors of which are written above, from today onward. I do not have anything of any kind in the world due from you for them from today onward. No one in the world, myself included, shall be able to exercise control over them from today onward.

6. [As for him who might come against] you regarding them, I will [make] him withdraw from you. If I do not make him withdraw from you, I will make him withdraw from you and I will clear them for you of every title deed or anything in the world. To you belong every document that was (ever) drawn up regarding them, every document that was (ever) drawn up for my father or my mother regarding them, and every document that was (ever) drawn up for me regarding them, and every document by which I am entitled to them. They belong to you together with the legal rights conferred by them. To you belongs that by which I am entitled to them. The oath or the court proof

7. [that might be] required of you in order to cause that I execute it concerning them, I shall perform it. You may go up (to) and down (from) the roof on the stairway of this aforesaid house and you may go in and out of the forehall, the main doorway and the (other) exits of this aforesaid house. And you shall make any alterations on it in proportion to your one-third share from today onward forever." Whereas the woman *Tȝy-ỉr≈w*, daughter of the god's sealer and embalmer *Pȝ-tỉ-Wsỉr*, whose mother is

8. [*Nȝ-nfr-*]*rnp.t* says: "Write! Do everything [aforesaid]. I am agreed thereto." She says also: "It is because I have claim on the god's sealer and embalmer *ʿnḫ-mr-wr*, son of *Pȝ-tỉ-nȝ-ntr.w*, whose mother is *Ta-Rnn.t*, above, through the legal right conferred by every docu-

ment that he has drawn up for me that I give the above consent, and he shall carry out the obligations conferred by them, and I shall carry out the obligations of the above consent. I relinquish to the woman *Ḥr-ʿnḫ*, daughter of the god's sealer and embalmer *Mȝʿ-Rʿ*, whose mother is *Nb.t-tȝ-ḥy*(?), the one-third of this house

9. [and the one-third of this] cell, the measurements and the neighbors of both of which are written above, from today onward. I have nothing at all in the world against you in respect to them from today onward." Written by *Pa-nȝ*(?), son of *Pȝ-tỉ-Ḥr-pȝ-šr-(n)-ỉs.t*.

GREEK DOCKETS

Year 8, Tybi 19, it (sc. the agreement) has been deposited in the (official) chest at Crocodilopolis of the Arsinoite (Nome) by Epiphanes, the agent of Rhodokles.

(Year) 8, Tybi 19, it has been deposited in the (official) chest, in the presence of Dionysios, the agent of Boethos.

COMMENTARY ON THE DEMOTIC TEXT

A The restoration is based on the Greek docket, which is dated to year 8, Tybi 19, corresponding to March 9, 239 B.C. during the reign of Ptolemy III Euergetes I. The annuity contract between the same individuals, Copenhagen Hawara Papyrus 1 (= P. Carlsberg 34), is dated to the same day.

B For the eponymous priest and Kanephoros, see Clarysse and van der Veken 1983: 10–11 (no. 51).

C From Chicago Hawara Papyrus 7 we know that in 245 B.C. *Pȝ-tỉ-nȝ-ntr.w*, the father of Party A in this text, *ʿnḫ-mr-wr*, had mortgaged this same one-third share of a house to a son of *Ḥr-ʿnḫ*, named *Sbk-ḥtp*.

Chicago Hawara Papyrus 9 provides the connection between the Chicago and Copenhagen Hawara papyri housed in the Institute of Egyptology of the University of Copenhagen. The background for this particular transaction is preserved in three Greek texts, published by Bülow-Jacobsen (1982: 12–16),[75] and two Demotic papyri, to be published by Erich Lüddeckens. Copenhagen Hawara Papyrus 1 (= P. Carlsberg 34), which bears a Greek docket dated to the same day as this Chicago Hawara Papyrus, March 9, 239 B.C., is an annuity contract drawn up between the same individuals, *ʿnḫ–mr-wr* and *Ḥr-ʿnḫ*. That annuity contract contains a consent clause in the name of *Tȝy-ỉr≠w*, daughter of *Pȝ-tỉ-Wsỉr* and *Nȝ-nfr-rnp.t*. The Copenhagen Hawara Papyrus 3 (= P. Carlsberg 36), written between July 17 and August 15, 233 B.C., is a deed of cession in which *ʿnḫ-mr-wr*, son of *Pȝ-tỉ-nȝ-ntr.w*, cedes to *Ḥr-ʿnḫ* the same one-third share of a house and the cell. The Chicago Hawara Papyrus 9 is indeed mentioned in Copenhagen Hawara Papyrus 3 (= P. Carlsberg 36), line 3, as the *sḫ-ḏbȝ-ḥḏ* for the transaction, giving the date as *ḥȝ.t-sp 8.t ỉbt 1 pr.t*.

The published Greek documents from Copenhagen are also helpful in understanding the financial relationship of the two parties.

---

75. The translations of the three Greek texts are based on those of Bülow-Jacobsen.

The earliest, P. Carlsberg 46, is dated to March 9, 239 B.C., precisely the day upon which this Chicago sale document and the Copenhagen annuity contract were written. P. Carlsberg 46 is translated as follows:

> "Year 8, Tybi 19. Socrates agrees that Aünchis (= *Ḥr-ᶜnḫ*), daughter of Marres, has paid at the bank of Python in Crocodilopolis, to the king, tax on mortgage of a third of a house and out-buildings[76] which are in Hawara in the division of Heracleides, the mortgagor Achomneuis, son of Petenenteris, being present, 40 drachmas, (of this) copper 4 obols, agio 5/8 obol."[77]

The situation seems to be analogous to that of Chicago Hawara Papyrus 7. Chicago Hawara Papyrus 9 records a conditional sale, in which the one-third share of a house becomes the possession of *Ḥr-ᶜnḫ*, if *ᶜnḫ-mr-wr* defaults on a loan. The Greek text published by Bülow-Jacobsen is parallel to the Chicago Hawara Greek Papyrus 7C; the Demotic text of Chicago Hawara Papyrus 9 corresponds to Chicago Hawara Papyrus 7A. We are lacking, however, the explicit mortgage agreement analogous to Chicago Hawara Papyrus 7B.

In P. Carlsberg 47, which seems to be dated to 237 B.C., *Ḥr-ᶜnḫ* pays the tax for renewing the mortgage:

> "Year 10(?), Tybi 10. Ptolemy agrees that Aünchis, daughter of Marres, has paid at the collection office in the town, to the king, tax on renewal of a mortgage of part of a house and buildings which are in Hawara and which Achomneuis, son of Petenonteris, has mortgaged to her, 60 drachmas and for interest of the 9th year and of the 10th year 40 drachmas, total 100 drachmas, (of this) copper 2, agio 1 1/2 obol."[78]

One year later, on May 17, 236 B.C., *Ḥr-ᶜnḫ* apparently took possession of the one-third share of the house, the loan having been presumably not repaid (P. Carlsberg 48):

> "Year 11, Phamenoth 29. Ptolemy agrees that Aünchis, daughter of Marres, has paid at the collection office in the town, to the king, tax on foreclosure for a third part of a house and buildings which are in Hawara, and which Achomneuis, son of Petenonteris, has mortgaged to her, 100 drachmas. She has made an additional payment of 60 drachmas. Total: 160 drachmas, (of this) copper 8, agio 5 obols."[79]

Note, however, that Copenhagen 3 (= P. Carlsberg 36), the Demotic deed of cession for this third part of a house, is dated some years later, namely, to July 17–August 15, 233 B.C.

D See figure 3 for the plans of the house and cell.

E Compare the neighbors of this property named in Chicago Hawara Papyrus 7A, lines 3–4.

F Restored on the basis of P. Copenhagen Hawara 3 (= P. Carlsberg 36), line 4.

---

76. Note that *ry.t* is rendered by οἰκήματα "out-buildings, rooms" in the Greek documents; for which, see Husson 1983: 183–86.

77. Although they all concern a mortgage for the same third part of a house and involve the same families, it is difficult to relate the amounts given in P. Carlsberg 46–48 with those in Chicago Hawara Papyri 7B and 7C, written some six years earlier. No "out-buildings" are mentioned in Chicago Hawara Papyri 7B and 7C. Bülow-Jacobsen (1983: 13) understands the total property as having "been evaluated at 1 talent," but compare the note to line 10 of Chicago Hawara Greek Papyrus 7C.

78. The agio is somewhat higher than the expected 10%.

79. The tax on this foreclosure transaction is 5% (the normal tax for a mortgage) and not the 2% of a conditional sale, as in Chicago Hawara Greek Papyrus 7C, P. Carlsberg 46 (approximate), and P. Carlsberg 47. On these taxes, see Pierce 1972: 132.

G This is probably a variant of *Pa-ḥy* (*Demot. Nb.*, p. 398).

H The writing of *nt nb* is odd.

I The scribe seems to have ligatured the *n* and the house determinative, but perhaps merely *r tb* is written.

J Compare Chicago Hawara Papyrus 5, lines 6–7.

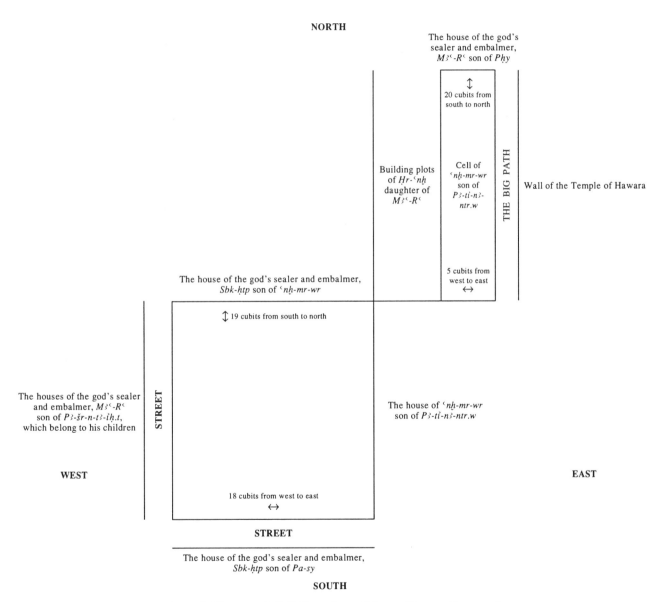

Figure 3. House and Cell Plans from Chicago Hawara Papyrus 9

K *Tȝy-ir=w*, who only appears here, does not specify the nature of the claim that she has on *ꜥnḫ-mr-wr*, but it is quite possibly based on an annuity contract. She might be the wife of *ꜥnḫ-mr-wr*.

L *Nȝ-nfr-rnp.t* is not in *Demot. Nb.*

M The reading of the name is uncertain; another possibility is *Ḥnꜣ*, as suggested to me by Rolf Wassermann. The same scribe wrote Copenhagen 1 (= P. Carlsberg 34; March 9, 239 B.C.), Copenhagen 3 (= P. Carlsberg 36; July 17–August 15, 233 B.C.), and the Rendell Papyrus.

N I am unable to read the first name, which perhaps is *Pꜣ-ky*. *Pꜣ-tı̓-Mn* seems possible for the father's name.

O *Pa-sy* is uncertain.

P *Pꜣ-ı̓gš* is not secure; compare *Demot. Nb.*, p. 160.

Q For *Pꜣ-nfr-ḥr*, see *Demot. Nb.*, pp. 192–93. The father's name might begin with *Pa*.

R The father's name perhaps begins with *Ḏḥwty*. The name of the grandfather might conclude the line. Carol Andrews (pers. comm.) reasonably proposes *Pa-wꜣ sꜣ Pꜣ-tı̓-Sbk*, comparing the first witness of the Rendell Papyrus, *Sbk-ḥtp sꜣ Pa-wꜣ sꜣ Pꜣ-tı̓-Sbk*(?).

S *Pꜣ-tı̓* is not certain.

T The father's name might include *hb*.

COMMENTARY ON THE GREEK DOCKETS

GENERAL REMARKS

There are two two-line dockets, apparently written in the same hand, below the extreme right of the Demotic texts, beginning ca. 23.0 cm in from the papyrus roll's right edge. The second docket, which is shorter, is indented at both left (3.0 cm) and right (5.5 cm) with respect to the first docket. Dockets made on the same date (below, note to line 1) and with the same personnel are found in Copenhagen Hawara Papyrus 1 (= P. Carlsberg 34).[80] The Copenhagen dockets have exactly the same configuration as the Chicago dockets, including the double indentation of the second docket. The Chicago dockets are better preserved, though the writing in both is somewhat faint.

COMMENTS ON LINES

1 (and 3). Year 8 (of Ptolemy III Euergetes I), Tybi 19 = March 9, 239 B.C. As mentioned above, Bülow-Jacobsen (1982: 14 = Rupprecht 1988: 91, no. 12342) has published the Greek receipt for the mortgage tax on this one-third of a house, dated to the same day.

4. Βοηθοῦ is a difficult reading, but the *beta* (a double-stroke *beta* with the strokes very close together; they are farther spread in the Copenhagen docket), *eta*, and *upsilon* are secure; the reading therefore seems unavoidable. Before *beta* there are perhaps traces of a letter, seemingly erased.

---

80. To be published by Erich Lüddeckens.

CHICAGO HAWARA PAPYRUS 10

Illustrations: Plates 56–57

Museum number: P. O.I. 25261

Maximum width: 21 cm

Maximum height: 34 cm

Physical description: The papyrus, light brown in color, was reconstructed by Hughes from numerous fragments. It comprises a single sheet of papyrus. The papyrus had been placed within Chicago Hawara Papyrus 2. The writing is parallel to the fibers.

Type: Confirmation of repayment of loan of one *deben*

Party A: *Mȝꜥ-Rꜥ*, son of *Nḫt-pȝ-Rꜥ* and *Tȝ-rmt.t-…*

Party B: *ꜥnḫ-mr-wr*, son of *Pa-se* (= *Pȝ-ti-Wsir*) and *Ḥr-ꜥnḫ*

Date: February 15–March 15, 221 B.C. during the reign of Ptolemy IV Philopator

Scribe: *Ḏḥwty-wȝḥ*, son of *Nḫt-ḥr-ḥb* and(?) *Mȝꜥ-…* , son of *Ḥr-…*

TRANSLITERATION

LINES 1–12

1. *ḥȝ.t-sp 1.t ỉbt 1 pr.t n Pr-ꜥȝ [Pt]lwmw[s] sȝ Pṭlwms ỉrm ȝrsyn* (sic) *tȝ mr-sn nȝ ntr.w sn.w*

2. *Brngȝ* **A** *wꜥb [ȝlgs]ȝntrws ỉrm nȝ ntr.w sn.w nȝ ntr.w mnḫ.w*

3. *Nqnr sȝ Bkys [ỉw ȝr]stmg tȝ šr.t Pṭlwmys fy*

4. *tn nb m-bȝḥ ȝrs[nȝ tȝ mr]-sn* **B** *ḏ wȝḥ-mw n Pr-ꜥȝ Mȝꜥ-Rꜥ Mȝꜥ-Rꜥ* **C**

5. *Mȝꜥ-Rꜥ sȝ Nḫt-pȝ-Rꜥ* **D** *mw.t≠f Tȝ-rmt.t-…* **E** *n ḥtmw-ntr wyt ꜥnḫ-mr-wr sȝ Pa-se*

6. *mw.t≠f Ḥr-ꜥnḫ* **F** *ti≠k n≠y ḥḏ 1 tȝy≠f pš.t qt 5 r ḥḏ 1 ꜥn n tȝy≠k tni.t pš ḥn ḥḏ 2*

7. *r-ỉr≠k n≠y sḫ r-r≠f ỉrm Nḫt sȝ Pȝ-[ti]-Sbk* **G** *šp≠y ḥḏ 1 nt ḥry n-ḏr.t≠k ḥȝ.t≠y mtre.w n-ỉm≠f*

8. *ỉw≠w mḥ ỉwty sp mn mtw≠[y] mt [nb] nt nb n pȝ tȝ ỉ-ỉr n≠k n rn pȝ sḫ rn≠f n*

9. *tȝy≠k tni.t pš [pȝ nt ỉw≠f r] ỉy [r-r≠k r-ḏbȝ].ṭ≠f ỉw≠y (r) ti.t wy≠f r-r≠k n ḥtr ỉwty mn*

10. *ỉw≠y m-sȝ Nḫt [sȝ Pȝ-ti]-Sbk n pȝ ḥ[ḏ 1 r-ḥ pȝ] sḫ nt ḥry* **H** *mn mtw≠y mt nb n pȝ tȝ*

11. *ỉ-ỉr n≠k n [r]n≠f ṭ [pȝ hrw r-ḥry…] … sḫ Ḏḥwty-wȝḥ sȝ Nḫt-Ḥr-ḥb(?)* **I**

12. *sḫ Mȝꜥ-[…]⌈… Ḥr-…⌉[…]* **J**

WITNESS LIST

1. *Sbk-…*

2. *Pa-ỉs.t sȝ Mȝꜥ-Rꜥ*

3. Check mark *Ḥr sȝ Pa-nȝ* **K**

4. *Mȝꜥ-Rꜥ sȝ Pa-sy*

5. Check mark *M3ʿ-Rʿ* ... [*s3*] *Pa-*...

6. *M3ʿ-Rʿ s3 Nḫt-*...

7. *M3ʿ-Rʿ s3 iy-m-ḥtp*

8. *M3ʿ-Rʿ s3*...

9. Check mark *M3ʿ(-Rʿ) s3* ⌈*Ḏ-B3st.t-iw≠f-ʿnḫ*⌉

10. *Nḫt-*[... *s3*] *iy-m-ḥtp*(?)

11. *P3-ti-Ḥr-p3-šr*[*-n-is.t... s3*] *Sy-Sbk*

12. Check mark *M3ʿ-Rʿ s3* [...]

TRANSLATION

1. Year 1, first month of the season *peret*, of Pharaoh [Pto]lemy, son of Ptolemy and Arsinoe Philadelphos (*sic*), the gods Adelphoi,

2. Berenike, the priest of [Alex]ander and the gods Adelphoi, the gods Euergetai, being

3. Nikanor, son of Bakkhios, while [Ari]stomakhe, the daughter of Ptolemaios, is the Kane-

4. phoros before Arsi[noe Phil]adelphos. Has declared the choachyte of Pharaoh *M3ʿ-Rʿ M3ʿ-Rʿ* (*sic*),

5. *M3ʿ-Rʿ*, son of *Nḫt-p3-Rʿ*, whose mother is [*T3*]*-rmt.t-*... , to the god's sealer and embalmer *ʿnḫ-mr-wr*, son of *Pa-se*,

6. whose mother is *Ḥr-ʿnḫ*: "You have given to me 1 silver (*deben*), its half being 5 *kite*, being 1 silver (*deben*) again, as your half share from the 2 silver (*deben*)

7. about which you wrote a document for me together with *Nḫt*, son of *P3-*[*ti*]*-Sbk*. I have received the 1 silver (*deben*) above from you. My heart is satisfied therewith,

8. they being paid in full, without remainder. [I] have nothing of [any]thing in the world against you on account of the aforementioned document with regard to

9. your half share. [As for him who might] come [against you concerning] it, I will make him withdraw from you of necessity, without delay,

10. I (still) having a claim on *Nḫt*, [son of *P3-ti*]*-Sbk*, with regard to the [1] sil[ver (*deben*) in accordance with the] document above. I have nothing in the world

11. against you on account [of] it from [today onward...]." ... *Ḏḥwty-w3ḥ*, son of *Nḫt-Ḥr-ḥb*(?), has written.

12. There has written *M3ʿ-*[...] ... *Ḥr-*...[...].

COMMENTARY

A The date is equivalent to February 15–March 15, 221 B.C. during the reign of Ptolemy IV Philopator. The scribe mistakenly wrote "Arsinoe" in the first line, but then corrected himself and added "Berenike," the actual mother of Ptolemy IV, in the second line.

B For the eponymous priests, see Clarysse and van der Veken 1983: 14–15 (no. 69B). The same individual appears some years later in P. BM 10071, published by Andrews 1988: 194. In that text, dated to July 12, 212 B.C., he is priest of Ptolemy I in the Theban Nome.

C Once again, the scribe seems to commit a blunder, writing *M3ꜥ-Rꜥ* twice after *pr-ꜥ3*. The Pharaoh Maare is presumably Amenemhet III. It is not surprising, of course, that there should be a "choachyte of *M3ꜥ-Rꜥ*" in the Fayum.

D *M3ꜥ-Rꜥ*, son of *Nḫt-p3-Rꜥ* (Party A), is not named in any of the other Chicago Hawara papyri. *Nḫt-p3-Rꜥ* is not in *Demot. Nb.* There could be more than merely *M3ꜥ-Rꜥ* at the beginning of this line (Carol Andrews, pers. comm.).

E The reading is uncertain.

F This *ꜥnḫ-mr-wr*, son of *Pa-se* (= *P3-ti-Wsir*) and *Ḥr-ꜥnḫ*, is to be identified with one of the two like-named brothers who are Parties A and B in the Rendell Papyrus.

G The document mentioned is not preserved among the Chicago papyri. *Nḫt*, son of *P3-ti-Sbk*, who borrowed the money together with *ꜥnḫ-mr-wr*, does not seem to be any relation to the latter.

H Evidently, *Nḫt*, son of *P3-ti-Sbk*, has not yet paid his debt. The reading of [*P3-ti*]-*Sbk n p3 ḥ*[*d*] is uncertain.

I Perhaps rather *Ḏḥwty-ms*. *Nḫt-Ḥr-ḥb*(?) is not in *Demot. Nb.*

J The reading of the entire line is uncertain. It is unclear why two scribes have signed their names to this text.

K Note the apparent check marks before this name as well as those in lines 5, 9, and 12. Compare witness 16 in the Rendell Papyrus, who might be identical with this man.

———————————

APPENDIX

RENDELL PAPYRUS

Illustrations: Plates 58–62[81]

Demotic papyrus published in Rendell and Rendell 1979: 98

Length: 101 cm (according to the catalog description)

Height: 33 cm (according to the catalog description)

Type: Donation of a house, various shares of other real estate, and sources of income

Party A: ꜥnḫ-mr-wr, the elder, son of Pꜣ-tï-Wsïr and Ḥr-ꜥnḫ

Party B: ꜥnḫ-mr-wr, the younger, son of Pꜣ-tï-Wsïr and Ḥr-ꜥnḫ

Date: August 16–September 14, 232 B.C. during the reign of Ptolemy III Euergetes I. The Greek docket is dated to September 5, 232 B.C. (dated according to the financial year).

Scribe: Pa-nꜣ(?), son of Pꜣ-tï-Ḥr-pꜣ-šr-n-ïs.t

TRANSLITERATION

LINES 1–12

1. ḥꜣ.t-sp 15 ïbt 3 šmm (n) Pr-ꜥꜣ Ptlw[m]ys ꜥnḫ ḏ.t sꜣ Ptlwmys ïrm ꜣrsn tꜣ mr-sn nꜣ ntr.w sn.w **A** wꜥb n ꜣrgsꜣntrws ïrm nꜣ ntr.w sn.w nꜣ ntr.w mnḫ.w Qrsmws sꜣ ꜣrstn ïw Brngꜣ tꜣ šr.t n Srtn fy tn nb m-bꜣḥ ꜣrsn tꜣ mr-sn **B**

2. ḏ ḥtmw-ntr wyt ꜥnḫ-mr-wr pꜣ ꜥꜣ sꜣ Pꜣ-tï-Wsïr mw.t⸗f Ḥr-ꜥnḫ n ḥtmw-ntr wyt ꜥnḫ-mr-wr pꜣ ḫm sꜣ Pꜣ-tï-Wsïr mw.t⸗f Ḥr-ꜥnḫ **C** tï⸗y n⸗k tꜣ pš n pr(?)**D** n pꜣy ꜥ.wy nt qt ïw⸗f grg n sy sbꜣ nt ïr mḫ-ntr 25 n rs r mḫt ïw⸗f ïr mḫ-ntr 17 n ïmnt (r) ꜣꜣbt **E**

3. [ḥnꜥ tꜣ pš] n tꜣ ḫry.t **F** nt ïr n⸗f ꜣꜣbt(?) nt ïr mḫ-ntr 21 n rs r mḫt ïw⸗s ïr mḫ-ntr 2 (n) ïmnt (r) ꜣꜣbt ḥnꜥ tꜣ pš n pꜣy ïnḫ **G** nt ïr n⸗f mḫt ꜣꜣbt nt ïr mḫ-ntr 9 n rs r mḫt ïw⸗f ïr mḫ-ntr 8 n ïmnt (r) ꜣꜣbt ḥnꜥ tꜣ pš (n) tꜣ nsy.t **H** nt ïr n⸗w ïmnt ḥr pꜣy⸗w mꜣꜥ rs ḫry ḫry nt n Ḥ.t-wr.t ḫn pꜣ tš

4. ꜣrsn nt wn mtw⸗y tꜣy⸗w k.t pš ḥr pꜣy⸗w mꜣꜥ mḫt ḫry ḫry nꜣy⸗w hyn.w rs nꜣ ꜥ.wy.w n ḥtmw-ntr wyt Sbk-ḥtp sꜣ Pꜣ-tï-Wsïr nt ḫr nꜣy⸗f ḫrṭ.w r pꜣ ḥr ïwt⸗w **I** mḫt nꜣ ꜥ.wy.w n ḥtmw-ntr wyt Sbk-ḥtp sꜣ ꜥnḫ-mr-wr **J** ḥnꜥ nꜣ ꜥ.wy.w n... sꜣ Pa-sy **K** nt ḫr nꜣy⸗f ḫrṭ.w ḫn n⸗w ïmnt nꜣ ꜥ.wy.w n ḥtmw-ntr wyt

5. [...] ... sꜣ ... ḥnꜥ nꜣ wrḥ.w ... Pa-wꜣ(?) r pꜣ ḥr ïwt⸗w **L** ꜣꜣbt pꜣ ꜥ.wy n Pꜣ-tï-Rnn.t sꜣ Ḥr ḥnꜥ tꜣy⸗y ry.t ḫn n⸗w **M** ḥnꜥ tꜣ pš n nꜣy⸗y mꜣꜥ.w nꜣ wrḥ.w nt ḫn⸗w **N** nt ïr mḫ-ntr 20 n

---

81. This edition is made on the basis of photographs alone.

rs r mḥt iw=w ir mḥ-ntr 36 n imnt (r) iꜣbt nt n Ḥ.t-wr.t nꜣy=w hyn.w rs nꜣ ꜥ.wy.w ḥtmw-ntr wyt Mꜣꜥ-Rꜥ sꜣ...^O *nt ḫr nꜣy=f ḥrṭ.w...*^P

6. [...] *...*^Q *mḥt nꜣ ꜥ.wy.w n Pꜣ-ti-Sbk sꜣ Pꜣ-šr-n-tꜣ-iḥ.t(?)*^R *ḥn n=w imnt pꜣ ꜥ.wy (n) gl-šr*^S *Pa-wꜣ sꜣ ir.t-Ḥr-r-r=w ḥn n=w iꜣbt nꜣ ꜥ.wy.w n ḥtmw-ntr wyt Sbk-ḥtp sꜣ Pꜣ-ti-Wsir nt ḫr nꜣy=f ḥrṭ.w r pꜣ ḫr iwt=w ḥnꜥ pꜣ 1/3 1/15 n nꜣ št.w (n) nꜣ ḥ.wt nꜣ qs.w*^T *n ḥtmw-ntr wyt Psy nt iw=w ḏ n=f Pꜣ-ti-Wsir sꜣ ꜥnḫ-mr-wr*

7. *mw.t=f Nꜣ-nfr-ib-Ptḥ*^U *pꜣy=y it pꜣy=k it ḥnꜥ nꜣy=w št.w ḥnꜥ nꜣy=w ꜣḫ.w ḥnꜥ nt nb nt mtw=w(?) ḥnꜥ nꜣ nt šp r-r=w ḥnꜥ nꜣ nt iw=w mḥ n-im=w ḥnꜥ nꜣ nt iw=w r wꜣḥ r-r=w ḥnꜥ nt nb nt pr n-im=w ḥnꜥ nꜣy=w ḥn.w*^V *n mꜣꜥ nb mtw=k tꜣ pš.t n pꜣy ꜥ.wy tꜣy ḥry.t pꜣy inḥ tꜣy nsy.t nt ḥry ḥr pꜣy=w mꜣꜥ rs ḥry ḥry ḥnꜥ tꜣ pš n nꜣy mꜣꜥ.w nꜣ wrḥ.w nt m-sꜣ=w*^W

8. *[nt iw] nꜣy=w ḥy.w nꜣy=w hyn.w sḫ r-ḥry ḥnꜥ pꜣ 1/3 1/15 n nꜣ št.w (n) nꜣ ḥ.wt nꜣ qs.w*^X *n ḥtmw-ntr wyt Psiy sꜣ ꜥnḫ-mr-wr mw.t=f Nꜣ-nfr-ib-Ptḥ pꜣy=y it pꜣy=k it nt ḥry ṭ pꜣ hrw r-ḥry r-ti=y n=k n tꜣy=k tni.t sꜥnḫ n nt nb nk nb nt mtw*^Y *ḥtmw-ntr wyt Psiy sꜣ ꜥnḫ-mr-wr mw.t=f Nꜣ-nfr-ib-Ptḥ*

9. *[pꜣy]=y it pꜣy=k it ḥnꜥ nt nb nk nb nt mtw*^Z *s-ḥm.t Ḥr-ꜥnḫ sꜣ.t n ḥtmw-ntr wyt Mꜣꜥ-Rꜥ mw.t=s Nb.t-tꜣ-ḥy(?)*^{AA} *tꜣy=y mw.t tꜣy=k mw.t mn mtw=y mt nb nt nb n pꜣ tꜣ i-ir n=k rn=w n ṭ pꜣ hrw r-ḥry pꜣ nt iw=f r iy r-r=k r-ḏbꜣ.ṭ=w n rn=y n rn pꜣy=y it tꜣy=y mw.t iw=y r ti.t wy=f r-r=k n ḥtr iwty mn iwty ḏ qnb.t nb mt nb (n) pꜣ tꜣ*

10. *mtw=k šm r-ḥry ḥry r tbn pꜣ trt n ⌜nꜣ⌝*^{BB} *mꜣꜥ.w nt ḥry mtw=k pr r-ḫn r bnr n tꜣ ḥyt pꜣ rꜣ ꜥꜣ nꜣ rꜣ.w n pr n nꜣy mꜣꜥ.w nt ḥry mtw=k ir n(?) ḥy nb n-im=w irm nꜣy=k rmt.w nꜣy=k nk.w n ṭ pꜣ hrw r-ḥry šꜥ ḏ.t iw*^{CC} *s-ḥm.t Ḥr-ꜥnḫ sꜣ.t n ḥtmw-ntr wyt Mꜣꜥ-Rꜥ mw.t=s Nb.t-tꜣ-ḥy(?) tꜣy=w mw.t ḏ sḫ i-iry mt nb nt ḥry ḥꜣ.t=y*

11. *mtr.w n-im=w my ir=w r-ḫ mt nb nt ḥry ḥꜣ.t=y mtr n-im=w ꜥnḫ-mr-wr pꜣ ꜥꜣ sꜣ Pa-sy ḥnꜥ ꜥnḫ-mr-wr pꜣ ḥm sꜣ Pa-sy nꜣy=y ḥrṭ.w nt ḥry nꜣ nb.w nt nb nk nb nt pꜣy=w wn sḫ r-ḥry n ṭ pꜣ hrw r-ḥry mn mtw=y mt nb nt nb n pꜣ tꜣ i-ir n=w n rn=w n ṭ pꜣ hrw r-ḥry šꜥ ḏ.t iw*^{DD} *s-ḥm.t Nb.t-tꜣ-ḥy(?) sꜣ.t n ḥtmw-ntr wyt Pꜣ-ti-Wsir*

12. *mw.t=s Ḥr-ꜥnḫ ḏ sḫ i-iry mt nb nt ḥry ḥꜣ.t=y mtr.w n-im=w mn mtw=y mt nb nt nb n pꜣ tꜣ i-ir ꜥnḫ-mr-wr pꜣ ꜥꜣ sꜣ Pa-sy ḥnꜥ ꜥnḫ-mr-wr pꜣ ḥm nt ḥry r-ḏbꜣ.ṭ=w(?)*^{EE} *nt nb nk nb nt pꜣy=w wn sḫ r-ḥry n ṭ pꜣ hrw r-ḥry šꜥ ḏ.t sḫ Pa-nꜣ(?) sꜣ Pꜣ-ti-Ḥr-pꜣ-šr-n-is.t*^{FF}

GREEK DOCKET

1. (῎Ετους) ις Ἐπεὶφ κᾱ πέπτωκεν εἰς κιβωτὸν

2.   τὸ συνάλλαγμα ἐν Αὐήρῃ τοῦ Ἀρσινοίτου νομοῦ

3.   διὰ Φιλήμονος τοῦ παρ᾽ Ἀράτου μετοχῆς ἡμίσους οἰκίας καὶ αὐλῆς καὶ τρίτου καὶ ιέ´ ταριχήας Ἀχομνεῦις μέγας Πάσιτος Ἀχομνεύει μικρῶι τῶι ἀδελφῶι.

CRITICAL APPARATUS

3. Read ταριχείας.

WITNESS LIST

1. *Sbk-ḥtp s3 Pa-w3 s3 P3-tỉ-Sbk(?)*^{GG}

2. *...s3 ...*^{HH}

3. Check mark *Ḏ-Ptḥ-ỉw=f-ʿnḫ...*^{II}

4. *Ḏḥwty-Ḥp s3 Ḥr-wḏ3*

5. *S-n-Wsr*^{JJ} *(s3) Ḥr-m-ḥb*

6. Check mark *Ḥr-wḏ3 s3 Pa-w3*

7. *Pa-sy s3 Pa-ḥy(?)*

8. Check mark *M3ʿ-Rʿ-... s3 Sy-Sbk*^{KK}

9. *Pa-ỉs.t s3... r3*^{LL}

10. *P3-tỉ-Wsỉr s3 M3ʿ-Rʿ*

11. *Pa-Ḏḥwty(?)*^{MM} *s3 Ḥr-s3-ỉs.t*

12. Check mark *Wn-nfr s3...*

13. Check mark *Pa-sy s3 M3ʿ-Rʿ(?)*

14. Check mark *Pa-sy s3...*

15. *Nḫt-Ḥr s3 Pa-ỉs.t*

16. Check mark *Ḥr s3 Pa-n3(?)*^{NN}

TRANSLATION

1. Year 15, third month of the season *shemu*, of Pharaoh Ptolemy, who lives forever, son of Ptolemy and Arsinoe Philadelphos, the gods Adelphoi, the priest of Alexander and of the gods Adelphoi and of the gods Euergetai being *Qrsmws*, son of Ariston, while Berenike, daughter of S(t)raton, is the Kanephoros before Arsinoe Philadelphos.

2. The god's sealer and embalmer *ʿnḫ-mr-wr*, the elder, son of *P3-tỉ-Wsỉr*, whose mother is *Ḥr-ʿnḫ*, has declared to the god's sealer and embalmer *ʿnḫ-mr-wr*, the younger, son of *P3-tỉ-Wsỉr*, whose mother is *Ḥr-ʿnḫ*: "I have given to you the half house share(?) of this house which is built, it being provided with beam and door, which measures 25 god's cubits from south to north, while measuring 17 god's cubits from west (to) east;

3. [together with the half] of the lane which is on the east(?) of it, which measures 21 god's cubits from south to north, while measuring 2 god's cubits (from) west (to) east; together with the half of this courtyard which is on its northeast, which measures 9 god's cubits from south to north, while measuring 8 god's cubits from west (to) east; together with the half of the bench which is on their west, on their southern part, below and above, which are in Hawara in the Nome of

4. Arsinoe; of which I own their other half on their northern part, below and above. Their neighbors are: south, the houses of the god's sealer and embalmer *Sbk-ḥtp*, son of *P3-tỉ-Wsỉr*, which are in the possession of his children, the street being between them; north, the houses of the god's sealer and embalmer *Sbk-ḥtp*, son of *ʿnḫ-mr-wr*, and the houses of ...

son of *Pa-sy*, which are in the possession of his children, adjoin them; west, the houses of the god's sealer and embalmer

5. [...] ... son of ... together with the building plots ... *Pa-wȝ*(?), the street being between them; east, the house of *Pȝ-ti̯-Rnn.t*, son of *Ḥr*, and my cell adjoins them; together with the half of my places of the building plots which are among them, which measure 20 god's cubits from south to north, while measuring 36 god's cubits from west (to) east, which are in Hawara. Their neighbors: south, the houses of the god's sealer and embalmer *Mȝꜥ-Rꜥ*, son of ... , which are in the possession of his children ...

6. [...] ... ; north, the houses of *Pȝ-ti̯-Sbk*, son of *Pȝ-šr-n-tȝ-iḥ.t*(?), adjoin them; west, the house of the *kalasiris Pa-wȝ*, son of *ir.t-Ḥr-r-rꝫw*, adjoins them; east, the houses of the god's sealer and embalmer *Sbk-ḥtp*, son of *Pȝ-ti̯-Wsir*, which are in the possession of his children, the street being between them. Together with the two-fifths of the incomes from the tombs and the burials of the god's sealer and embalmer *Psy*, who is called *Pȝ-ti̯-Wsir*, son of *ꜥnḫ-mr-wr*,

7. whose mother is *Nȝ-nfr-ib-Ptḥ*, my father and your father, together with their incomes and their property and everything that pertains to them and those things which are received with respect to them and those which are paid and those which will be added to them and everything which proceeds from them and their revenues anywhere. Yours are the half of this house, this lane, this courtyard, and this bench aforesaid on their southern part, below and above, together with the half of these places of the building plots which pertain to them,

8. the measurements and neighbors [of which] are written above, together with two-fifths of the incomes from the tombs and burials of the god's sealer and embalmer *Psi̯y*, son of *ꜥnḫ-mr-wr*, whose mother is *Nȝ-nfr-ib-Ptḥ*, my father and your father aforesaid, from today onward, which I have given to you as your share of the annuity from all of everything that belonged to the god's sealer and embalmer *Psi̯y*, son of *ꜥnḫ-mr-wr*, whose mother is *Nȝ-nfr-ib-Ptḥ*,

9. [m]y father and your father, together with all of everything that belonged to the woman *Ḥr-ꜥnḫ*, daughter of the god's sealer and embalmer *Mȝꜥ-Rꜥ*, whose mother is *Nb.t-tȝ-ḥy*(?), my mother and your mother. I do not have anything at all in the world due from you on their account from today onward. As for him who might come against you concerning them in my name or in the name of my father or my mother, I will make him withdraw from you of necessity without delay, without any lawsuit or anything (in) the world.

10. You may go up (to) and down (from) the roof on the stairway of the aforesaid places, and you may go in and out of the forehall (by) the main door and the exit doors of these aforesaid places, and you are to make any alterations in them with your men and your materials from today on forever." Whereas the woman *Ḥr-ꜥnḫ*, daughter of the god's sealer and embalmer *Mȝꜥ-Rꜥ*, whose mother is *Nb.t-tȝ-ḥy*(?), their mother, says: "Write. Do everything above. My heart

11. is satisfied therewith. Cause that it be done in accordance with everything above. My heart is satisfied therewith. *ꜥnḫ-mr-wr*, the elder, son of *Pa-sy*, and *ꜥnḫ-mr-wr*, the younger, son of *Pa-sy*, my children aforesaid, are the owners of everything of all the property, of which

the list is written above, from today onward. I do not have anything at all in the world due from them with respect to it from today onward forever." Whereas the woman, *Nb.t-t3-ḥy*(?), daughter of the god's sealer and embalmer *P3-tỉ-Wsỉr*,

12. whose mother is *Ḥr-ˁnḥ*, says: "Write! Do everything aforesaid. My heart is satisfied therewith. I do not have anything at all in the world due from *ˁnḥ-mr-wr*, the elder, son of *Pa-sy*, and *ˁnḥ-mr-wr*, the younger, aforesaid, on account of all of everything, of which the specification is written above from today onward forever." Written by *Pa-n3*(?), son of *P3-tỉ-Ḥr-p3-šr-n-ỉs.t*.

GREEK DOCKET

(Year) 16, Epeiph 21, the agreement has been deposited in the (official) chest at Hawara of the Arsinoite Nome by Philemon, the agent of Aratos, for sharing of half a house and courtyard and 1/3 and 1/15 [= 2/5] (sc. share) of mummification (sc. mummification business or shop?): Achomneuis, the elder son of Pasis, to Achomneuis, the younger, his brother.

COMMENTARY ON THE DEMOTIC TEXT

A The date is equivalent to August 16–September 14, 232 B.C. during the reign of Ptolemy III Euergetes I. The Greek docket is dated precisely to September 5, 232 B.C.

B For the eponymous priests, see Clarysse and van der Veken 1983: 12–13 (no. 58). *Qrsmws* is presumably the Greek personal name Khruse(r)mos. The father's name in P. Cairo 30604, line 1, is *L3n* (see Thissen 1984b: 235), while *3rstn* is written in this papyrus. There seems to have been some confusion among the Egyptian scribes concerning the name of the eponymous priest of this year.

C One of these brothers is Party B in Chicago Hawara Papyrus 10 (dated to 221 B.C.). In that document the father is called *Psỉy*, but in this text the scribe has thoughtfully written "*Psy* who is called *P3-tỉ-Wsỉr*, son of *ˁnḥ-mr-wr*, whose mother is *N3-nfr-ỉb-Ptḥ*" (lines 6–7). On the personal name *Pa-sy* (*Demot. Nb.*, p. 412) as an abbreviation of *P3-tỉ-Wsỉr*, see Parker 1972: 134–35; Quaegebeur 1987: 79.

D *pš n pr* or *pš (n) pr* does seem to be the most likely transliteration. This appears to be a compound "half house share" or similar, though I know of no other attestations. It occurs only here; later the scribe writes just *pš(.t)*.

E See figure 4 for the plan of this house.

F Although *Glossar*, p. 390, translates *ḥr.t* as "Futterplatz," *ḥry.t* is probably to be rendered "lane"; see El-Amir 1955: 135–38; Andrews 1990: 38 (line 3).

G The writing of *ỉnḥ* is rather odd, as one expects the initial *ỉ* to be written before the *ỉn*-sign.

H For *nsy.t* "bench," see note H to Chicago Hawara Papyrus 7A.

I If "children" here means "descendants," *Sbk-ḥtp*, son of *P3-tỉ-Wsỉr*, could be identical to the witness of Chicago Hawara Papyrus 2, column 1, line 16, dated to 331 B.C.

J This is the house of *Sbk-ḥtp*, son of *ʿnḫ-mr-wr*, restored in Chicago Hawara Papyrus 9, line 4, on the basis of Copenhagen Hawara Papyrus 3 (= P. Carlsberg 36), line 4.

K Perhaps *Mȝʿ-Rʿ*, son of *Pa-sy*. However, the writing of *Mȝʿ-Rʿ* would be quite atypical.

L The reading of the beginning of this line is quite obscure. On the basis of Copenhagen Hawara Papyrus 3 (= P. Carlsberg 36), line 4, one expects that the western boundary of this property is formed by the house of *Mȝʿ-Rʿ*, son of *Pȝ-šr-n-tȝ-iḥ.t*. However, in that text, dated to 233 B.C., there is no mention of "building plots" to the west.

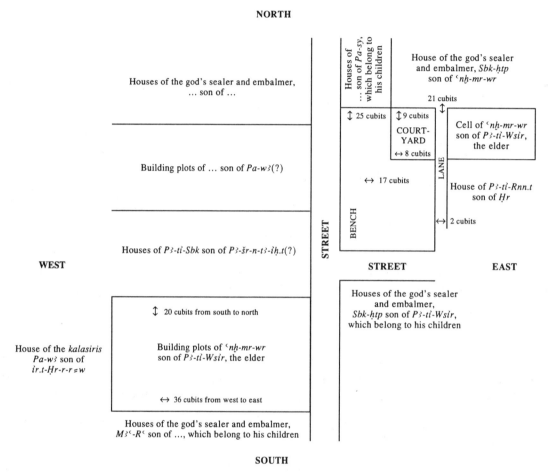

Figure 4. House Plan from Rendell Papyrus

M The same individual appears in Copenhagen Hawara Papyrus 3 (= P. Carlsberg 36), line 4; see *Demot. Nb.*, p. 321.

N The precise meaning of the phrase "my places of the building plots which are among them" is unclear. An alternative translation is "my places (and) the building plots which are among them." What has been read as *ḫn≠w* here is more like *m-sȝ≠w* in the same phrase in line 7.

O I am unable to read the name of the father.

P The papyrus is damaged. One expects a parenthetical remark such as *r pȝ ḫr iwt≠w*, and the reading *r pȝ ḫr* at the end of the line is possible.

Q Perhaps *iwt[≠w]* "between them"; compare the writing of *iwt* in line 5.

R *P3-šr-n-t3-iḥ.t* is quite uncertain.

S For *gl-šr* "*kalasiris*," see the remarks of Vleeming 1991: 114–15.

T For a discussion of the various meanings of *qs.t*, see M. Smith 1987: 27–28.

U The name of the grandmother of both parties is definitely *N3-nfr-ib-Ptḥ*. Her name occurs in Chicago Hawara Papyri 3/1, 4/1, and 6/1.

V This is the same word rendered "festival offerings" by Reymond (1973: 116 [P. Ashm. D. Hawara 16, line 3] with discussion on p. 118).

W In line 5 the same phrase *n3 m3ˁ.w n3 wrḥ.w* concludes with *ḫn≠w*, but here *m-s3≠w* seems to be written.

X The relationship between *št.w* and *ḥ.wt* must be genitival with unwritten *n*, while *ḥ.wt* and *qs.w* must be coordinate nouns.

Y *mtw* is strangely formed; the ink seems to have flaked off here or the papyrus is damaged.

Z Here, too, the *mtw* is somewhat unusual.

AA On this name, see note C to Chicago Hawara Papyrus 6.

BB There is perhaps a trace of the *n3*.

CC There are two consents in this document. In the first consent, the mother of the two parties, *Ḥr-ˁnḫ*, affirms that they are indeed the lawful owners of the property which forms the subject in this transaction.

DD In the second consent the sister of the two parties, named after her grandmother, also declares that she has no claim on the property transferred in this text.

EE *r-ḏb3.ṯ≠w* is oddly written.

FF For this scribe, see note M to Chicago Hawara Papyrus 9.

GG *P3-ti-Sbk* is an uncertain reading. See note R to Chicago Hawara Papyrus 9.

HH I am unable to decipher this line satisfactorily. The first name seems to conclude with the seated-goddess determinative. *Pa-t3-ntr.t* is a possible reading, but I can quote no other example of this name.

II Perhaps *s3 M3y-ḥs* follows the first name.

JJ There might also be a check mark in front of this name. For the name *S-n-Wsr*, see Zauzich 1976: 129.

KK Perhaps read *M3ˁ-Rˁ-p3-3w*, an otherwise unattested variant of *M3ˁ-Rˁ-p3-w3* (*Demot. Nb.*, p. 580).

LL *r3* in the second name seems secure, but I cannot interpret the first part of the group.

MM *Pa-Ḏḥwty* is uncertain; perhaps read *M3ˁ-Rˁ*.

NN The reading *Pa-n3*(?) was suggested by Carol Andrews (pers. comm.); compare Chicago Hawara Papyrus 10, witness 3. The two could be identical.

COMMENTARY ON THE GREEK DOCKET

GENERAL REMARKS

The Greek docket is written at the lower left of the Demotic text. Line 1 of the Greek begins at the Demotic document's left margin and continues toward the end of line 12 of the Demotic text (the Greek being written left to right, the Demotic right to left). Line 1 of the Greek text stops short of line 12 of the Demotic, but the next Greek line carries a short way into the end of line 12 of the Demotic. The tops of some of the Greek letters (beginning with the first *omicron* of Ἀρσινοίτου) overlap the bottoms of some of the Demotic signs. The third line of Greek continues from the left margin below and roughly to the midpoint of line 12 of the Demotic text. Thus, the first two lines in Greek are very short (with line 2 somewhat longer than line 1) and the third line is proportionately very long.

COMMENTS ON LINES

1. Year 16 (of Ptolemy III Euergetes I), Epeiph 21. The same variation between the Demotic contract (year 15) and the Greek registration (year 16) is found in the nurse contract P. Cairo 30604, published by Thissen (1984b: 235–44). That papyrus is dated to the same year as this one, 232 B.C. Year 15 refers to the Egyptian regnal year; year 16 refers to the financial year; see Thissen 1984b: 239. On the dating problems connected with documents of this period, and specifically 232/231 B.C., see Kramer 1991: 90–95.

2. νομοῦ is not impossibly νομωῦ, with *omega* for second *omicron*.

3. Ἀράτου might be too short for the space; read perhaps Ἀραταίου.
   μετοχῆς has a small blank space between the *epsilon* and *tau*.

SELECTIVE INDEX OF WORDS AND PHRASES
DISCUSSED IN THE COMMENTARIES

GLOSSARY

DEITIES

ỉmn "Amun," 1 vso. 1/8

Ptḥ "Ptah," 1/1 (2×), 2 (2×); 2/1 (2×), 2, 3; 3/1, 2, 3 (2×); 6/2 (2×), 3 (2×); 8/2, 3, 4, 5

N.t "Neith," 3, witness copy 1, 1; 5/3 (2×)

Sbk "Sobek," 1/4, vso. 1/13 (2×), 2/19; 4/1, 2; 5/2 (*Sbk-Rʿ*; 2×), 3, 4; 7A/3, 9; 8/2, 6

TITLES, OCCUPATIONS, AND EPITHETS

ỉmy-wnw.t "astronomer," 1/4; 7A/9; 8/6

ỉtnw "deputy," 1 vso. 2/19 (2×)

ʿ-n-ỉr-ḥbs.w "chief tailor," 5/3, 4

wꜣḥ-mw " choachyte," 10/4

wyt "embalmer," 1/1 (2×), 3 (2×); 2/1 (2×); 3/1 (2×); 4/1 (2×), 3; 5/1 (2×), 8, 9; 6/1, 2; 7A/2 (2×), 3, 4 (2×), 8 (2×), 9; 7B/3; 9/2 (2×; once restored), 3 (2×), 4 (2×), 7, 8 (2×); 10/5; Rendell Papyrus 2 (2×), 4 (3×), 5, 6 (2×), 8 (2×), 9, 10, 11

wʿb "priest," 1 vso. 2/20(?); 6/1; 7A/1; 8/1; 9/1; 10/2; Rendell Papyrus 1

wpṯ(y).w "judges," 1/3; 2/4; 3/4; 6/4; 8/6

wḥy (n) tꜣ mre "fisherman (of) the lake," 8/2

bꜣk "male servant," 1/2; 2/2, 3; 3/2; 4/5; 6/2; 8/2, 3

bꜣk.t "female servant," 1/2; 2/2, 3; 3/2; 4/5; 6/2; 8/3

pr-ʿꜣ "pharaoh," 1/1; 2/1; 3/1; 4/1; 5/1(restored); 6/1; 7A/1; 7B/1; 8/1; 9/1(restored); 10/1, 4; Rendell Papyrus 1

fy tn nb "Kanephoros," 6/1; 7A/1; 8/1; 9/1; 10/3-4; Rendell Papyrus 1

fkṯ (priestly title), 1 vso. 1/9, 2/35

mr-sn "Philadelphos," 6/1; 7A/2; 8/2; 9/1 (2×); 10/1, 4; Rendell Papyrus 1 (2×)

mr-šn "lesonis," 1 vso. 2/25(?)

nꜣ ntr.w mnḫ.w "the gods Euergetai," 9/1; 10/2; Rendell Papyrus 1

nt ntr.w sn.w "the gods Adelphoi," 6/1; 7A/1 (2×); 7B/3; 8/1 (2×); 9/1 (2×); 10/1, 2; Rendell Papyrus 1 (2×)

ḥm "servant," 3, witness copy 1, 1; 5/3 (2×)

ḥm-ntr "prophet," 1 vso. 1/2, 3 (2×), 4 (2×), 5, 6, 7, 8, 9, 10, 11, 12, 13, 16 (2×), 18, 2/20 (2×), 21 (2×), 22 (2×), 28, 29, 31, 35 (2×), 36; 2 vso. 1/5, 7, 12; 4/vso. 1

ḥm-sʿnḫ n ḥ.t-ntr "temple sculptor," 5/2

TITLES, OCCUPATIONS, AND EPITHETS (*cont.*)

ḥtmw-ntr "god's sealer,"   1/1 (2×), 3 (2×), vso. 1/13; 2/1 (2×); 3/1 (2×); 4/1 (2×), 3; 5/1 (2×), 8, 9;
6/1, 2; 7A/2 (2×), 3, 4 (2×), 8 (2×), 9; 7B/3; 9/2 (2×; once restored), 3 (2×), 4 (2×), 7, 8 (2×);
10/5; Rendell Papyrus 2 (2×), 4 (3×), 5, 6 (2×), 8 (2×), 9, 10, 11

sẖ "scribe,"   1 vso. 1/12, 13

šwt "merchant,"   5/3

gl-šr "*kalasiris,*"   Rendell Papyrus 6

TOPOGRAPHY

Wȝḥ-r-qr(?),   4/3

Wynn.w "Greeks,"   7A/1

Pȝ-bw-n-ym,   4/2

Mr-wr "Moeris,"   7A/3

Ḥ.t-wr.t "Hawara,"   4/2 (2×), 3; 7A/3; 7B/7; 9/5; Rendell Papyrus 3, 5

MEASUREMENTS

mḥ-ntr "divine cubit,"   4/2 (4×); 5/2 (2×); 7A/2 (2×); 9/2 (2×), 3 (2×); Rendell Papyrus 2 (2×), 3
(4×), 5 (2×)

hn "*hin*-measure,"   1/2 (3×); 2/2 (3×); 6/3 (3×); 8/4 (3×)

MONEY

ḥmt "copper,"   7B/13

ḥḏ "silver, money,"   1/1 (3×), 2 (3×); 2/1 (3×), 2 (2×), 3; 3/1, 2 (2×), 3 (3×); 4/4 (2×); 5/1, 2; 6/2
(3×), 3 (3×); 7A/2, 3; 7B/8, 9, 13, 14, 15 (3×), 16 (2×), 19, 24, 25 (2×), 27; 8/2 (3×), 4 (3×);
9/2; 10/6 (3×), 7, 10. See also *pr-ḥḏ, sẖ n ḏbȝ ḥḏ*

sttr(*.t*) "*stater,*"   4/4 (3×); 7B/8 (2×), 10, 13

qt "*kite,*"   1/1, 2 (2×); 2/1, 2, 3; 3/2, 3 (3×); 6/2, 3 (3×); 7B/8, 9, 13, 14, 15 (2×), 16 (2×), 19; 8/2, 4
(3×); 10/6

ḏbꜥ.t "obol,"   7B/9, 10, 13

GENERAL VOCABULARY

ȝ

ȝḥ "field,"   1/2; 2/2, 3; 3/2; 6/2; 8/3

ȝḥ.w "property,"   Rendell Papyrus 7

ȝḥ.t see *ìbt*

ì

ì-ìr "from,"   4/3

ì-ìr "against,"   Rendell Papyrus 12

    ì-ìr n⸗k   7A/9; 10/8, 11; Rendell Papyrus 9

    r-ìr n⸗k   7B/18

    ì-ìr n⸗t   9/5, 9

G<small>ENERAL</small> V<small>OCABULARY</small> (*cont.*)

  i-ir n≠s 5/9

  i-ir n≠w Rendell Papyrus 11

i3w.t "office," 3/2; 6/2; 8/3

i3w.t "cattle, animal," 1/2; 2/2, 3; 6/2

i3bt "east," 4/2; 5/2, 4; 7A/3, 4; 9/2, 3, 4, 5 (restored); Rendell Papyrus 2, 3 (4×), 5 (2×), 6

iy "come," 4/4; 5/5; 7A/5; 9/6 (restored); 10/9; Rendell Papyrus 9

iw3.t "security, pledge, guarantee," 1/3; 2/4; 3/3; 6/3; 8/5

iwt "between," 5/3; 7A/4; 9/3, 4, 5; Rendell Papyrus 4, 5, 6

iwty "without," 4/4;10/8, 9; Rendell Papyrus 9 (2×)

ibt "month," 5/1 (restored); 7B/10 (2×), 11

  ibt 2 3ḥ.t "second month of the season *akhet*," 1/1; 3/1

  ibt 1 pr.t "first month of the season *peret*," 4/1; 9/1 (restored); 10/1

  ibt 2 šmm "second month of the season *shemu*," 7A/1; 7B/1, 11; 8/1

  ibt 3 šmm "third month of the season *shemu*," 6/1; Rendell Papyrus 1

  ibt 4 šmm "fourth month of the season *shemu*," 2/1

imnt "west," 4/2; 5/2, 3; 7A/3, 4, 5; 9/2, 3, 4 (2×); Rendell Papyrus 2, 3 (3×), 4, 5, 6

in "bring," 4/3

inḥ "courtyard," 1/2; 2/2, 3; 3/2; 6/2; 7A/4, 7; 8/3; Rendell Papyrus 3, 7

ir "make, do, amount to, execute," 1/4 (2×); 3/4 (2×); 4/2 (4×), 4 (2×); 5/2 (2×), 4, 5 (3×), 6 (2×), 7, 8 (2×); 6/4 (2×); 7A/1, 2 (2×), 5 (2×), 6 (4×), 7 (2×), 8 (3×); 7B/1, 3, 10 (2×), 12, 24; 8/2, 3, 4, 6 (2×); 9/2 (2×), 3 (3×), 5, 6 (3×), 7 (3×), 8 (5×); 10/7; Rendell Papyrus 2 (2×), 3 (7×), 5 (2×), 10, 11

  i-ir(y) (imperative) "Do!," 1/4; 5/8, 10; 7A/8; 7B/21; 9/8; Rendell Papyrus 10, 12

irm "and," 5/7; 6/1 (2×); 7A/1 (2×), 7; 7B/2, 4, 14, 25; 8/1 (2×); 9/1 (2×); 10/1, 2, 7; Rendell Papyrus 1 (2×), 10

iḥ.t "cow," 2/2, 3; 3/2; 8/3

it "father," 1/3; 4/3; 5/5; 7A/6; 9/6; Rendell Papyrus 7 (2×), 8 (2×), 9 (3×)

it "barley," 1/2; 2/2; 3/3; 6/3; 8/4

  ꜥ

ꜥ.wy "house," 1/2, 3; 2/3, 4; 3/3, 4; 4/1 (2×), 2 (3×); 5/1, 2 (3×), 3 (2×), 4 (2×), 6, 7, 9; 6/3, 4; 7A/2, 3 (2×), 4 (3×), 7 (2×), 9; 7B/6; 8/5, 6; 9/2, 3 (4×), 4 (4×), 5, 7 (2×), 8; Rendell Papyrus 2, 4 (4×), 5 (2×), 6 (3×), 7

ꜥ.wy (in the compound *r-ꜥ.wy*) "be due from," 1/2; 2/3; 3/3; 6/3; 8/5

ꜥ3 "elder, great, large, main," 1/3; 4, right margin; 5/7; 7A/7; 8/4 (2×); 9/5, 7; Rendell Papyrus 2, 10, 11, 12

ꜥ3 "ass," 2/2, 3; 3/2; 6/2; 8/3

ꜥn "again, also," 1/1, 2, 4; 2/1, 2, 3; 3/2, 3 (2×); 4/4; 5/10; 6/2, 3 (2×); 7A/7, 9; 7B/9, 12, 24, 27; 8/3, 4, 5; 9/8; 10/6

GENERAL VOCABULARY (*cont.*)

ꜥnḫ "live," 7A/1; 7B/2; 8/1; 9/1; Rendell Papyrus 1

ꜥnḫ "oath," 1/3; 2/4; 3/4; 5/6; 6/4; 7A/6; 8/6; 9/6

ꜥḥꜥ-rt "court proof," 5/6; 7A/6; 9/6

ꜥš "consent," 7A/8; 9/8 (2×)

ꜥq-ḥbs "subsistence," 1/2 (2×); 2/3 (2×); 3/3; 6/3 (2×); 8/5 (2×)

ꜥt "shore," 7A/3

w

w3ḥ "to add," Rendell Papyrus 7

wy "be far, cede," 5/5 (3×), 8; 7A/5 (3×), 9; 9/6 (3×), 8; 10/9; Rendell Papyrus 9. See also *sḫ n*
    wy

wꜥ "one," 4/4

wꜥb "be clear," 5/5; 7A/5; 9/6

wn "specification, listing," 4/1, 4; 7B/14; Rendell Papyrus 11, 12

wn "exist," 7B/5; Rendell Papyrus 4

wrḥ "building plot," 1/2; 2/2, 3; 3/2; 6/2; 8/3; 9/4; Rendell Papyrus 5 (2×), 7

wḫ3 "desire," 1/3; 2/4; 3/4; 6/4; 8/6

wtḫ "refined," 1/1 (2×), 2 (2×); 2/1 (2×), 2, 3; 3/1, 2, 3 (2×); 6/2 (2×), 3 (2×); 8/2, 3, 4, 5

wḏ3(.t) "arrear(s)," 1/2; 2/3; 3/3; 6/3; 8/5

b

b3ḥ (in the compound *m-b3ḥ*) "before," 6/1; 7A/2; 8/2; 9/1; 10/4; Rendell Papyrus 1

bnr "out of, out, except," 1/3; 2/4; 4/4; 5/5, 7; 7A/5, 7; 9/5, 7; Rendell Papyrus 10

bt "emmer," 1/2 (2×); 2/2 (2×); 3/2, 3; 6/3 (2×); 8/4 (2×)

p

pr "house, temple, domain," 1/2, vso. 1/13; 2/2, 3; 3/2; 5/3, 4, 6; 6/2; 8/3; Rendell Papyrus 2(?).
    See also *myt pr, tbn*

pr-ḥḏ "treasury," 1/1 (2×), 2 (2×); 2/1 (2×), 2, 3; 3/1, 2, 3 (2×); 6/2 (2×), 3 (2×); 8/2, 3, 4, 5

pr "go out," 5/6; 7A/7; 9/7 (2×); Rendell Papyrus 7, 10 (2×)

pr.t see *ibt*

pš(.t) "half," 4/2 (2×), 3 (4×); 8/3 (3×), 4 (2×), 5 (2×); 10/6 (2×), 9; Rendell Papyrus 2, 3 (3×;
    once restored), 4, 5, 7 (2×)

m

m see *sḫ*

m3ꜥ "place, part," 5/2, 4, 9; 7A/3, 4, 9; 9/5; Rendell Papyrus 3, 4, 5, 7 (3×), 10 (2×)

m3ꜥ "be justified, entitled," 5/6 (2×); 7A/6 (2×); 9/6 (2×)

m3y "new," 9/3

mi-nn "like-titled," 7B/4 (restored)

m / n-mi.t "likewise," 5/4; 7A/5; 9/5

GENERAL VOCABULARY (*cont.*)

my (imperative of "give, cause"), 7B/23; Rendell Papyrus 11

myt "path," 9/5

myt pr "house-path," 5/7

mw.t "mother," 5/5; 7A/6; 9/6; Rendell Papyrus 9 (2×), 10

    mw.t⸗f   1/1, 3 (2×); 2/1; 3/1; 4/1 (2×); 5/1, 8; 6/1; 7A/2 (2×), 8; 8/2; 9/2, 8; 10/5, 6; Rendell Papyrus 2 (2×), 7, 8 (2×)

    mw.t⸗s   1/1; 2/1; 3/1; 5/1, 8, 9; 6/2; 7A/8; 8/2; 9/2, 7, 8; Rendell Papyrus 9, 10, 12

mn "delay," 4/4; 10/9; Rendell Papyrus 9

mn "there exists not," 7B/22. See also under *Negative Possession*

mre "lake," See *wḥy (n) tꜣ mre* in *Titles, Occupations, and Epithets*

mr "to desire, wish," 1/2; 2/3; 3/3; 6/3; 8/5

mḥ "total, complete," 5/8; 7B/7, 13, 15; 10/8; Rendell Papyrus 7

  (as noun) *mḥ* "completion," 7B/11, 17, 20

mḥt "north, northern," 4/2; 5/2, 3; 7A/2, 3, 4; 9/2, 3 (3×), 4; Rendell Papyrus 2, 3 (3×), 4 (2×), 5, 6

ms "bear," 1/1; 2/2; 3/2; 6/2; 8/3, 4

ms.t "interest," 7B/15, 25

mt "matter, contract, thing," 1/2, 4; 2/2, 3; 3/2; 5/5, 8, 9, 10; 6/3; 7A/6, 8, 9; 7B/18, 21; 8/3; 9/5, 6, 8, 9; 10/8, 10; Rendell Papyrus 9 (2×), 10, 11 (2×), 12 (2×)

mtr(e) "witness," 1/3; 2/4; 3, witness copies 1–4, line 1

mtr "be satisfied," 1/1, 4; 2/1; 3/1; 5/1, 8, 10; 6/2; 7A/2, 8; 7B/22; 8/2; 9/2, 8; 10/7; Rendell Papyrus 11 (2×), 12

mdꜣ.t-ntr "divine book," 1 vso. 1/12

n

n (genitive adjective), *passim*

n (dative), *passim*

    n⸗y   1/1; 2/2; 3/2, 4 (2×); 4/3; 5/5, 8; 6/2, 4 (2×); 7A/6, 8 (2×); 7B/8, 20; 8/3, 4, 6 (2×); 9/6, 8 (2×); 10/6, 7

    n⸗t   1/2, 3 (2×), 4 (2×); 2/2, 4 (2×); 3/2, 3; 5/5; 6/3 (2×), 4 (2×); 8/4, 5 (2×), 6; 9/6

    n⸗k   4/1, 4; 7A/3, 5; 7B/16, 19, 24, 25; Rendell Papyrus 2, 8

    n⸗f   1/1 (2×), 3; 7A/4 (2×), 5; Rendell Papyrus 3 (2×), 6

    n⸗s   9/4

    n⸗w   5/3 (2×), 4; 9/4 (3×); Rendell Papyrus 3, 4, 5, 6 (2×)

    See also *i-ir*

n "in, from," *passim*

    n-im⸗f   1/3; 2/4 (2×); 3/4 (2×); 5/4, 6 (2×), 7; 6/4 (2×); 7A/6; 8/6 (2×); 9/7; 10/7

    n-im⸗w   1/4; 4/4; 5/8, 10; 7A/5, 6, 8; 7B/22; 9/5, 6, 8; Rendell Papyrus 7 (2×), 10, 11 (2×), 12

nb "every, any," *passim*

GENERAL VOCABULARY (*cont.*)

nb "owner, master," 8/4; Rendell Papyrus 11

nmḥ(w) "freeman, free," 1/2. See also *rmt-nmḥ(w)*

nḥ.ṯ "be authorized, certified, empowered," 1/2; 3/3; 6/3; 8/5

nsy.t "bench," 7A/4, 9; 7B/7; Rendell Papyrus 3, 7

nk "property, thing, material," 2/2, 3; 4/3; 5/7; 6/2, 3; 7A/7; 8/3 (2×), 4 (2×), 5; Rendell Papyrus 8, 9, 10, 11, 12

ntr "god," see *ḥm-ntr, ḫtmw-ntr* in *Titles, Occupations, and Epithets*

r

r "to, about, equaling," *passim*

    r-ḥr=y   7B/9

    r-r=k   4/4; 7A/5 (4×); 10/9 (2×; once restored); Rendell Papyrus 9 (2×)

    r-ḥr=t   5/5 (4×); 9/6 (4×)

    r-r=f   10/7

    r-r=w   5/5 (3×); 7A/6 (3×); 9/6 (3×); Rendell Papyrus 7 (2×)

    See also *(r-)ḥry, (r-)ḫn*

r꜄ "gate, door," 5/7; 7A/7 (2×); 9/7 (2×); Rendell Papyrus 10 (2×)

ry.t "cell, room, hut," 9/3, 4, 5, 9; Rendell Papyrus 5

rmt "man," 4/4; 5/4, 7; 7A/5, 7; 9/5; Rendell Papyrus 10

rmt-nmḥ(w) "freeman," 2/2; 3/2; 6/3; 8/3

rn "name," 5/6 (3×), 9; 7A/6 (3×), 9; 7B/18; 9/5, 6 (2×), 7, 9; 10/8 (2×), 11; Rendell Papyrus 9 (3×), 11

rnp.t "year," 1/2; 2/3; 3/3; 6/3; 7B/11, 12, 17; 8/5

rḫ "know, be able," 1/3 (2×); 2/4 (2×); 3/4; 4/3; 5/4; 6/4; 7A/5; 8/5; 9/5

rs "south, southern," 4/2; 5/2 (2×), 4, 7, 9; 7A/2, 3 (2×), 4, 9; 9/2, 3 (2×), 4, 5; Rendell Papyrus 2, 3 (3×), 4, 5 (2×), 7

h

hy "expenditure(s)," 5/7; 7A/7; 9/7; Rendell Papyrus 10

hyn.w "neighbors," 5/2, 4, 9; 7A/3, 5, 9; 9/3, 4, 5, 9; Rendell Papyrus 4, 5, 8

hp "legal obligation, right, legal claim," 1/4; 4/4; 5/6, 8 (3×); 7A/6, 8, 9; 7B/19, 21; 9/6, 8 (2×)

hn "agreement," 7B/3, 8, 22

hn "to adjoin," 5/3 (2×), 4; 7A/4 (2×); 9/4 (5×); Rendell Papyrus 4, 5, 6 (2×)

hrw "day," 4/2, 3 (2×), 4 (4×), 5; 5/4, 5, 7, 9; 7A/5 (2×), 7, 9; 7B/24; 9/5 (3×), 7, 9 (2×); 10/11 (restored); Rendell Papyrus 8, 9, 10, 11 (2×), 12. See also *sw-hrw*

ḥ

ḥ.t "tomb," Rendell Papyrus 6, 8

ḥ.t-ntr "temple," 4/1; 5/2 (3×); 9/5. See also *ḥm-sꜥnḫ n ḥ.t-ntr* in *Titles, Occupations, and Epithets*

GENERAL VOCABULARY (*cont.*)

ḥ₃.t-sp "year, regnal year,"   1/1; 2/1; 3/1; 4/1; 5/1 (restored); 6/1; 7A/1 (2×); 7B/1 (2×), 10 (2×); 8/1; 9/1 (restored); 10/1; Rendell Papyrus 1

ḥ₃.t (in the compound [*n*] ḥ₃.t) "before," 7B/26

ḥ₃.t "heart,"   1/1, 4; 2/1; 3/1; 5/1, 8, 10; 6/2; 7A/2, 8; 7B/22; 8/2; 9/2, 8; 10/7; Rendell Papyrus 10, 11, 12

ḥw "increase, gain," 7B/9, 12, 14

ḥwt "male," 4/5

ḥbs "clothing," see ˁq-ḥbs

ḥm.t "wife," 7B/23

ḥny "canal," 7A/3

ḥnˁ "together with, and,"   1/1, 2, 3; 2/2, 3, 4; 3/2, 3; 4/2 (5×), 3 (5×), 4, 5; 5/2, 3, 5 (2×), 6 (2×), 7, 8; 6/2, 3; 7A/4, 6 (4×), 9; 7B/18, 20; 8/3, 4, 5; 9/3 (restored), 5, 6 (4×); Rendell Papyrus 3 (3×; once restored), 4, 5 (3×), 6, 7 (9×), 8, 9, 11, 12

ḥr "on,"   4/3; 5/2, 4, 6, 9; 7A/3 (2×), 4, 7, 9; 7B/8, 9; 9/7; Rendell Papyrus 3, 4, 7

ḥry "above,"   1/3 (3×), 4 (2×); 2/4 (3×); 3/3; 4/4; 5/2 (2×), 4 (2×), 6, 7 (2×), 8 (2×), 9 (3×), 10; 6/4 (2×); 7A/3 (2×), 4 (2×), 5, 7 (3×), 8 (3×), 9 (3×); 7B/5 (2×), 12, 17 (2×), 18, 19, 20 (2×), 21, 22 (supplied), 23, 26 (2×), 27; 8/5; 9/3 (2×), 5, 7 (2×), 8 (4×); 10/7, 10; Rendell Papyrus 3, 4, 7 (2×), 8, 10 (3×), 11 (2×), 12 (2×)

(*r-*)ḥry "onwards,"   4/2, 3 (2×), 4 (3×), 5; 5/4 (2×), 5, 6, 7, 9 (2×); 7A/5 (3×), 7 (2×), 9 (2×); 9/5 (4×), 7 (2×), 9 (3×); 10/11 (restored); Rendell Papyrus 8 (2×), 9, 10 (2×), 11 (3×), 12 (2×)

ḥtr (in the compound *n* ḥtr) "of necessity,"   4/4; 10/9; Rendell Papyrus 9

ḫ

ḫ₃s.t "necropolis," 4/2 (2×), 3 (2×)

ḫpr "to become,"   1/1, 2, 3; 2/2, 3 (2×), 4; 3/2, 3 (2×); 4/2, 3 (2×); 6/2, 3 (2×); 7B/16, 19; 8/3, 4, 5 (2×)

ḫm "younger," 9/vso. 4, 8; Rendell Papyrus 2, 11, 12

ẖ

ẖ(.t) (in the compound preposition *r-*ẖ[.*t*]) "in accordance with,"   5/7; 7A/7; 9/7; 10/10 (restored); Rendell Papyrus 11

ẖy.w "measurements,"   5/4, 9; 7A/5, 9; 9/5, 9; Rendell Papyrus 8 (written ẖy.w)

ẖyt "forehall,"   5/7; 7A/7; 9/7; Rendell Papyrus 10

(*r-*)ẖn "in, from, out of,"   4/4; 5/6; 7A/3, 7; 7B/25, 27; 8/4; 9/7; 10/6; Rendell Papyrus 3, 5, 10

ẖn.w "revenue," Rendell Papyrus 7

ẖr "per, for, in the possession of,"   1/2; 2/3; 3/3; 5/3 (3×); 6/3; 7A/4; 7B/10 (2×); 8/5; 9/4; Rendell Papyrus 4 (2×), 5, 6

ẖry "below,"   5/2, 4, 6, 9; 7A/3, 4, 7, 9; 9/3, 5, 7; Rendell Papyrus 3, 4, 7, 10

ẖr "street,"   5/3, 7; 7A/3; 9/3, 4; Rendell Papyrus 4, 5, 6

GENERAL VOCABULARY (*cont.*)

ḥry.t "lane," Rendell Papyrus 3, 7

ẖrṭ.w "children," 1/1; 2/2; 3/2; 5/3 (3×); 6/2; 7A/4; 8/3, 4; 9/4; Rendell Papyrus 4 (2×), 5, 6, 11

s

s "man," 7B/21

s꜄ (in the compound preposition *m-s꜄*) "after, pertaining to," 1/3; 2/4; 3/4; 4/4; 5/6, 8; 6/4; 7A/6, 8; 7B/9; 8/6; 9/7, 8; 10/10; Rendell Papyrus 7

s꜄ "son," *passim*

s꜄.t "daughter," *passim*

sy "beam," 4/1; 5/2; 7A/2; 9/2; Rendell Papyrus 2

sꜥnḫ "annuity, endowment," 1/1, 3 (2×), 4; 2/2, 4 (2×); 3/2, 3, 4; 6/2, 3, 4; 8/3, 5, 6; Rendell Papyrus 8. See also *ḥm sꜥnḫ n ḥ.t-ntr* in *Titles, Occupations, and Epithets; sḫ (n) sꜥnḫ*

sw "day," 1/3; 2/4; 3/4; 6/4; 7A/1 (*sw* 2); 7B/1(*sw* 2), 12, 20; 8/6

sw-hrw "date, deadline," 7B/26

sb꜄ "door," 4/1; 5/2; 7A/2; 9/2; Rendell Papyrus 2

sbt "wall," 9/5 (restored)

sp "remainder," 10/8

sp-2 "twice," 7B/15

sn "brother," See *mr-sn, n꜄ ntr.w sn.w* in *Titles, Occupations, and Epithets*

s-ḥm.t "woman, female," 1/1; 2/1; 3/1; 4/5; 5/1, 7, 9; 6/2; 7A/4, 8; 7B/23; 8/2; 9/2, 7, 8; Rendell Papyrus 9, 10, 11

sḫ(r)y "authority," 4/4; 5/4; 7A/5; 9/5

sḫ "to write," 3/4; 4/4; 5/4, 8, 9, 10; 7A/5, 8, 9; 7B/21; 9/5, 8, 9; 10/11, 12; Rendell Papyrus 8, 10, 11, 12 (3×)

   m-sḫ   1/4; 2/4; 4/5; 5/10; 6/4; 7A/9; 7B/27; 8/6

   r-sḫ   6 (below Greek docket); 9/9 (N.B. it is often difficult to distinguish between *m-sḫ* and *r-sḫ*)

sḫ "document," 1/3; 2/4; 3/2; 5/5 (3×), 6 (restored), 8; 6/2; 7A/6 (4×); 7B/7, 18, 20, 23; 8/3; 9/6 (4×), 8; 10/7, 8, 10

   sḫ n wy   "document of cession," 7B/6

   sḫ (n) sꜥnḫ   "document of annuity," 1/4; 5/8; 7A/8

   sḫ n ḏb꜄-ḥḏ   "document of payment," 5/8; 7B/6

sḫ "hinder, obstruct," 4/4

š

šꜥ "until," 5/7; 7B/11, 17, 20; 9/7; Rendell Papyrus 10, 11, 12

šp "to receive," 1/3 (2×); 2/4; 3/4; 6/4; 7B/26; 8/6; 10/7; Rendell Papyrus 7

šm "to go," 5/6, 7; 7A/7; 9/7; Rendell Papyrus 10

šmw see *ibt*

GENERAL VOCABULARY (*cont.*)

 šr "son," 1/3; 4/1, 4; 6/1; 8/4 (2×)

 šr.t "daughter," 9/1; 10/3; Rendell Papyrus 1

 št "income," Rendell Papyrus 6, 7, 8

q

 qnb.t "title deed," 1/2; 2/2, 3; 5/5; 6/2; 7A/6; 8/3; 9/6; Rendell Papyrus 9

 qrf "subterfuge," 7B/22

 qs "burial," Rendell Papyrus 6, 8

 qt "to build," 4/1; 5/2 (restored); 7A/2; 9/2; Rendell Papyrus 2

g

 grg "to furnish, provide," 4/1; 5/2 (restored); 7A/2; 9/2; Rendell Papyrus 2

k

 k.t "other," Rendell Papyrus 4

t

 tꜣ "world," 1/2; 2/2, 3; 3/2; 4/4 (2×); 5/4, 5, 9; 6/3; 7A/5, 6, 9; 7B/18; 8/3; 9/5 (2×), 6, 9; 10/8, 10; Rendell Papyrus 9 (2×), 11, 12

 tỉ "to cause, give," 1/1 (2×), 2 (2×), 3 (4×); 2/1, 2 (2×), 3 (2×), 4 (2×); 3/1, 2 (2×), 3 (2×), 4 (2×); 4/1, 2, 3 (3×), 4; 5/1, 2, 5 (4×), 6 (2×); 6/2 (2×), 3 (3×), 4 (2×); 7A/2, 3, 5 (4×), 6 (2×); 7B/7, 8, 16, 19, 20, 24, 25, 27; 8/2, 3, 4 (2×), 5 (2×), 6 (2×); 9/2, 6 (4×), 7 (2×); 10/6, 9; Rendell Papyrus 2, 8, 9

 tbn (also in the compound *tbn n pr*) "roof(?)," 5/6; 7A/7; 9/7; Rendell Papyrus 10

 tp-n-ỉꜣw.t "animal," 2/2, 3; 3/2; 6/2; 8/3

 tm (negative verb), 4/4; 5/5; 7A/5; 9/6

 tmỉ "town," 4/2; 7A/3

 tn "at the rate of," 7B/9, 13

 tnỉ.t "share, piece," 1/1 (2×), 2 (2×); 2/1 (2×), 2, 3; 3/1, 2, 3 (2×); 4/1 (2×), 2 (4×), 3 (4×), 4 (2×); 5/1, 7; 6/2 (2×), 3 (2×); 7A/2, 7; 8/2 (2×), 4; 9/2, 3 (restored), 7; 10/6, 9; Rendell Papyrus 8

 trt "stairway," 5/6; 7A/7; 9/7; Rendell Papyrus 10

 tš "nome," 7A/3; Rendell Papyrus 3

ṯ

 ṯ "since, from," 4/2, 3 (2×), 4 (2×), 5; 5/4, 5, 7, 9; 7A/5 (2×), 7, 9; 7B/10; 9/5 (3×), 7, 9 (2×); 10/11; Rendell Papyrus 8, 9, 11 (2×), 12

 ṯ "to take," 7B/27

GENERAL VOCABULARY (*cont.*)

ḏ

    ḏ "to declare, say, call," 1/1 (3×), 3 (3×), 4; 2/1, 4; 3/1, 4; 4/1; 5/1, 8, 10; 6/1, 4; 7A/2, 8; 7B/5, 8, 21, 22 (supplied), 24; 8/2, 5; 9/2 (restored), 8 (2×); 10/4; Rendell Papyrus 2, 6, 9, 10, 12

    ḏ.t "eternity," 5/7; 7A/1; 7B/2; 8/1; 9/1, 7; Rendell Papyrus 1, 10, 11, 12

    ḏꜣḏꜣ "principal," 7B/14, 15

    r-ḏbꜣ "on account of," 4/4; 5/2, 5; 7A/3, 5; 9/6; 10/9; Rendell Papyrus 9, 12. See also *sḥ n ḏbꜣ-ḥḏ*

    ḏr.t "hand," 7B/7 (in *r-ḏr.t* "to"), 26 (in *n-ḏr.t* "from"); 10/7 (in *n-ḏr.t* "from")

AUXILIARIES, GRAMMATICAL ITEMS, AND NUMERALS

First Present

tw≠y	5/8; 9/8
st	2/4; 7B/9

Relative Present

nt iw≠y	4/2 (written *nt iw≠y r;* probably for *nt iw*); 5/6 (2×); 7A/6 (2×); 9/6 (2×)

Second Tense

i-ir≠y	7A/8; 9/8

Relative Converter

nt	*passim*
nt iw	1/2, 3; 2/4; 3/3, 4; 4/4; 5/4, 9; 6/3, 4; 7A/5, 9; 8/5, 6; 9/5 (partly supplied); Rendell Papyrus 8 (restored)
nt iw≠w	Rendell Papyrus 6, 7

Circumstantial

iw (also written *r*)	1/3; 5/3, 7; 6/1, 4(?); 7A/1, 3, 8; 7B/4, 19, 22 (supplied); 8/1; 9/1, 3, 4, 5, 7; Rendell Papyrus 1, 4, 5, 6, 10, 11
iw≠y	5/8; 7A/8, 9; 9/8; 10/10
iw≠k	4/4
iw≠f	1/4; 3, witness copies 1–4, 1; 4/2 (2×); 5/2 (2×; once restored); 7A/2 (2×); 7B/24; 9/2 (2×); Rendell Papyrus 2 (2×), 3
iw≠s	5/9; 9/3, 8; Rendell Papyrus 3
iw≠w	4/1; 7B/21; 10/8; Rendell Papyrus 5

Possession

mtw≠y	1/1, 2; 2/2 (2×), 3 (2×); 3/2 (2×), 3; 4/2, 4, 5; 6/2, 3 (2×); 8/3 (2×), 4, 5; Rendell Papyrus 4
mtw≠n	7B/22

AUXILIARIES, GRAMMATICAL ITEMS, AND NUMERALS (*cont.*)

mtw≠w   Rendell Papyrus 7(?)

mtw   1/1; 2/2; 6/2; 8/3; Rendell Papyrus 8, 9

Negative Possession

mn mtw≠y 5/9; 7A/9; 7B/17; 9/5, 9; 10/8, 10; Rendell Papyrus 9, 11, 12

Future II

ꞽ-ꞽr≠t r   3/4; 6/4; 8/6

Future III

ꞽw≠y r   1/3; 2/4; 3/4; 5/5 (2×), 6; 6/4; 7A/5 (2×), 6–7; 8/6; 9/6 (2×; once restored), 7; 10/9; Rendell Papyrus 9

ꞽw≠k r   7B/20

ꞽw≠f r   4/4

ꞽw≠w r   7B/26

Relative Future III

nt ꞽw≠y r   1/1, 3; 2/2, 3; 3/2, 3; 4/2, 3 (2×); 6/2, 3; 7B/24, 25; 8/3, 4, 5

nt ꞽw≠t r   1/1; 2/2; 3/2; 6/2 (*nt ꞽ-ꞽr≠t r*); 8/3, 4

nt ꞽw≠f r   4/4 (2×); 5/5; 7A/5; 9/6 (restored); 10/9 (restored); Rendell Papyrus 9

nt ꞽw≠s r   1/2; 2/3; 3/3; 6/3; 8/5

nt ꞽw≠w r   5/6; 7A/6; 9/7 (restored); Rendell Papyrus 7

Negative Future III

bn ꞽw≠y   1/3 (2×); 2/4 (2×); 3/3; 6/4 (possibly circumstantial negative future); 8/5

bn ꞽw   4/3; 5/4; 7A/5; 9/5

Aorist

ḫr   7B/12

Circumstantial Negative Past

ꞽw bn-pw≠y 7B/16

Conditional

ꞽw≠y   5/5; 7A/5; 9/6

ꞽw≠f   7B/16, 19

ꞽw≠w   3/4; 6/4; 8/6

Conjunctive

mtw≠y   1/2 (2×); 2/2, 3; 3/2, 3; 5/5; 6/3 (2×); 7A/5; 8/4, 5; 9/6, 8

mtw≠k   7A/7 (3×); Rendell Papyrus 10 (3×)

AUXILIARIES, GRAMMATICAL ITEMS, AND NUMERALS (*cont.*)

Conjunctive (*cont.*)

mtw≠t	5/6 (2×), 7; 9/7 (2×)
mtw≠f	1/4; 7A/8; 9/8
mtw≠w	7B/27

Relative Form

r-	4/3; 5/2, 5 (3×); 6 (below Greek docket); 7A/3, 6 (3×), 8; 7B/3; 9/6 (3×), 8, 9; 10/7

Definite Articles

pꜣ	*passim*
tꜣ	*passim*
nꜣ	*passim*

Possessive Articles

pꜣy≠y	1/3; 4/1, 2, 3; 5/5; 7A/4, 6; 8/4; 9/3, 4 (2×), 6; Rendell Papyrus 7, 8, 9 (2×)
pꜣy≠k	Rendell Papyrus 7, 8, 9
pꜣy≠t	1/1, 2, 3 (3×); 2/2, 3 (2×), 4 (3×); 3/2, 3 (3×), 4 (2×); 6/2, 3 (3×), 4 (2×); 8/3, 4, 5 (3×), 6 (2×)
pꜣy≠f	1/3, 4; 5/2, 4, 7, 9; 6/1; 7A/3 (2×), 4, 9; 9/5
pꜣy≠w	4/1, 4 (2×); 5/6, 8; 7A/6, 9; 7B/12, 14, 18, 20; 9/6, 8; Rendell Papyrus 3, 4, 7, 11, 12
tꜣy≠y	4/1; 5/1, 5; 7A/2, 4, 6; 7B/23; 9/2, 3 (2×; once restored), 6; Rendell Papyrus 5, 9 (2×)
tꜣy≠k	7A/7; 10/6, 9; Rendell Papyrus 8, 9
tꜣy≠t	5/7; 9/7
tꜣy≠f	7B/25; 10/6
tꜣy≠w	Rendell Papyrus 4, 10
nꜣy≠y	4/1 (2×), 2, 5 (2×); Rendell Papyrus 5, 11
nꜣy≠k	7A/7 (2×); Rendell Papyrus 10 (2×)
nꜣy≠t	5/7 (2×); 9/4
nꜣy≠f	5/3 (3×), 4 (2×), 9 (2×); 7A/4; 9/4; Rendell Papyrus 4 (2×), 5, 6
nꜣy≠w	7A/5 (2×), 9 (2×); 9/5 (2×), 9 (2×); Rendell Papyrus 4, 5, 7 (3×), 8 (2×)

Demonstrative Adjectives

pꜣy	4/1; 5/1, 2, 4, 6, 7, 9; 7A/2, 3, 4, 7 (2×), 8, 9; 7B/16, 19, 26; 9/2, 3, 5, 7 (2×), 8 (2×); Rendell Papyrus 2, 3, 7 (2×)
tꜣy	Rendell Papyrus 7 (2×)
nꜣy	Rendell Papyrus 7, 10

Demonstrative Pronouns

nꜣy/nꜣw	2/2, 3; 3, witness copy 1/4; 3, witness copy 2/4; 3, witness copy 3/5; 3, witness copy 4/7

Auxiliaries, Grammatical Items, and Numerals (*cont.*)

Indefinite Articles

wꜥ	4/4; 7B/6 (3×)
wꜥ.t	7B/6, 10, 13

Qualitative Endings

k	5/6 (2×), 8; 7A/6 (2×); 9/6 (2×), 8
ṯ	7A/9
w	1/4; 5/8, 10; 7A/8; 7B/22; 9/8; 10/7; Rendell Papyrus 11, 12

Copula

pꜣy	8/4 (2×)
nꜣw	3/3

Suffix Pronouns

passim

Dependent Pronouns

passim

Independent Pronouns

ink	5/4; 7A/5; 9/5
mtwꞇk	4/3, 4, 5; 7A/4, 6 (3×); Rendell Papyrus 7
mtwꞇt	1/2; 2/3; 3/2 (2×), 3; 5/4, 5, 6; 6/3; 8/5; 9/5, 6 (3×)

Numerals

1/60	1/1 (2×), 2 (2×); 2/1 (2×), 2 (2×); 3/2 (2×), 3 (2×); 6/2 (2×), 3 (2×); 8/2 (2×), 4 (2×)
1/30	1/1, 2; 2/1, 2; 3/2, 3; 6/2, 3; 8/2, 4
1/18	5/1, 4, 7, 9
1/15	Rendell Papyrus 6, 8
1/10	1/1, 2; 2/1, 2; 3/2, 3; 6/2, 3; 8/2, 4
1/6	1/1, 2
1/4	7B/9
1/3	7A/2, 3, 4 (2×), 7, 9 (2×); 7B/6, 11; 9/2, 3 (restored), 5, 7, 8, 9 (restored); Rendell Papyrus 6, 8
1/2	7B/9
2/3	1/1, 2; 4/1, 2 (2×), 5 (2×)
5/6	2/1, 2; 3/2, 3; 6/2, 3; 8/2, 4
1	1/2 (2×); 2/2 (2×), 3; 3/3 (2×); 6/3 (4×); 7B/8, 9, 13, 15 (2×); 8/4 (3×); 10/6 (2×), 7, 10 (restored)

AUXILIARIES, GRAMMATICAL ITEMS, AND NUMERALS (*cont.*)

Numerals (*cont.*)

1.*t*	2/1; 10/1
2	1/2 (2×); 2/2, 3; 3/3 (2×); 5/8; 6/3 (2×); 7B/7, 13, 14, 15, 16 (2×), 19, 21; 10/6; Rendell Papyrus 3
2.*t*	7A/1; 7B/1, 10, 11, 12, 17
3.*t*	7A/1; 7B/1, 10
4.*t*	8/1
5	9/3; 10/6
6	7B/8, 9, 10, 15
7	3/1; 8/4
7.*t*	3, witness copy 1/1; 3, witness copy 2/1; 3, witness copy 3/1; 3, witness copy 4/1
8	7B/8, 14, 16 (2×), 19; 8/4 (2×); 9/1 (restored); Rendell Papyrus 3
9	1/1; 2/1 (2×); 3/2 (2×); 6/2 (2×); 8/2; Rendell Papyrus 3
10	2/1 (2×); 3/1, 2; 4/4; 6/2 (2×)
13	4/1
15	Rendell Papyrus 1
17	1/1; Rendell Papyrus 2
18	4/2; 7A/2; 9/2
19	4/2; 7A/3; 9/2
20	8/2; 9/3; Rendell Papyrus 5
21	4/2; 8/2 (2×); Rendell Papyrus 3
22	4/2
24	1/2; 2/2; 3/3; 5/2; 6/3; 7B/11, 13; 8/4
25	5/2; Rendell Papyrus 2
26	6/1
29	1/1
30	1/1 (2×)
36	1/2 (2×); 2/2 (2×); 3/2, 3; 6/3 (2×); 8/4 (2×); Rendell Papyrus 5
40	1/2 (3×); 2/2 (3×); 3/2, 3 (3×); 6/3 (3×); 8/4 (3×)
100	4/4 (2×)
500	4/4

Unread

… title(?)	1 vso. 2/35

INDEX OF PERSONAL NAMES

EGYPTIAN PERSONAL NAMES (*cont.*)

ꜥnḫ-mꜣꜥ-Rꜥ son of *Ḥr-Ḏḥwty*, 1 vso. 2/34

ꜥnḫ-mr-wr son of *ꜥnḫ-Ḥp* and *Ta-ỉmn*, 1/1, 3; 2/1

ꜥnḫ-mr-wr father of *Pꜣ-tỉ-ỉs.t*, 1 vso. 1/1

ꜥnḫ-mr-wr son of *Pꜣ-tỉ-Wsỉr*(?), 4, right margin

ꜥnḫ-mr-wr(the elder) son of *Pꜣ-tỉ-Wsỉr* (=*Pa-se/Pa-sy*), 10/5(?); Rendell Papyrus 2, 11, 12

ꜥnḫ-mr-wr(the younger) son of *Pꜣ-tỉ-Wsỉr* (=*Pa-se/Pa-sy*), Rendell Papyrus 2, 11, 12

ꜥnḫ-mr-wr son of *Pꜣ-tỉ-nꜣ-ntr.w* and *ꜥnḫ.t*, 3/1; 4/1; 6/1; 7A/2, 8; 7B/4, 5; Rendell Papyrus 6, 8 (2×), 11

ꜥnḫ-mr-wr son of *Pa-tr* (= *Pꜣ-tỉ-nꜣ-ntr.w*) and *Ta-Rnn.t*, 9/2, 8

ꜥnḫ-mr-wr father of *Sbk-ḥtp*, 9/4 (restored); Rendell Papyrus 4

ꜥnḫ-mr-wr father of *Tꜣ-ḥnꜣ*, 7A/4

ꜥnḫ-mr-wr son of *Ṯ-Ḥp-n-ỉm꞊w*, 5/3

ꜥnḫ-mr-wr son of ... , 9/vso. 13

ꜥnḫ-nꜣ-... son of *Tỉ-Bꜣst.t-ỉꜣw*(?), 1 vso. 2/25

ꜥnḫ-⌐nb.t⌐-ḥ.t son of *Mꜣꜥ-Rꜥ*, 2 vso. 1/10

ꜥnḫ-Ḥp father of *ꜥnḫ-mr-wr* and *Psṯ*, 1/1, 3

ꜥnḫ-Ḥp father of *Wꜣḥ-ỉb-Rꜥ-mr-N.t*, 1 vso. 2/24

ꜥnḫ-Ḥp father of *Pꜣ-tỉ-Wsỉr*, 2/1

ꜥnḫ-Ḥp son of *Mꜣꜥ-Rꜥ*, 9/vso. 14

ꜥnḫ-Ḥp father of *Ḥr-wḏꜣ*, 2 vso. 1/8

ꜥnḫ-Ḫnsw father of *Ḏ-Bꜣst.t-ỉw꞊f-ꜥnḫ*(?), 1 vso. 2/31

ꜥnḫ꞊s mother of *Smꜣ-tꜣ.wy*, 8/2

ꜥnḫ-smꜣ-tꜣ.wy father of *ỉy-m-ḥtp*, 6/vso. 1

ꜥnḫ-smꜣ-tꜣ.wy son of *ỉmn-m-ḥꜣ.t*, 3, witness copy 2/1

ꜥnḫ.t mother of *ꜥnḫ-mr-wr* and *ỉmn-m-ḥꜣ.t;* daughter of *ꜥnḫ-mr-wr* and *Psṯ*, 2/1; 3/1; 4/1; 5/1, 8

ꜥnḫ.t mother of *Psṯ*, 1/1

ꜥnḫ.t mother of *Pa-tr* (= *Pꜣ-tỉ-nꜣ-ntr.w*), 7A/2, 8

ꜥnḫ.t daughter of *S-n-Wsr.t* and *Ta-Rnn.t*, 5/1, 9

w

Wꜣḥ-ỉb-Rꜥ-mr-N.t son of *ꜥnḫ-Ḥp*, 1 vso. 2/24

Wn-nfr father of *Pa / Pꜣy-N.t-wr*(*.t*), 4/3, vso. 11

Wn-nfr father of *Pꜣy-Ḥr-sꜣ-ỉs.t*, 4/vso. 3

Wn-nfr father of *Ḥr-wḏꜣ*, 5/3

Wn-nfr father of *Ḥr-ḫb*, 4/vso. 5

Wn-nfr son of *Ḥr-Ḏḥwty*, 1 vso. 2/33

Wn-nfr son of *Ḥr-Ḏḥwty*(?), 4/vso. 7

Wn-nfr father of *Sbk-ḥtp*, 1 vso. 1/4

E<small>GYPTIAN</small> P<small>ERSONAL</small> N<small>AMES</small> (*cont.*)

  Wn-nfr(?) father of *Sbk-...* , 6/vso. 10

  Wn-nfr son of ... , Rendell Papyrus vso. 12

  Wsrkn son of *Mꜣꜥ-Rꜥ,* 1 vso. 1/18

  Wsrkn father of *Ḥr-ḫb,* 1 vso. 2/23

p

  Pꜣ-igš son of *Ḥr,* 9/vso. 7

  Pꜣ-nfr-ḥr son of ... , 9/vso. 10

  Pꜣ-Rꜥ-nt-rq(?) father of *Pꜣ-ti-Ḥr-pꜣ-šr-is.t,* 3, witness copy 3/1

  Pꜣ-rl father of ... , 6/vso. 13

  Pꜣ-ḥm-ntr-4.nw father of *Pꜣ-tỉ-Wsỉr,* 1 vso. 1/17

  Pꜣ-ḥtr father of *Pꜣy꓿f-iwiw,* 2 vso. 1/9

  Pꜣ-ḫꜣꜥ꓿s son of ... , 6/vso. 12

  Pꜣ-sn-ky son of *Mꜣꜥ-Rꜥ,* 1 vso. 1/1

  Pꜣ-š-mtre father of *Smꜣ-tꜣ.wy,* 8/2

  Pꜣ-šwṱ father of *Šty,* 8/2

  Pꜣ-šr-n-tꜣ-iḥ.t father of *ꜥnḫ-Ḥp,* 1/3

  Pꜣ-šr-n-tꜣ-iḥ.t(?) father of *Pꜣ-tỉ-Sbk,* Rendell Papyrus 6

  Pꜣ-šr-(n)-tꜣ-iḥ.t father of *Mꜣꜥ-Rꜥ,* 7A/4; 9/4

  Pꜣ-gwr(?) son of *Twt*(?), 6/vso. 15

  Pꜣ-tỉ-imn father of *Pa-gꜣy,* 4/3

  Pꜣ-tỉ-in-ḥr.t son of *Nb-wꜥb,* 5/2

  Pꜣ-tỉ-is.t son of *ꜥnḫ-mr-wr,* 1 vso. 1/1

  Pꜣ-tỉ-Wsỉr, 1/1. See *ꜥnḫ-Ḥp*

  Pꜣ-tỉ-Wsỉr son of *ỉy-m-ḥtp,* 6 (below Greek docket)

  Pꜣ-tỉ-Wsỉr (= *Psy* / *Psiy* / *Pa-se* / *Pa-sy*) son of *ꜥnḫ-mr-wr* and *Nꜣ-nfr-ib-Ptḥ,* 4/1; 6/1; 10/5; Rendell Papyrus 2, 6, 8 (2×), 11 (3×), 12

  Pꜣ-tỉ-Wsỉr(?) father of *ꜥnḫ-mr-wr,* 4 (right margin)

  Pꜣ-tỉ-Wsỉr son of *ꜥnḫ-Ḥp,* 2/1

  Pꜣ-tỉ-Wsỉr son of *Pꜣ-ḥm-ntr-4.nw,* 1 vso. 1/17

  Pꜣ-tỉ-Wsỉr son of *Mꜣꜥ-Rꜥ,* Rendell Papyrus vso. 10

  Pꜣ-tỉ-Wsỉr father of *Sbk-i-ir-ti-s*(?), 1 vso. 2/26

  Pꜣ-tỉ-Wsỉr father of *Sbk-iw,* 2 vso. 1/13

  Pꜣ-tỉ-Wsỉr son of *Sbk-pꜣ-ym,* 2 vso. 1/5

  Pꜣ-tỉ-Wsỉr father of *Sbk-ḥtp,* 2 vso. 1/16

  Pꜣ-tỉ-Wsỉr father of *Sbk-ḥtp,* Rendell Papyrus 4, 6

  Pꜣ-tỉ-Wsỉr father of *Sṯꜣ꓿w-tꜣ-wty,* 7A/10; 7B/28; 8/6

  Pꜣ-tỉ-Wsỉr father of *Tꜣy-ir꓿w,* 9/7

EGYPTIAN PERSONAL NAMES (*cont.*)

P3-tỉ-p3-R^c(?) father of *Sbk-ḥtp*, 4/vso. 12

P3-tỉ-Mn(?) father of … , 9/vso. 1

P3-tỉ-n3-ntr.w father of *^cnḫ-mr-wr* and *ỉmn-m-h3.t*, 3/1; 4/1, 3; 5/1, 8

P3-tỉ-n3-ntr.w (= *Pa-tr*) son of *^cnḫ-mr-wr* and father of *^cnḫ-mr-wr*, 7A/2, 8; 7B/3, 4, 22 (supplied); 9/2, 8

P3-tỉ-n3-ntr.w father of *Ḏḥwty-ỉw*, 3, witness copy 4/1

P3-tỉ-Rnn.t son of *Ḥr*, Rendell Papyrus 5

P3-tỉ-Rnn.t father of *Sbk-Ḥ^cpy*, 4/vso. 8

P3-tỉ-Ḥr son of *ỉy-m-ḥtp*, 9/vso. 9

P3-tỉ-Ḥr father of *Nḫt-Ḥr*(?), 4/5

P3-tỉ-Ḥr-p3-šr-ỉs.t father of *ỉy-m-ḥtp*, 5/3

P3-tỉ-Ḥr-p3-šr-ỉs.t son of *P3-R^c-nt-rq*(?), 3, witness copy 3/1

P3-tỉ-Ḥr-p3-šr-(n)-ỉs.t father of *Pa-n3*(?), 9/9; Rendell Papyrus 12

P3-tỉ-Ḥr-p3-šr-ỉs.t father of *Ḥm-n3y꞊f-šms.w*, 5/4

P3-tỉ-Ḥr-p3-šr[-n-ỉs.t] son of *Sy-Sbk*, 10/vso. 11

P3-tỉ-Ḥr-p3-šr-ỉs.t son of *Ḏ-B3st.t-ỉw꞊f-^cnḫ*, 2 vso. 1/2

P3-tỉ-Sbk son of *P3-šr-n-t3-ỉḥ.t*(?), Rendell Papyrus 6

P3-tỉ-Sbk(?) son of … , 2 vso. 2/22

P3-tỉ-Sbk(?) father of *Pa-w3*, Rendell Papyrus vso. 1

P3-[tỉ]-Sbk father of *Nḫt*, 10/7, 10

P3-tỉ-Sbk son of *Ḥr-s3-ỉs.t*(?), 6/vso. 2

P3-tỉ-Sbk-ḥtp father of *Sbk-ḥtp*, 2 vso. 1/6

P3-tỉ-Sbk-ḥtp father of *Ḏ-ḥr*(?), 5 (upper left)/4

P3-tỉ-… son of *Nḫt-nb꞊f*, 9/vso. 12

P3-tỉ꞊w father of *M3^c-R^c*(?), 4/vso. 6

P3-… son of *Sy-Sbk*(?), 6/vso. 3

P3-… son of *ỉy-m-ḥtp*, 9/vso. 15

Pa-ỉmn son of *Sy-Sbk*, 9/vso. 3

Pa-ỉs.t son of *M3^c-R^c*, 10/vso. 2

Pa-ỉs.t son of …*r3*, Rendell Papyrus vso. 9

Pa-ỉs.t father of *Nḫt-Ḥr*, Rendell Papyrus vso. 15

Pa-w3 son of *ỉr.t-Ḥr-r-r꞊w*, Rendell Papyrus 6

Pa-w3 son of *P3-tỉ-Sbk*(?), Rendell Papyrus vso. 1

Pa-w3 father of *Ḥr-wḏ3*, Rendell Papyrus vso. 6

Pa-w3 father of *Sbk-ḥtp*, 7A/2, 9; 7B/4, 5; Rendell Papyrus vso. 1

Pa-w3(?) father of … , Rendell Papyrus 5

Pa-Ptḥ father of *Ḥr-Ḏḥwty*, 1 vso. 2/27

Pa / P3y-N.t-wr(.t) son of *Wn-nfr*, 4/3, vso. 11

Egyptian Personal Names (*cont.*)

    Pa-nꜣ(?) son of *Pꜣ-ti-Ḥr-pꜣ-šr-n-is.t*, 9/9; Rendell Papyrus 12

    Pa-nꜣ father of *Ḥr*, 10/vso. 3; Rendell Papyrus vso. 16

    Pa-ḥy(?) father of *Pa-sy*, Rendell Papyrus vso. 7

    Pꜣy(= *Pa*)-*Ḥr-sꜣ-is.t* son of *Wn-nfr*, 4/vso. 3

    Pa-se (= *Pa-sy*) father of *ꜥnḫ-mr-wr*, see *Pꜣ-ti-Wsir* son of *ꜥnḫ-mr-wr*

    Pa-sy son of *Pa-ḥy*(?), Rendell Papyrus vso. 7

    Pa-sy father of *Mꜣꜥ-Rꜥ*, 10/vso. 4

    Pa-sy son of *Mꜣꜥ-Rꜥ*(?), Rendell Papyrus vso. 13

    Pa-sy(?) son of *Ḥr-sꜣ-is.t*, 9/vso. 2

    Pa-sy father of *Sbk-ḥtp*, 7A/3; 9/3

    Pa-sy father of ... , Rendell Papyrus 4

    Pa-sy son of ... , Rendell Papyrus vso. 14

    Pa-gꜣy son of *Pꜣ-ti-imn*, 4/3

    Pa-tr son of *ꜥnḫ-mr-wr*, see *Pꜣ-ti-nꜣ-ntr.w* son of *ꜥnḫ-mr-wr*

    Pa-Ḏḥwty(?) son of *Ḥr-sꜣ-is.t*, Rendell Papyrus vso. 11

    Pa-... father of *Mꜣꜥ-Rꜥ*... , 10/vso. 5

    Pꜣy-ꜥr-imn father of *Nꜣ-nfr-ib-Ptḥ* (written *Nꜣ-nfr-mn-ib-Ptḥ*), 3/1

    Pꜣy-N.t-wr(.t), see *Pa-N.t-wr*(.t)

    Pꜣy⸗f-iwiw son of *Pꜣ-ḥtr*, 2 vso. 1/9

    Pꜣy⸗f-iwiw father of *Mꜣꜥ-Rꜥ*, 5/3

    Prl son of *Mꜣꜥ-Rꜥ*, 5/10 (perhaps identical with the following individual)

    Prl father of *Ḏ-Ḥnsw-iw⸗f-ꜥnḫ*, 6/4 (perhaps identical with the preceding individual)

    Pḥy father of *Mꜣꜥ-Rꜥ*, 9/4

    Psiy see *Pꜣ-ti-Wsir* son of *ꜥnḫ-mr-wr*

    Psy see *Pꜣ-ti-Wsir* son of *ꜥnḫ-mr-wr*

    Psṭ daughter of *ꜥnḫ-Ḥp* and *ꜥnḫ.t*, 1/1, 3; 2/1

    Ptḥ-nfr father of *Mꜣꜥ-Rꜥ*, 1/4

m

    Mꜣꜥ-Rꜥ son of *iy-m-ḥtp*, 10/vso. 7

    Mꜣꜥ-Rꜥ father of *ꜥnḫ-⌈nb.t⌉-ḥ.t*, 2 vso. 1/10

    Mꜣꜥ-Rꜥ father of *ꜥnḫ-Ḥp*, 9/vso. 14

    Mꜣꜥ-Rꜥ father of *Wsrkn*, 1 vso. 1/18

    Mꜣꜥ-Rꜥ son of *Pꜣ-šr-*(*n*)-*tꜣ-iḥ.t*, 7A/4; 9/4

    Mꜣꜥ-Rꜥ(?) son of *Pꜣ-ti⸗w*, 4/vso. 6

    Mꜣꜥ-Rꜥ father of *Pꜣ-ti-Wsir*, Rendell Papyrus vso. 10

    Mꜣꜥ-Rꜥ father of *Pa-is.t*, 10/vso. 2

    Mꜣꜥ-Rꜥ son of *Pa-sy*, 10/vso. 4

EGYPTIAN PERSONAL NAMES (*cont.*)

M3ꜥ-Rꜥ(?) father of *Pa-sy*, Rendell Papyrus vso. 13

M3ꜥ-Rꜥ son of *P3y≠f-iwîw*, 5/3

M3ꜥ-Rꜥ father of *Prl*, 5/10

M3ꜥ-Rꜥ son of *Phy*, 9/4

M3ꜥ-Rꜥ son of *Ptḥ-nfr*, 1/4

M3ꜥ-Rꜥ son of *Nḫt-p3-Rꜥ*, 10/5

M3ꜥ-Rꜥ son of *Hry.w*(?), 1 vso. 1/1

M3ꜥ-Rꜥ father of *Ḥr*, 9/vso. 6

M3ꜥ-Rꜥ father of *Ḥr-ꜥnḫ*, 6/2; 9/2, 8; Rendell Papyrus 9, 10

M3ꜥ-Rꜥ son of *Ḥr-wḏ3*, 9/vso. 16

M3ꜥ-Rꜥ son of *Ḥr-s3-is.t*, 9/vso. 5

M3ꜥ-Rꜥ(?) father of *Ḥr-sy-Sbk*, 1 vso. 2/32

M3ꜥ-Rꜥ son of *Sbk-ḥtp*, 1 vso. 1/10

M3ꜥ-Rꜥ father of *Sbk-ḥtp*, 9/vso. 4

M3ꜥ-Rꜥ son of *Ḏ-B3st.t-iw≠f-ꜥnḫ*, 1 vso. 1/2, 7

M3ꜥ-Rꜥ son of *Ḏ-B3st.t-iw≠f-ꜥnḫ*, 2 vso. 2/20

M3ꜥ(-Rꜥ) son of ⌈*Ḏ-B3st.t-iw≠f-ꜥnḫ*⌉, 10/vso. 9

M3ꜥ-Rꜥ son of *Ḏ-Ḥnsw-iw≠f-ꜥnḫ*, 2/4

M3ꜥ-Rꜥ ... son of *Pa-...* , 10/vso. 5

M3ꜥ-Rꜥ(?) father of *[...]ḫ*, 6, signature on verso

M3ꜥ-Rꜥ son of *Nḫt-...* , 10/vso. 6

M3ꜥ-Rꜥ son of ... , 10/vso. 12

M3ꜥ-Rꜥ son of ... , 10/vso. 8

M3ꜥ-Rꜥ son of ... , Rendell Papyrus 5

M3ꜥ-Rꜥ(?) son of *...-t3.wy*(?), 5 (upper left)/7

M3ꜥ-Rꜥ-... son of *Sy-Sbk*, Rendell Papyrus vso. 8

M3ꜥ-Rꜥ-... father of *Sbk-...* , 2 vso. 2/21

M3ꜥ-Rꜥ-s3-Sbk father of *Ḏ-...* , 5 (upper left)/5

M3ꜥ-... son of ... , 10/12

Mnḫ-...-Ḥnsw father of *T3-ti-Wsir*, 5/7

n

N3-nfr-ib-Ptḥ (= *N3-nfr-mn-ib-Ptḥ*) daughter of *P3y-ꜥr-imn* and *Šty*, 3/1; 4/1; 6/1; Rendell Papyrus 7, 8 (2×)

N3-nfr-rnp.t mother of *T3y-ir≠w*, 9/8

N3-nfr-Sbk mother of *Ta-Rnn.t*, 7A/8

Nb-wꜥb father of *P3-ti-in-ḥr.t*, 5/2

Nb.t-t3-ḫy(?) daughter of *P3-ti-Wsir* and *Ḥr-ꜥnḫ*, Rendell Papyrus 11

E GYPTIAN P ERSONAL N AMES (*cont.*)

Nb.t-t3-ḥy(?) mother of *Ḥr-ʿnḫ*, 6/2; 9/2, 8; Rendell Papyrus 9, 10

Nḫt son of *P3-[ti]-Sbk*, 10/7, 10

Nḫt-p3-Rʿ father of *M3ʿ-Rʿ*, 10/5

Nḫt-nb⸗f father of *P3-ti-...*, 9/vso. 12

Nḫt-Ḥr(?) son of *P3-ti-Ḥr*, 4/5

Nḫt-Ḥr son of *Pa-is.t*, Rendell Papyrus vso. 15

Nḫt-Ḥr-ḥb(?) father of *Ḏḥwty-w3ḥ*, 10/11

Nḫt-Sbk(?) son of *...-Rnn.t*(?), 5 (upper left)/1

Nḫt-... son of ... , 6/vso. 7

Nḫt-[...] son of *iy-m-ḥtp*(?), 10/vso. 10

Nḫt-... father of *M3ʿ-Rʿ*, 10/vso. 6

Ns-B3st.t father of *Ḥtr*, 1 vso. 1/3

h

Hry.w(?) father of *M3ʿ-Rʿ*, 1 vso. 1/1

Hgr(?) father of ... , 4/vso. 10

ḥ

Ḥp-mn(?) son of *Sbk-ḥtp*, 2 vso. 1/7

Ḥm-ntr-3.nw son of *imn-m-ḥ3.t*, 2 vso. 2/17

Ḥr father of *P3-igš*, 9/vso. 7

Ḥr father of *P3-ti-Rnn.t*, Rendell Papyrus 5

Ḥr son of *Pa-n3*(?), 10/vso. 3; Rendell Papyrus vso. 16

Ḥr son of *M3ʿ-Rʿ*, 9/vso. 6

Ḥr father of *Ḥr-wd3*, 2 vso. 1/15

Ḥr son of *Ḥr-s3-is.t*, 9/vso. 8

Ḥr-ʿnḫ daughter of *M3ʿ-Rʿ*, 6/2; 7A/2; 8/2; 9/2, 8; 10/6; Rendell Papyrus 2, 9, 10, 12

Ḥr-wd3 father of *iʿḥ-i-ir-ti-s*, 4/vso. 2

Ḥr-wd3 father of *imn-m-ḥ3.t*, 2 vso. 2/18

Ḥr-wd3 father of *ʿnḫ-imn*, 1 vso. 2/21

Ḥr-wd3 son of *ʿnḫ-Ḥp*, 2 vso. 1/8

Ḥr-wd3 son of *Wn-nfr*, 5/3

Ḥr-wd3 son of *P3-sn-ky*, 1 vso. 1/1

Ḥr-wd3 son of *Pa-w3*, Rendell Papyrus vso. 6

Ḥr-wd3 father of *M3ʿ-Rʿ*, 9/vso. 16

Ḥr-wd3 son of *Ḥr-ḥb*, 1 vso. 2/35

Ḥr-wd3 son *Ḥr*, 2 vso. 1/15

Ḥr-wd3 son of *Sy-Sbk*, 1 vso. 1/12

EGYPTIAN PERSONAL NAMES (*cont.*)

Ḥr-wḏꜣ son of *Sbk-ỉ-ỉr-tỉ-s*(?), 1 vso. 2/26

Ḥr-wḏꜣ son of *Sbk-ỉw*, 2 vso. 1/13

Ḥr-wḏꜣ father of *Sbk-ḥtp*, 3, witness copy 1/1

Ḥr-wḏꜣ father of *Smꜣ-tꜣ.wy-tꜣy=f-nḫt*, 1 vso. 1/16

Ḥr-wḏꜣ son of *Ḏ-Bꜣst.t-ỉw=f-ꜥnḫ*, 2 vso. 2/19

Ḥr-wḏꜣ father of *Ḏḥwty-Ḥp*, Rendell Papyrus vso. 4

Ḥr-m-ḥb father of *S-n-wsr*, Rendell Papyrus vso. 5

Ḥr-ḫb, father of *ꜥꜣ-ỉmn*, 1 vso. 2/36

Ḥr-ḫb son of *Wn-nfr*, 4/vso. 5

Ḥr-ḫb son of *Wsrkn*, 1 vso. 2/23

Ḥr-ḫb father of *Ḥr-wḏꜣ*, 1 vso. 2/35

Ḥr-ḫb son of *Ḥr-Ḏḥwty*, 4/vso. 1

Ḥr-ḫb son of *Sy-Sbk*, 1 vso. 2/22

Ḥr-ḫb father of *Sbk-mn*, 1 vso. 1/11

Ḥr-ḫb father of *Sbk-ḥtp*, 1 vso. 1/9

Ḥr-ḫb son of *Sbk-ḥtp*(?), 6/vso. 4

Ḥr-sꜣ-ỉs.t(?) father of *Pꜣ-tỉ-Sbk*, 6/vso. 2

Ḥr-sꜣ-ỉs.t father of *Pa-sy*(?), 9/vso. 2

Ḥr-sꜣ-ỉs.t father of *Pa-Ḏḥwty*(?), Rendell Papyrus vso. 11

Ḥr-sꜣ-ỉs.t father of *Mꜣꜥ-Rꜥ*, 9/vso. 5

Ḥr-sꜣ-ỉs.t father of *Ḥr*, 9/vso. 8

Ḥr-sꜣ-ỉs.t son of … , 6/vso. 9

Ḥr-sy-Sbk son of *Mꜣꜥ-Rꜥ*(?), 1 vso. 2/32

Ḥr-sy-Sbk father of *Sbk-mn*, 1 vso. 1/13

Ḥr-Ḏḥwty father of *ꜥnḫ-mꜣꜥ-Rꜥ*, 1 vso. 2/34

Ḥr-Ḏḥwty father of *Wn-nfr*, 1 vso. 2/33

Ḥr-Ḏḥwty(?) father of *Wn-nfr*, 4/vso. 7

Ḥr-Ḏḥwty son of *Pa-Ptḥ*, 1 vso. 2/27

Ḥr-Ḏḥwty father of *Ḥr-ḫb*, 4/vso. 1

Ḥr-Ḏḥwty father of *Sbk-ḥtp*, 1 vso. 1/14

⌜*Ḥr-*…⌝ father of … , 10/12

Ḥtr son of *Ns-Bꜣst.t*, 1 vso. 1/3

ḫ

Ḫyrk(?) father of *Sṯꜣ-ỉr.t-bn*, 5 (upper left)/2

Ḫm-nꜣy=f-šms.w son of *Pꜣ-tỉ-Ḥr-pꜣ-šr-ỉs.t*, 5/4

EGYPTIAN PERSONAL NAMES (*cont.*)

    Sbk-ḥtp son of *Mꜣꜥ-Rꜥ*, 9/vso. 4

    Sbk-ḥtp father of *Ḥp-mn*(?), 2 vso. 1/7

    Sbk-ḥtp son of *Ḥr-wḏꜣ*, 3, witness copy 1/1

    Sbk-ḥtp son of *Ḥr-ḫb*, 1 vso. 1/9

    Sbk-ḥtp(?) father of *Ḥr-ḫb*, 6/vso. 4

    Sbk-ḥtp son of *Ḥr-Ḏḥwty*, 1 vso. 1/14

    Sbk-ḥtp son of *Sy-Sbk*, 1 vso. 2/19

    Sbk-ḥtp son of *Sy-Sbk*, 1 vso. 2/30

    Sbk-ṯꜣy father of *Iꜥḥ-ms*, 1 vso. 1/5

    Sbk-... son of *Mꜣꜥ-Rꜥ,* 2 vso. 2/21

    Sbk-... son of ... , 10/vso. 1

    Sbk-... son of *Wn-nfr*(?), 6/vso. 10

    Sbk-... son of *Ḏḥwty...*(?), 6/vso. 8

    Smꜣ-tꜣ.wy son of *Inp*, 4/vso. 9

    Smꜣ-tꜣ.wy son of *Pꜣ-š-mtre*, 8/2

    Smꜣ-tꜣ.wy-tꜣy⸗f-nḫt son of *Ḥr-wḏꜣ*, 1 vso. 1/16

    Sṯꜣ-ir.t-bn son of *Ḫyrk*(?), 5 (upper left)/2

    Sṯꜣ⸗w-tꜣ-wty son of *Pꜣ-ti-Wsir*, 7A/10; 7B/28; 8/6

  š

    Šty daughter of *Pꜣ-šwṱ* and *Ḥr-ꜥnḫ*, 8/2

    Šty mother of *Nꜣ-nfr-ib-Ptḥ* (= *Nꜣ-nfr-mn-ib-Ptḥ*), 3/1

  t

    Tꜣ-rmt.t-Bꜣst.t mother of *Tꜣ-ti-Wsir*, 5/8

    Tꜣ-rmt.t-... mother of *Mꜣꜥ-Rꜥ*, 10/5

    Tꜣ-ḫnꜣ daughter of *ꜥnḫ-mr-wr*, 7A/4

    Tꜣ-ti-Wsir daughter of *Mnḫ-...-Ḫnsw*, 5/7

    Ta-imn mother of *ꜥnḫ-mr-wr*, 1/1, 3

    Ta-Rnn.t mother of *ꜥnḫ.t*, 5/1, 9

    Ta-Rnn.t daughter of *Sbk-iw* and *Nꜣ-nfr-Sbk*, 7A/8; 7B/23; 9/2, 8

    Tꜣy-ir⸗w daughter of *Pꜣ-ti-Wsir*, 9/7

    Tꜣy-nḫt-r-r⸗w(?) father of *ir.t⸗w-r-r⸗w*, 1 vso. 1/6

    Ti-Bꜣst.t-iꜣw(?) father of *ꜥnḫ-nꜣ-...*, 1 vso. 2/25

    Ti-Bꜣst.t-iꜣw(?) father of *Sy-Sbk*, 1 vso. 2/20

    Ti-n⸗y-iꜣw(?) father of *Tꜣy-nḫt-r-r⸗w*(?), 1 vso. 1/6

    Twt(?) father of *Pꜣ-gwr*(?), 6/vso. 15

    Trkm(?) son of *Mꜣꜥ-Rꜥ*, 1 vso. 1/18, 2/23

EGYPTIAN PERSONAL NAMES (*cont.*)

ṯ

Ṯ-Ḥp-n-im≠w father of *ʿnḫ-mr-wr*, 5/3

ḏ

Ḏ-Bȝst.t-iw≠f-ʿnḫ father of *iy-m-ḥtp*, 2 vso. 1/14

Ḏ-Bȝst.t-iw≠f-ʿnḫ son of *iw≠f-iw*, 1 vso. 1/8

Ḏ-Bȝst.t-iw≠f-ʿnḫ son of *ʿȝ-imn*, 1 vso. 2/36

Ḏ-Bȝst.t-iw≠f-ʿnḫ(?) son of *ʿnḫ-Ḫnsw*, 1 vso. 2/31

Ḏ-Bȝst.t-iw≠f-ʿnḫ father of *Pȝ-ti-Ḥr-pȝ-šr-is.t,* 2 vso. 1/2

Ḏ-Bȝst.t-iw≠f-ʿnḫ father of *Mȝʿ-Rʿ*, 1 vso. 1/2, 7

Ḏ-Bȝst.t-iw≠f-ʿnḫ father of *Mȝʿ-Rʿ*, 2 vso. 2/20

⌜*Ḏ-Bȝst.t.-iw≠f-ʿnḫ*⌝(?) father of *Mȝʿ(-Rʿ)*, 10/vso. 9

Ḏ-Bȝst.t-iw≠f-ʿnḫ father of *Ḥr-wḏȝ*, 2 vso. 2/19

Ḏ-Ptḥ-iw≠f-ʿnḫ son of ... , Rendell Papyrus vso. 3

Ḏ-ḥr(?) son of *Pȝ-ti-Sbk-ḥtp*, 5 (upper left)/4

Ḏ-Ḫnsw-iw≠f-ʿnḫ son of *Prl*, 6/4

Ḏ-Ḫnsw-iw≠f-ʿnḫ father of *Mȝʿ-Rʿ*, 2/4

Ḏḥwty-i-ir-ti-s(?) father of ... , 6/vso. 5

Ḏḥwty-iw son of *Pȝ-ti-nȝ-ntr.w*, 3, witness copy 4/1

Ḏḥwty-wȝḥ son of *Nḫt-Ḥr-ḥb*(?), 10/11

Ḏḥwty-Ḥp son of *Ḥr-wḏȝ*, Rendell Papyrus vso. 4

Ḏḥwty-...(?) father of *Sbk-...* , 6/vso. 8

GREEK PERSONAL NAMES

ȝ

ȝntytwtws father of *ȝrystwbwlws*, 8/1

ȝntrwgtws father of *Mȝṱlȝ*, 6/1

ȝrystwbwlws son of *ȝntytwtws*, 8/1

ȝrsynȝ daughter of *Pwlmwqrts*, 7A/1

ȝrstmg daughter of *Pṱlwmys*, 10/3

ȝrstn father of *Qrsmws*, Rendell Papyrus 1

ȝrkylws son of *ṱymȝ*, 7A/1

y

Ymnȝ daughter of *Hprbsȝ*, 8/1

GREEK PERSONAL NAMES (*cont.*)

b

    Brngꜣ daughter of *Srtn*, Rendell Papyrus 1

    Bkys father of *Nqnr*, 10/3

p

    Pwlmwqrts father of *ꜣrsynꜣ*, 7A/1

    Prwn father of *Nwmstws*, 9/1

    Pṱlwmys father of *ꜣrstmg*, 10/3

m

    Mꜣṱlꜣ daughter of *ꜣntrwgtws*, 6/1

    Mꜣts son of *Lmpn*, 6/1

n

    Nwmstws son of *Prwn*, 9/1

    Nqnr son of *Bkys*, 10/3

l

    Lmpn father of *Mꜣts*, 6/1

h

    Hprbsꜣ father of *Ymnꜣ*, 8/1

s

    Srtn father of *Brngꜣ*, Rendell Papyrus 1

q

    Qrsmws son of *ꜣrstn*, Rendell Papyrus 1

g

    Glwtrtꜣ daughter of *Gtsgls*, 9/1

    Gtsgls father of *Glwtrtꜣ*, 9/1

t

    ṱymꜣ father of *ꜣrkylws*, 7A/1

DAMAGED AND UNREAD NAMES

    … father of *Sbk-ṱꜣy*, 1 vso. 1/5

    ꜥr…(?) father of *Sbk-… ḥ…* , 1 vso. 1/15

    Sbk-…ḥ… son of ꜥr…(?), 1 vso. 1/15

DAMAGED AND UNREAD NAMES (*cont.*)

...-*mn* father of ... , 2 vso. 1/1

... son of ...-*mn*, 2 vso. 1/1

... father of *Pꜣ-tỉ-Sbk*(?), 2 vso. 2/22

... son of ... (two unread names), 2 vso. 2/23

... son of ... (two unread names), 2 vso. 2/24

... son of *Hgr*(?), 4/vso. 10

...-*Rnn.t*(?) father of *Nḫt-Sbk*(?), 5 (upper left)/1

... son of ... (two unread names), 5 (upper left)/3

Ḏ-... son of *Mꜣꜥ-Rꜥ-sꜣ-Sbk*(?), 5 (upper left)/5

... son of ... (two unread names), 5 (upper left)/6

... -*tꜣ.wy*(?) father of *Mꜣꜥ-Rꜥ*(?), 5 (upper left)/7

Pꜣ-... son of *Sy-Sbk*(?), 6/vso. 3

... son of *Ḏḥwty-ỉ-ỉr-tỉ-s*(?), 6/vso. 5

... son of ... (two unread names), 6/vso. 6

... father of *Nḫt*-... , 6/vso. 7

... father of *Ḥr-sꜣ-ỉs.t*, 6/vso. 9

... son of ... (two unread names), 6/vso. 11

... father of *Pꜣ-ḫꜣꜥ≠s*, 6/vso. 12

... son of *Pꜣ-rl*, 6/vso. 13

... son of ... (two unread names), 6/vso. 14

[...]ḥ son of *Mꜣꜥ-Rꜥ*(?), 6, signature on vso.

... son of *Pꜣ-tỉ-Mn*(?), 9/vso. 1

... father of *Pꜣ-nfr-ḥr*, 9/vso. 10

... father of *Sbk-Ḥp*, 9/vso. 11

... father of *ꜥnḫ-mr-wr*, 9/vso. 13

... father of *Sbk*-... , 10/vso. 1

... father of *Mꜣꜥ-Rꜥ*, 10/vso. 8

... son of *Pa-sy*, Rendell Papyrus 4

... son of ... (two unread names), Rendell Papyrus 5

... son of *Pa-wꜣ*(?), Rendell Papyrus 5

... father of *Mꜣꜥ-Rꜥ*, Rendell Papyrus 5

... son of ... (two unread names), Rendell Papyrus vso. 2

... father of *Ḏ-Ptḥ-ỉw≠f-ꜥnḫ*, Rendell Papyrus vso. 3

... *rꜣ* father of *Pa-ỉs.t*, Rendell Papyrus vso. 9

... father of *Wn-nfr*, Rendell Papyrus vso. 12

... father of *Pa-sy*, Rendell Papyrus vso. 14

ROYAL NAMES

   M3ꜥ-Rꜥ (= Amenemhet III),   10/4

   Nektanebo (I),   1/1

   Alexander (the Great),   2/1; 3/1; 6/1; 7A/1; 8/1; 9/1; 10/2; Rendell Papyrus 1

   Alexander IV son of Alexander the Great,   3/1

   Ptolemy I Soter,   4/1

   Arsinoe Philadelphos,   6/1; 7A/1, 2, 3; 7B/2; 8/1, 2; 9/1 (2×); 10/1, 4; Rendell Papyrus 1 (2×), 4

   Ptolemy II Philadelphos,   5/1; 6/1; 7A/1; 7B/2; 8/1; 9/1; Rendell Papyrus 1

   Ptolemy III Euergetes I,   6/1; 7A/1; 7B/1; 8/1; 9/1; 10/1; Rendell Papyrus 1

   Ptolemy IV Philopator,   10/1

   Berenike,   10/2

EPONYMOUS PRIESTS AND PRIESTESSES

   3rystwbwlws son of *3ntytwtws*,   8/1 (priest of Alexander and the gods Adelphoi)

   3rsyn3 daughter of *Pwlmwqrts*,   7A/1 (Kanephoros before Arsinoe Philadelphos)

   3rstmg daughter of *Pṯlwmys*,   10/3 (Kanephoros before Arsinoe Philadelphos)

   3rkylws son of *ṯym3*,   7A/1 (priest of Alexander and the gods Adelphoi)

   Ymn3 daughter of *Hprbs3*,   8/1 (Kanephoros before Arsinoe Philadelphos)

   Brng3 daughter of *Srtn*,   Rendell Papyrus 1 (Kanephoros before Arsinoe Philadelphos)

   M3ts son of *Lmpn*,   6/1 (priest of Alexander and the gods Adelphoi)

   M3ṯl3 daughter of *3ntrwgtws*,   6/1 (Kanephoros before Arsinoe Philadelphos)

   Nwmstws son of *Prwn*,   9/1 (priest of Alexander, the gods Adelphoi, and the gods Euergetai)

   Nqnr son of *Bkys*,   10/3 (priest of Alexander, the gods Adelphoi, and the gods Euergetai)

   Qrsmws son of *3rstn,*   Rendell Papyrus 1 (priest of Alexander, the gods Adelphoi, and the gods Euergetai)

   Glwtrt3 daughter of *Gtsgls*,   9/1 (Kanephoros before Arsinoe Philadelphos)

PLATES

Chicago Hawara Papyrus 1 (P. O.I. 17481)

Plate 1

Plate 2

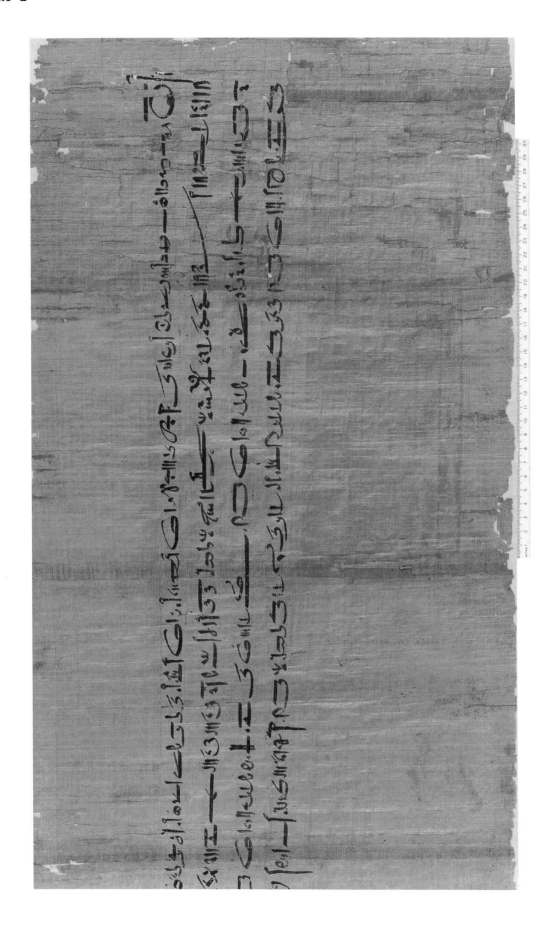

Chicago Hawara Papyrus 1 (P. O.I. 17481). Lines 1–4

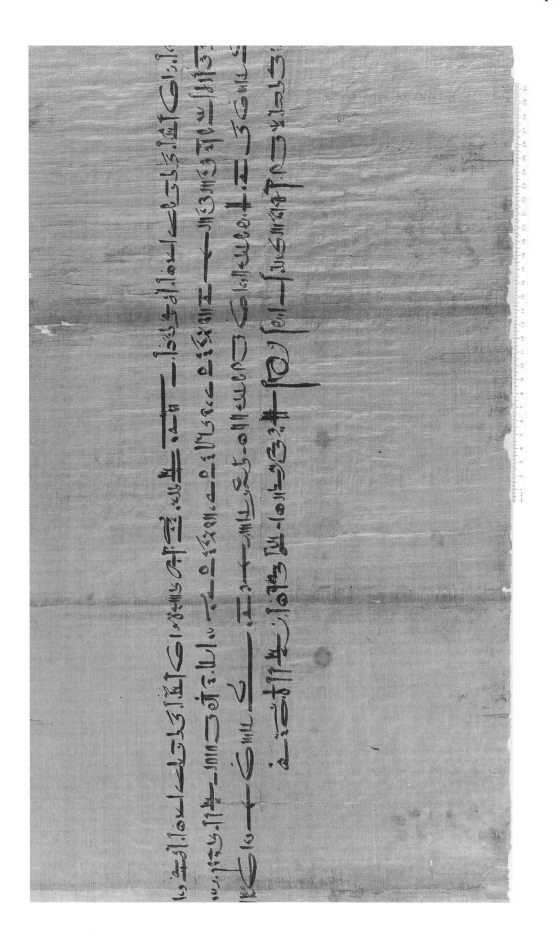

Chicago Hawara Papyrus 1 (P. O.I. 17481). Lines 1–4 (*cont.*)

Plate 3

Plate 4

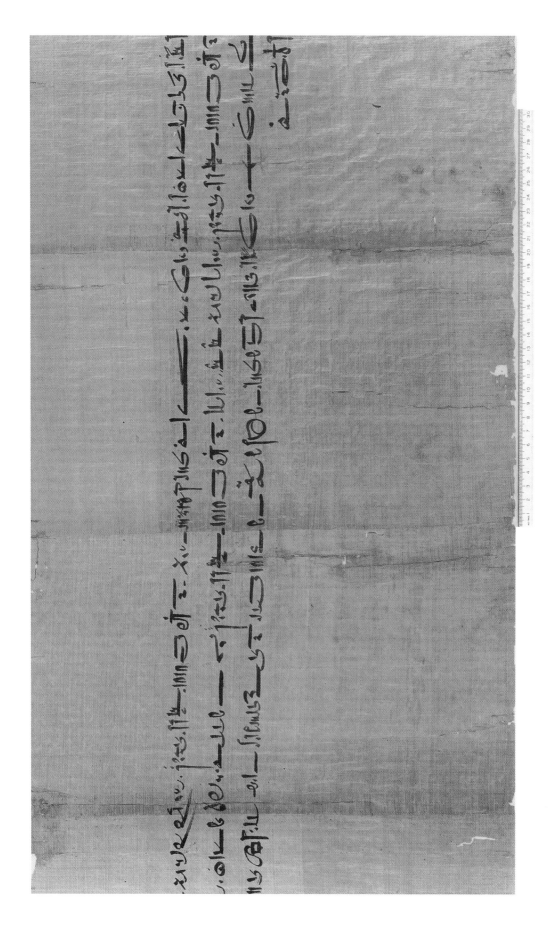

Chicago Hawara Papyrus 1 (P. O.I. 17481). Lines 1–4 (*cont.*)

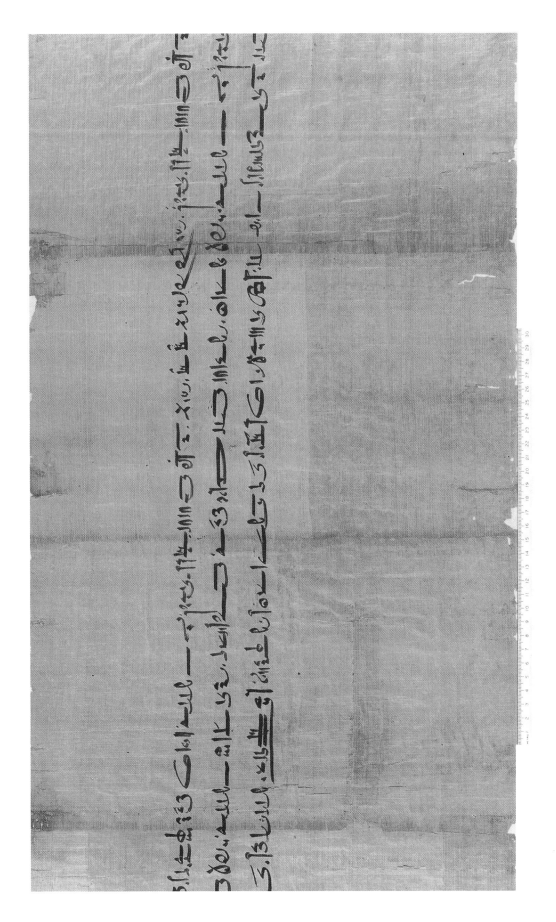

Chicago Hawara Papyrus 1 (P. O.I. 17481). Lines 1–3 (*cont.*)

Plate 5

Plate 6

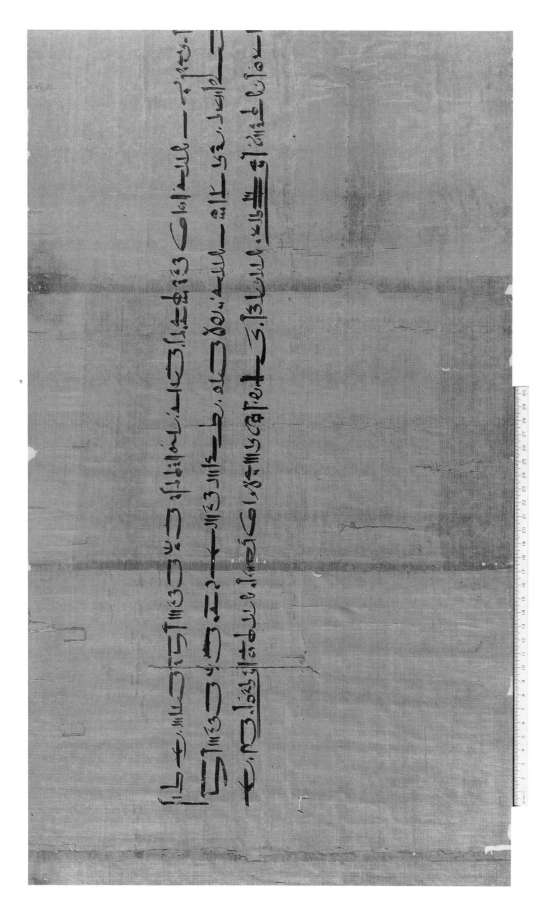

Chicago Hawara Papyrus 1 (P. O.I. 17481). Lines 1–3 (*cont.*)

Plate 7

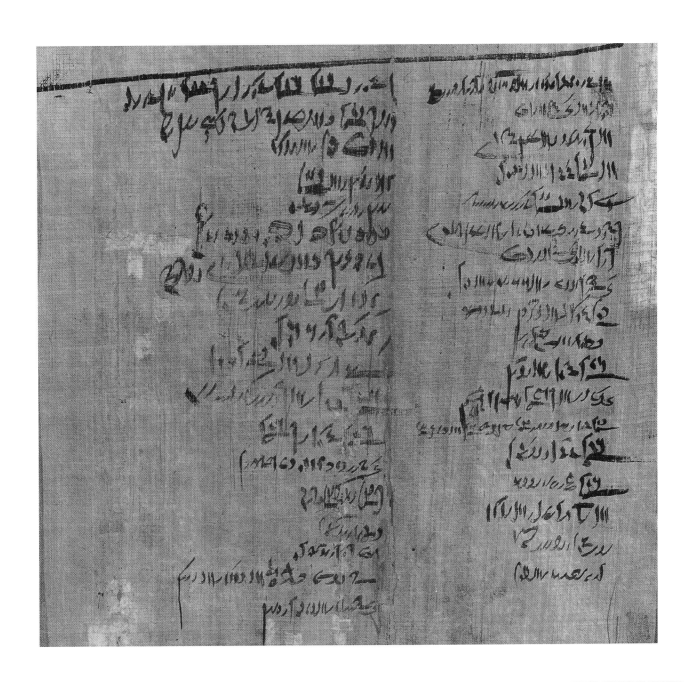

Chicago Hawara Papyrus 1 (P. O.I. 17481). Verso. Witness List

Plate 8

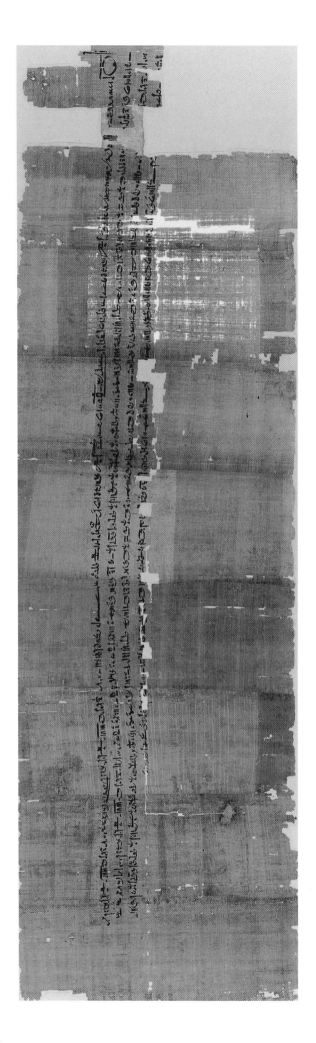

Chicago Hawara Papyrus 2 (P. O.I. 25257)

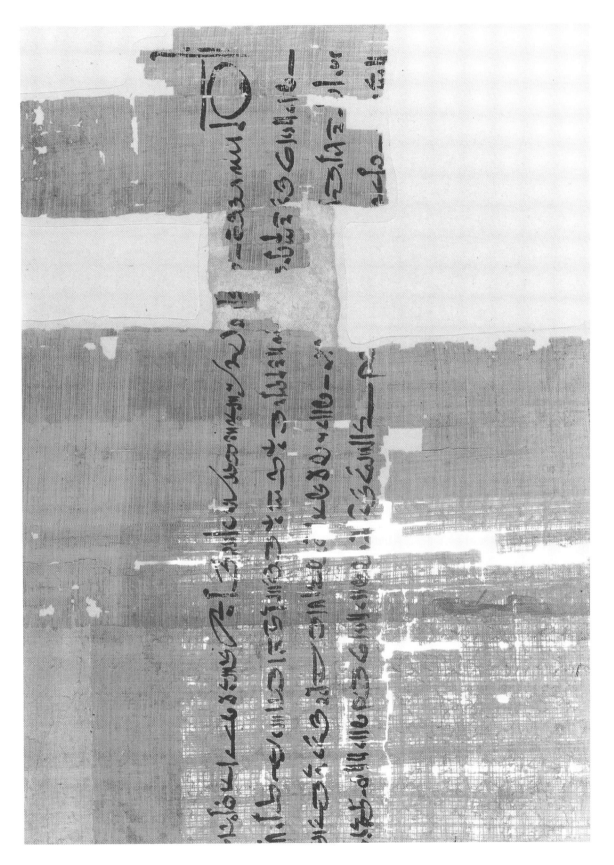

Plate 9

Chicago Hawara Papyrus 2 (P. O.I. 25257). Lines 1–4

Plate 10

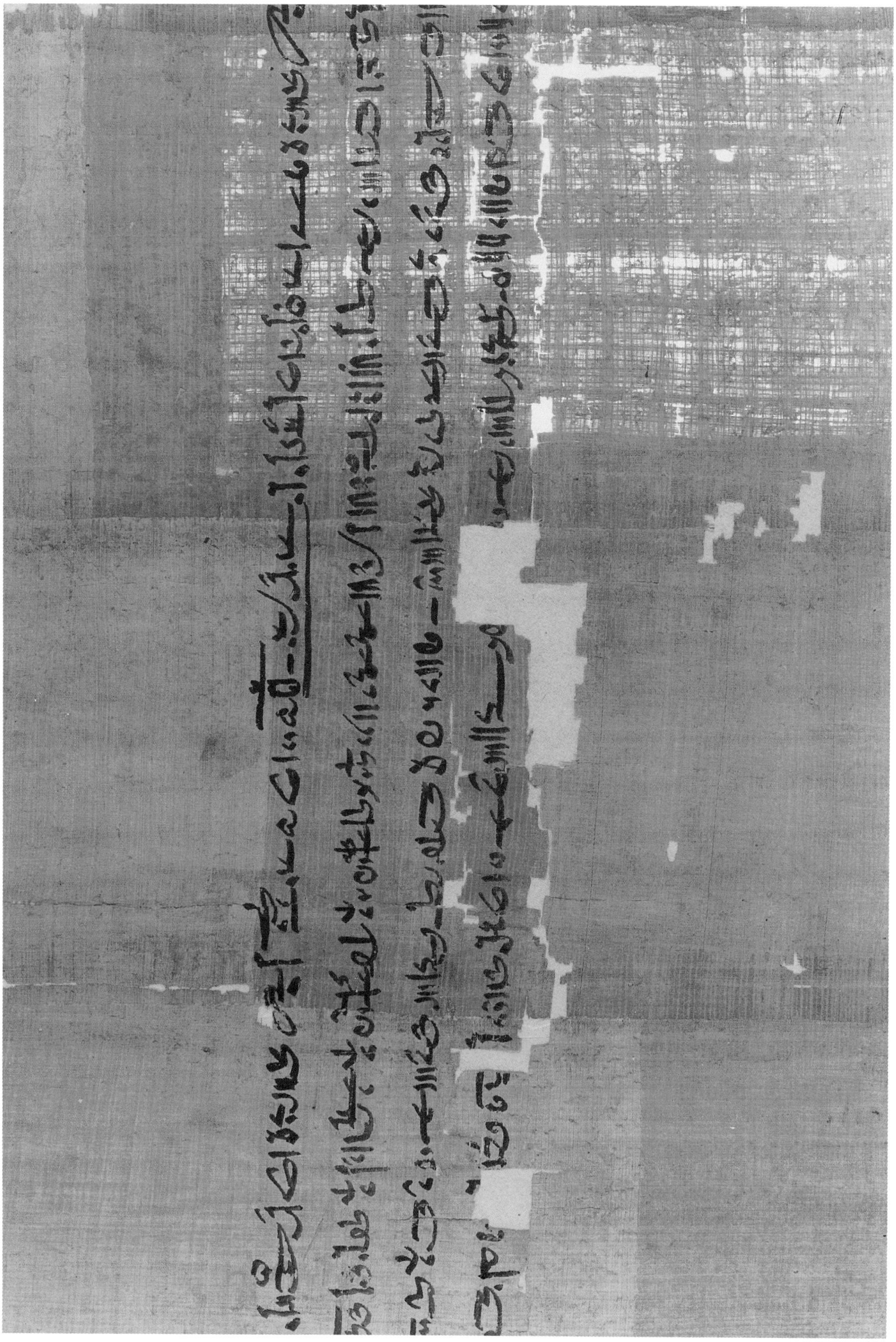

Chicago Hawara Papyrus 2 (P. O.I. 25257). Lines 1–4 (*cont.*)

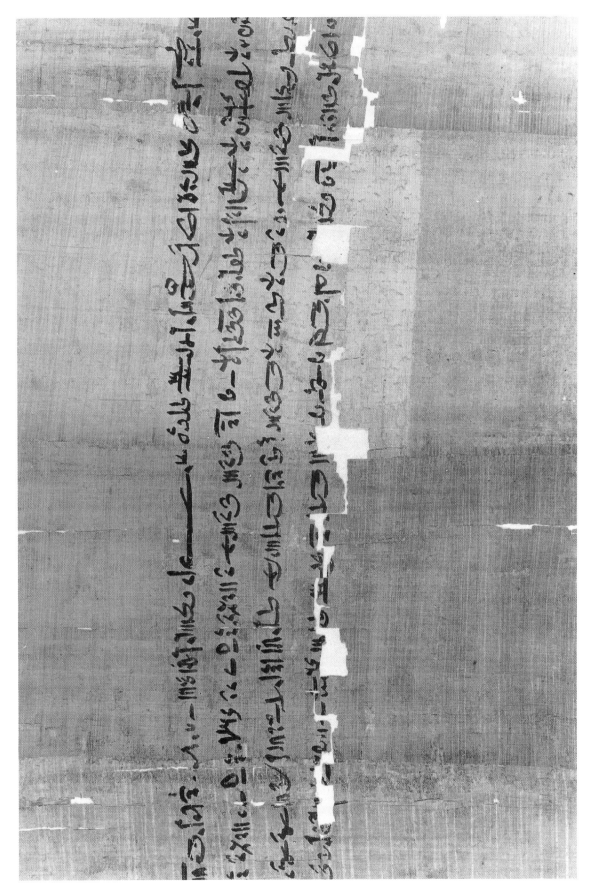

Plate 11

Chicago Hawara Papyrus 2 (P. O.I. 25257). Lines 1–4 (*cont.*)

Plate 12

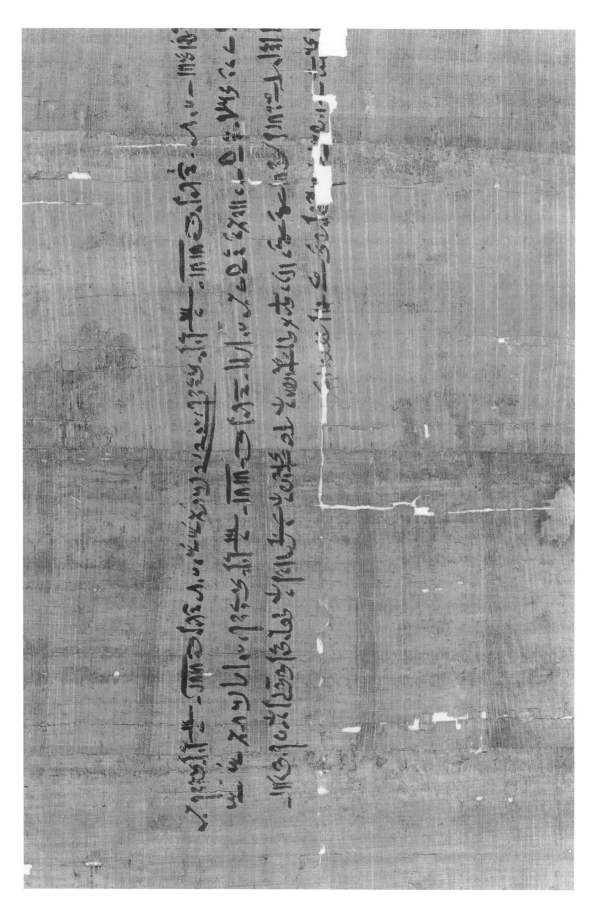

Chicago Hawara Papyrus 2 (P. O.I. 25257). Lines 1–4 (*cont.*)

Plate 13

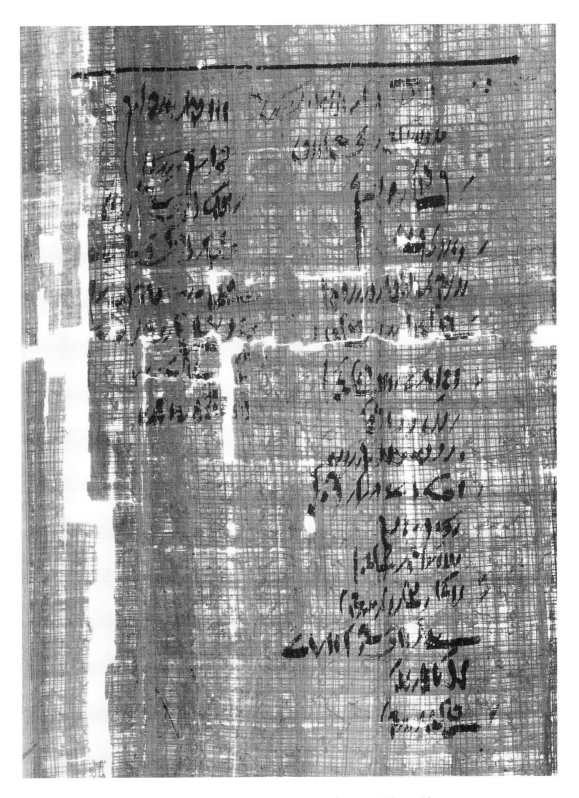

Chicago Hawara Papyrus 2 (P. O.I. 25257). Verso. Witness List

Plate 14

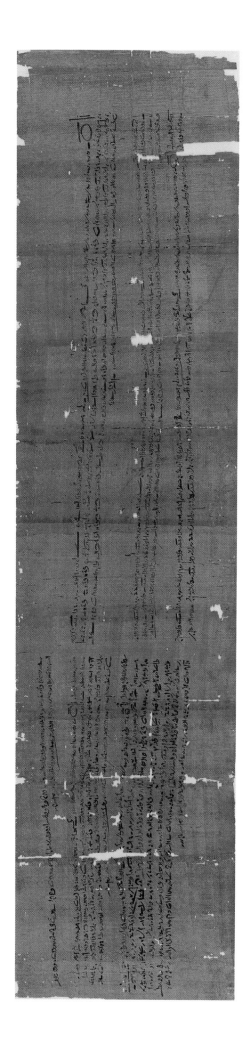

Chicago Hawara Papyrus 3 (P. O.I. 25259)

Plate 15

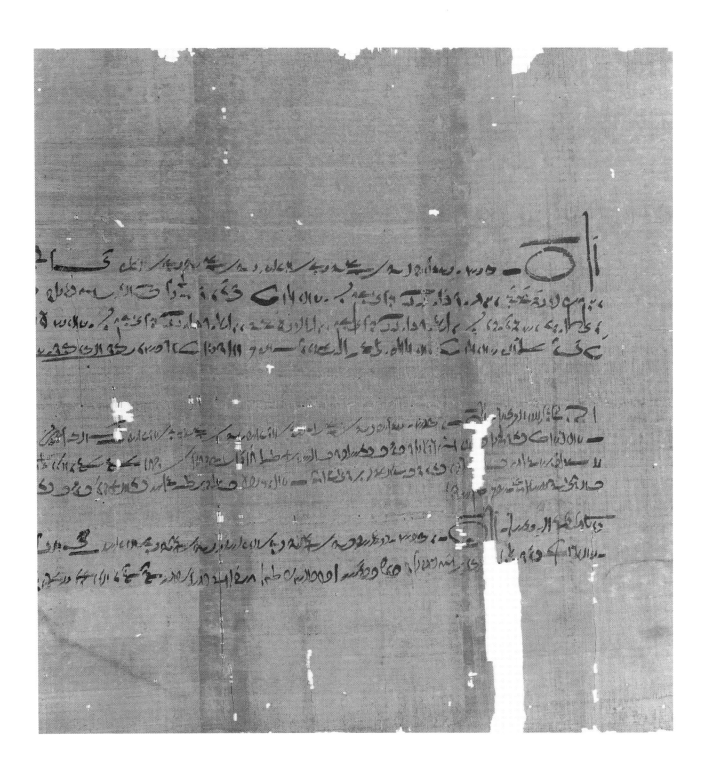

Chicago Hawara Papyrus 3 (P. O.I. 25259). Lines 1–4 and Witness Copies 1–2

Plate 16

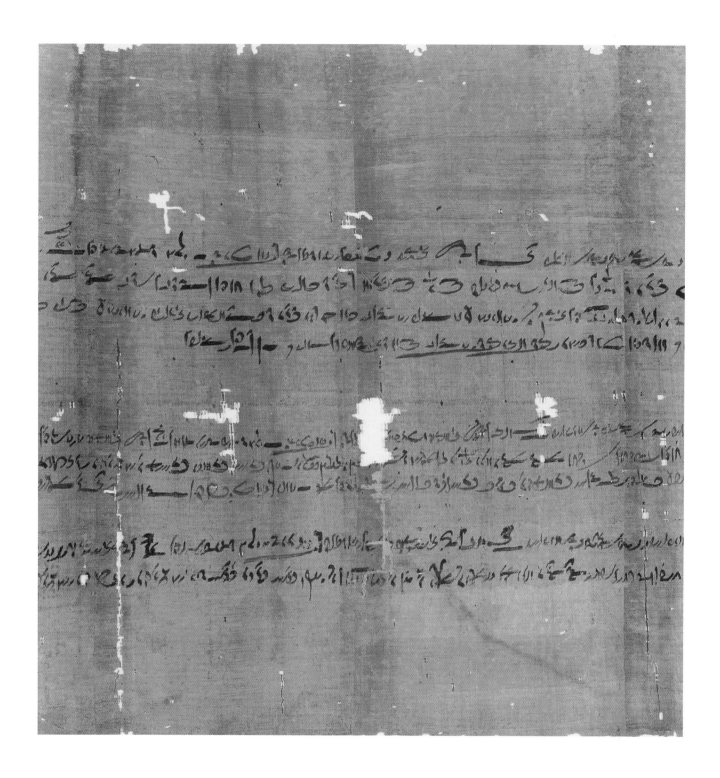

Chicago Hawara Papyrus 3 (P. O.I. 25259). Lines 1–4 and Witness Copies 1–2 (*cont.*)

Plate 17

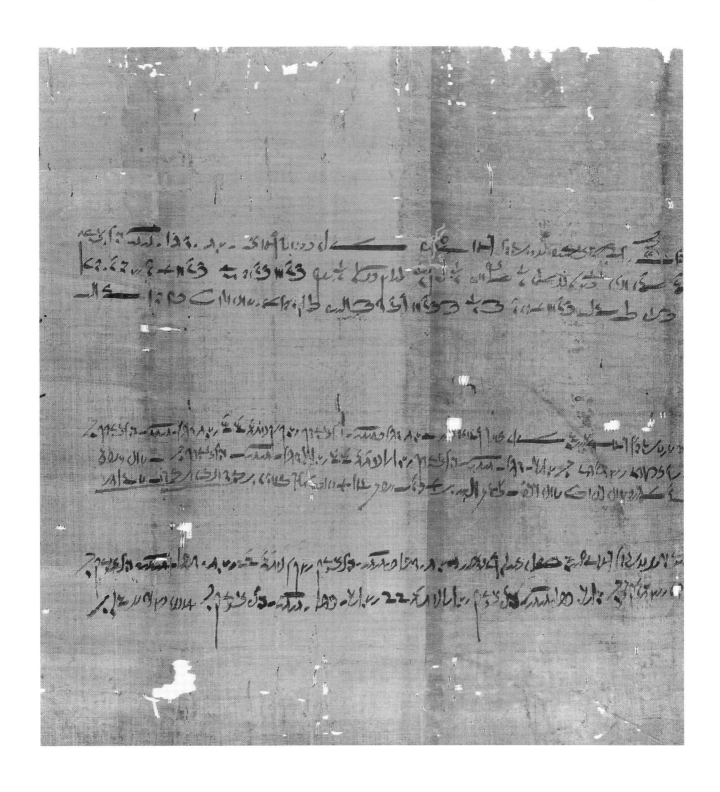

Chicago Hawara Papyrus 3 (P. O.I. 25259). Lines 1–3 and Witness Copies 1–2 (*cont.*)

Plate 18

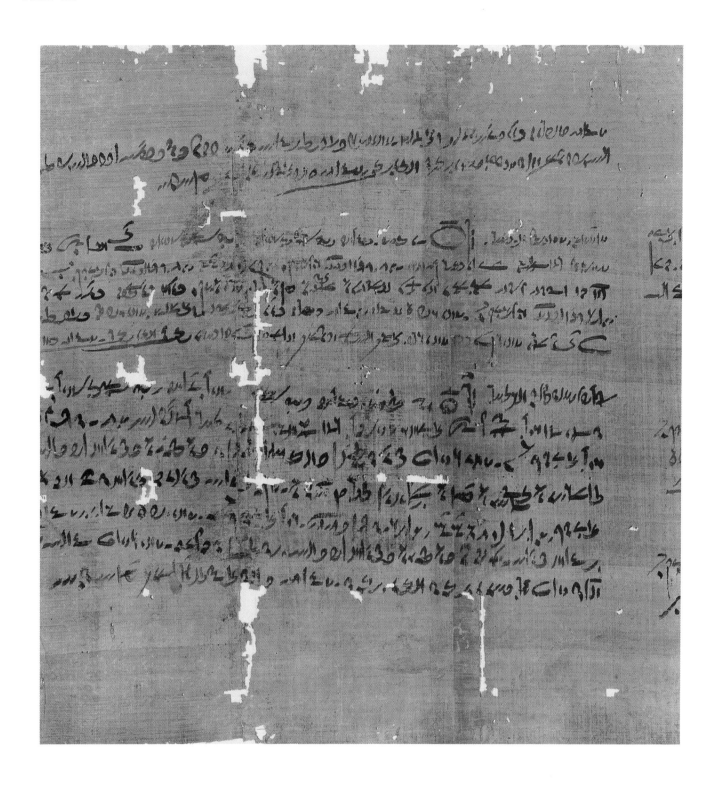

Chicago Hawara Papyrus 3 (P. O.I. 25259). Witness Copies 2–4

Plate 19

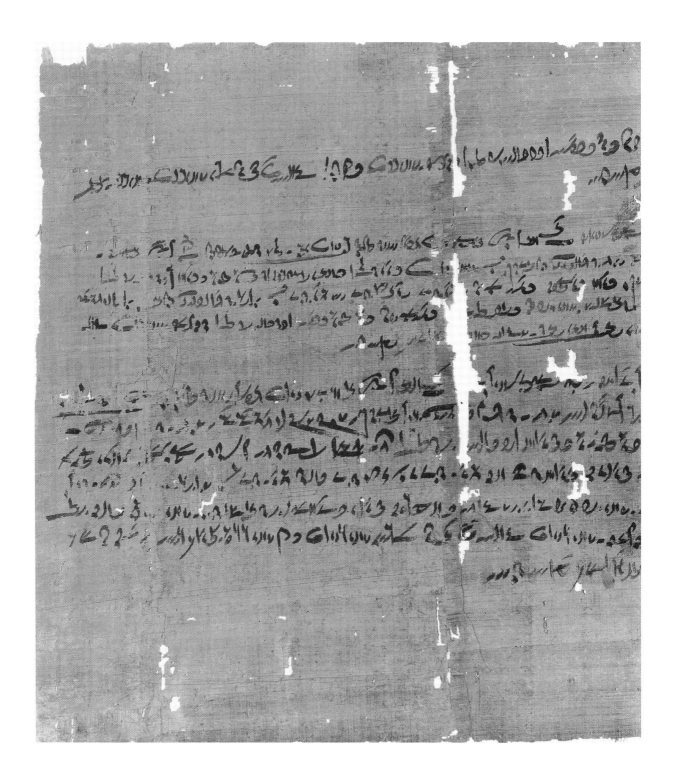

Chicago Hawara Papyrus 3 (P. O.I. 25259). Witness Copies 2–4 (*cont.*)

Plate 20

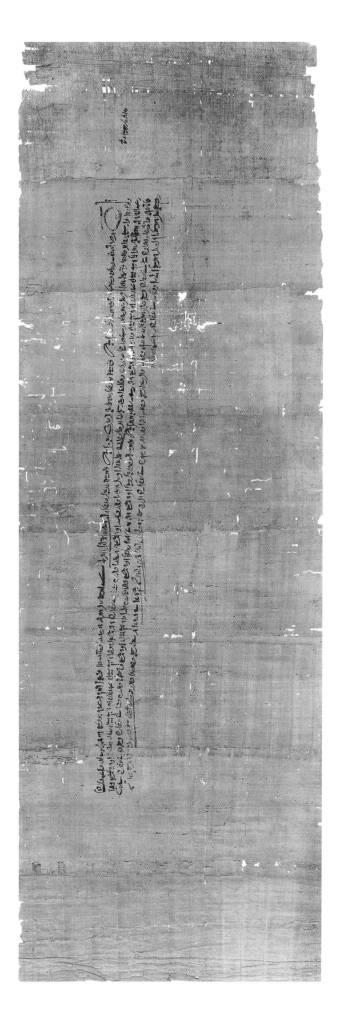

Chicago Hawara Papyrus 4 (P. O.I. 25262)

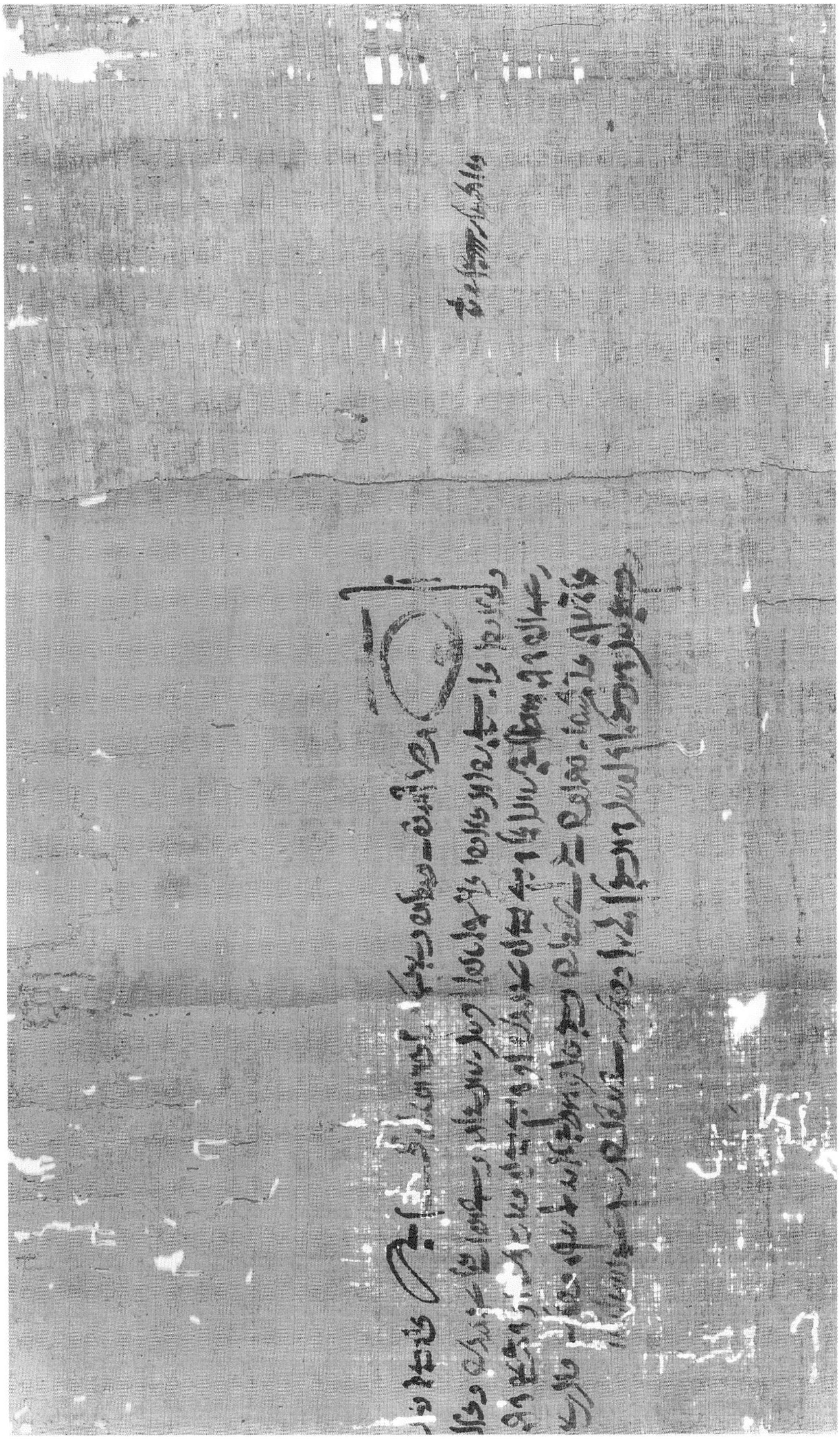

Plate 21

Chicago Hawara Papyrus 4 (P. O.I. 25262). Lines 1–5

Plate 22

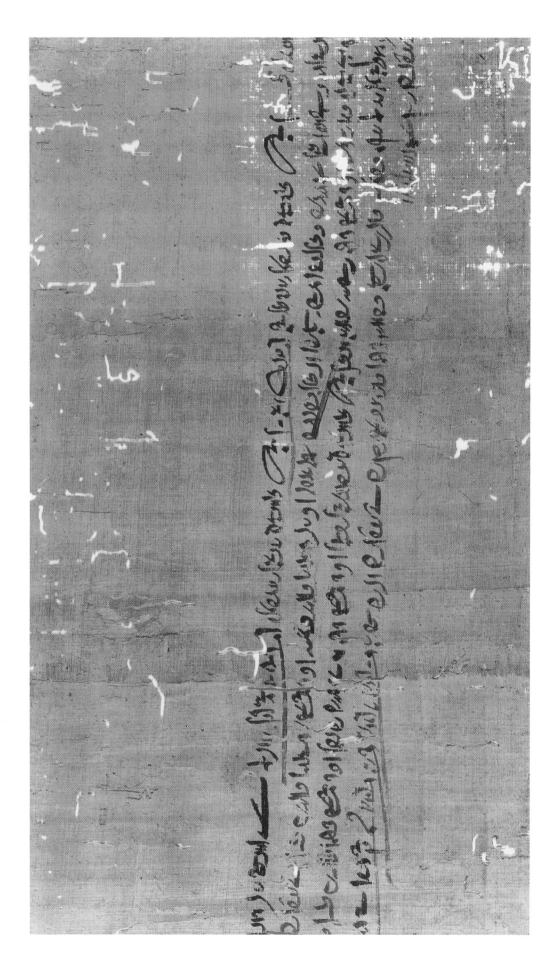

Chicago Hawara Papyrus 4 (P. O.I. 25262). Lines 1–5 (*cont.*)

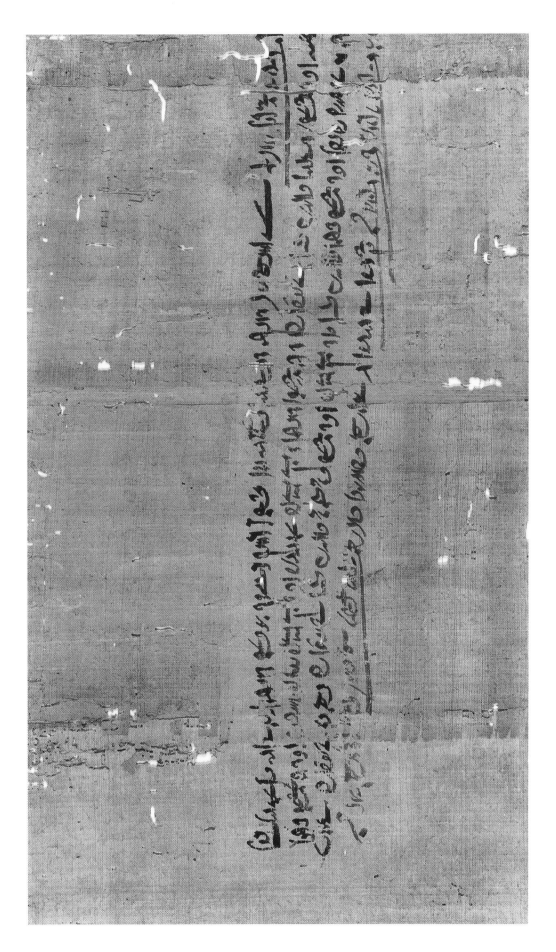

Plate 23

Chicago Hawara Papyrus 4 (P. O.I. 25262). Lines 1–4 (*cont.*)

Plate 24

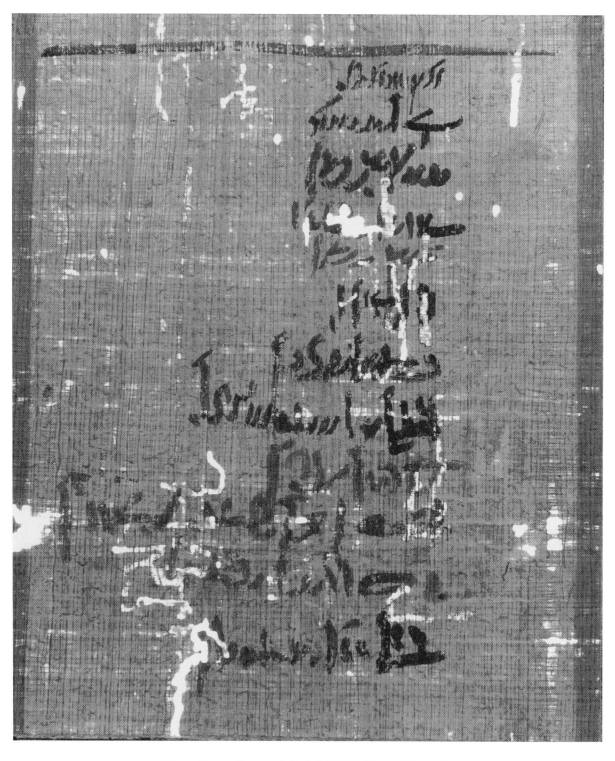

Chicago Hawara Papyrus 4 (P. O.I. 25262). Verso. Witness List

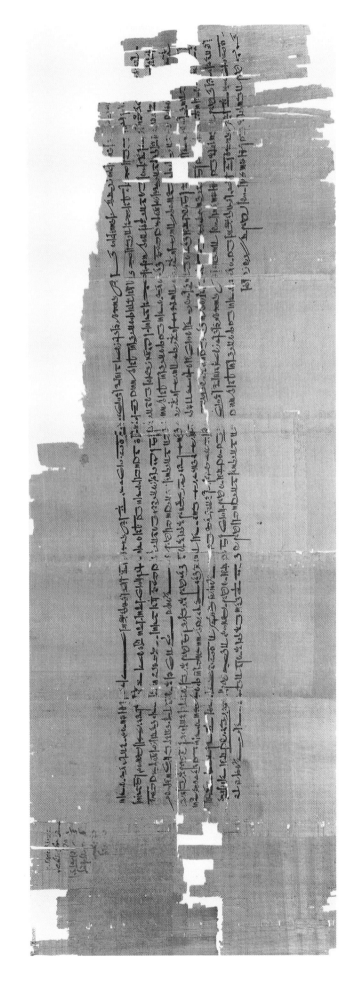

Plate 25

Chicago Hawara Papyrus 5 (P. O.I. 25258)

Plate 26

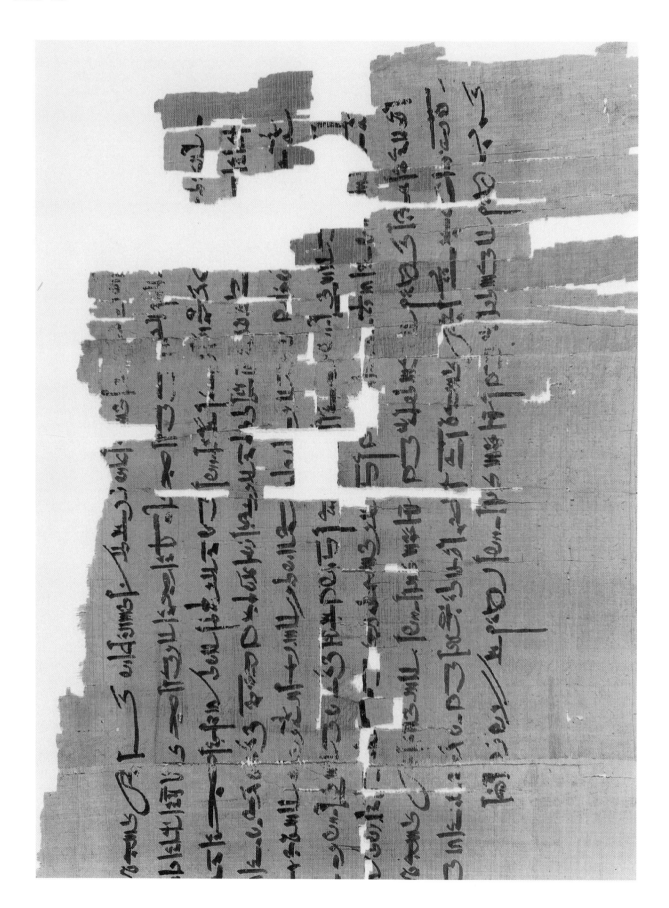

Chicago Hawara Papyrus 5 (P. O.I. 25258). Lines 1–10

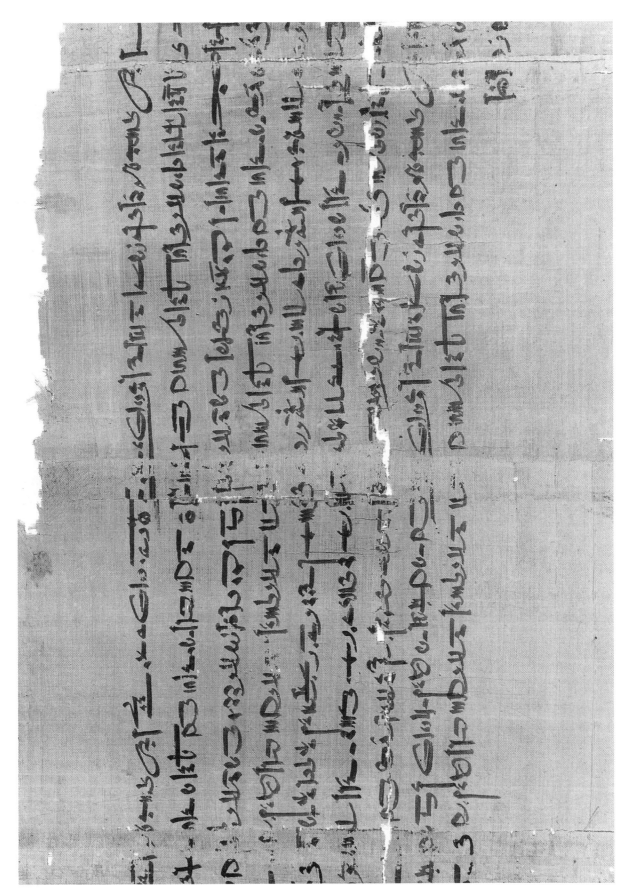

Plate 27

Chicago Hawara Papyrus 5 (P. O.I. 25258). Lines 1–10 (*cont.*)

Plate 28

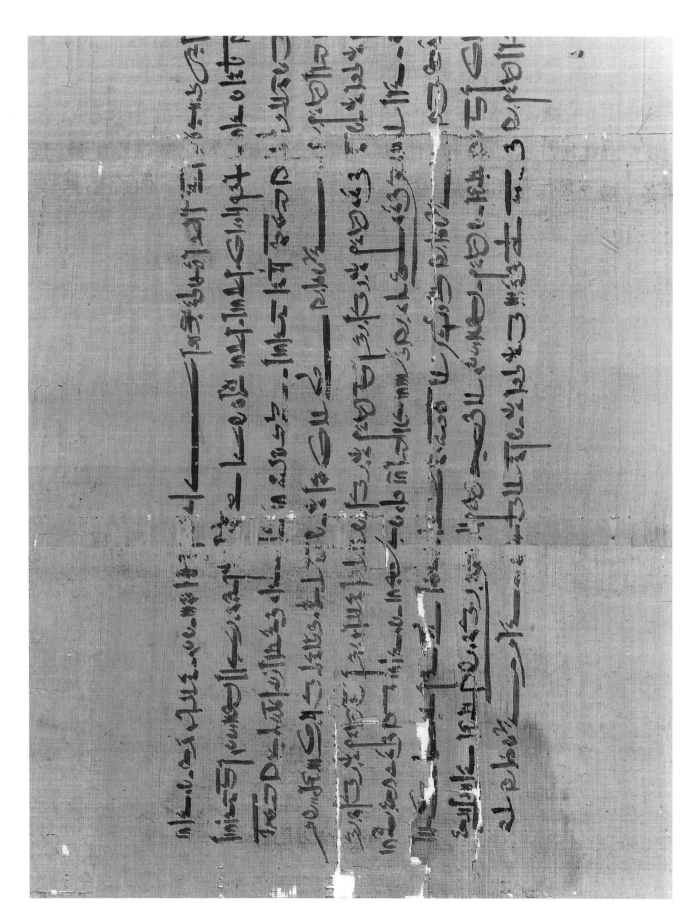

Chicago Hawara Papyrus 5 (P. O.I. 25258). Lines 1–9 (cont.)

Plate 29

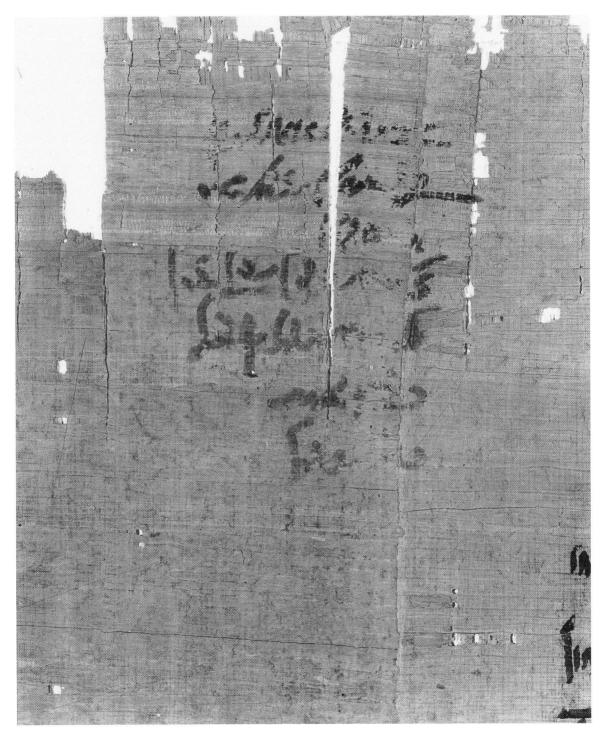

Chicago Hawara Papyrus 5 (P. O.I. 25258). Upper Left End of Papyrus. Witness List

Plate 30

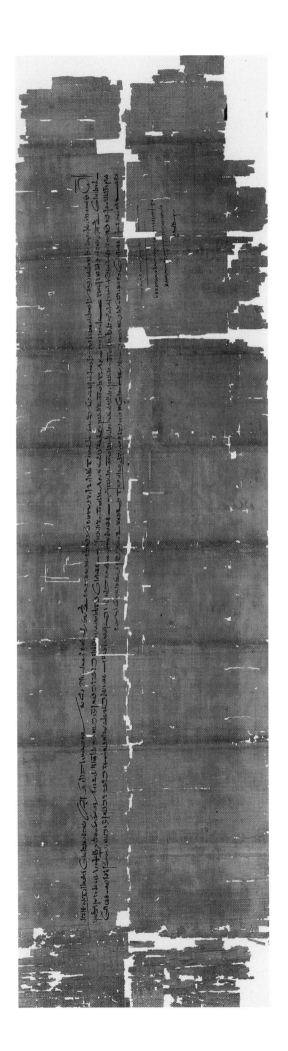

Chicago Hawara Papyrus 6 (P. O.I. 25388)

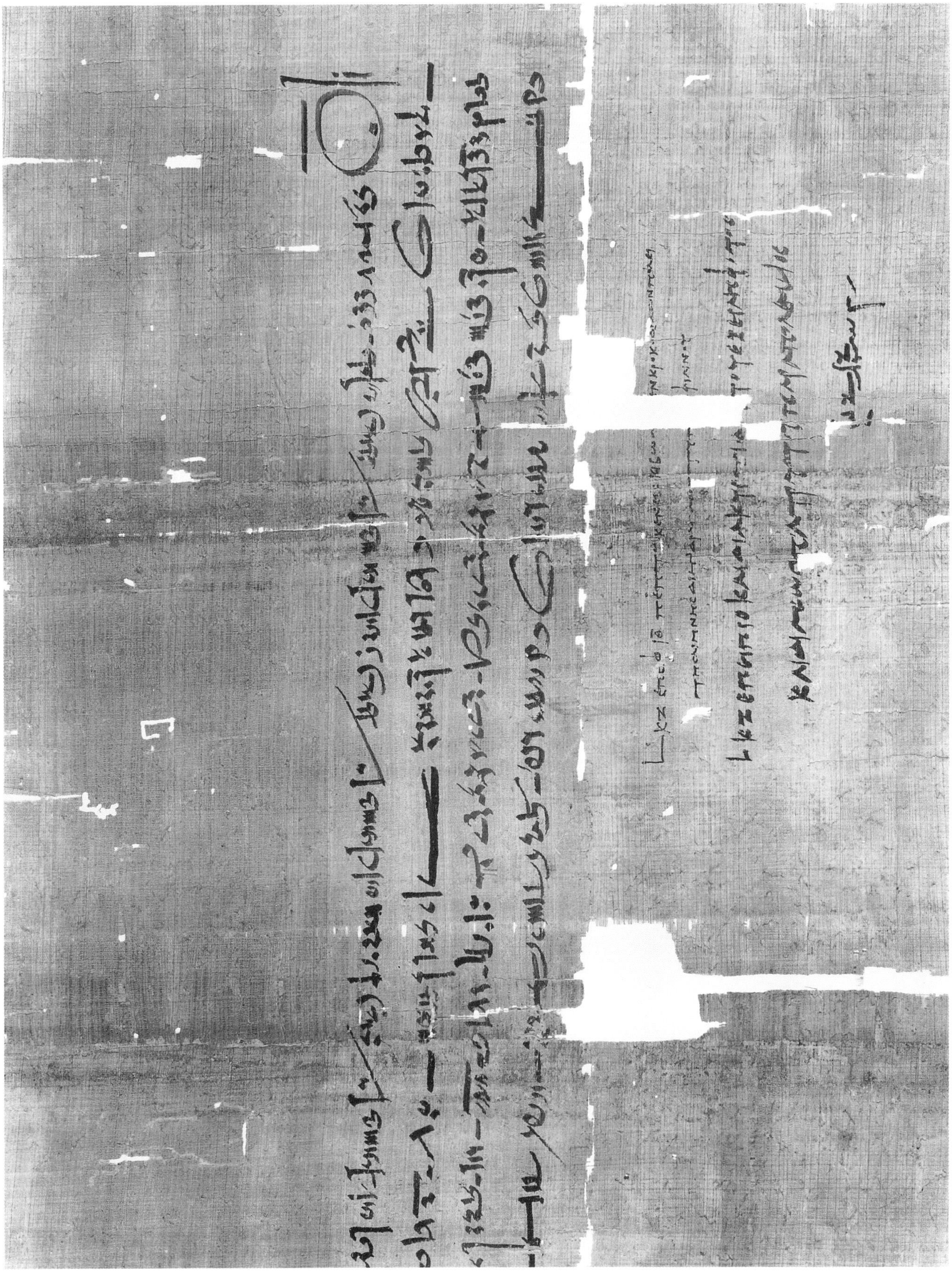

Plate 31

Chicago Hawara Papyrus 6 (P. O.I. 25388). Lines 1–4

Plate 32

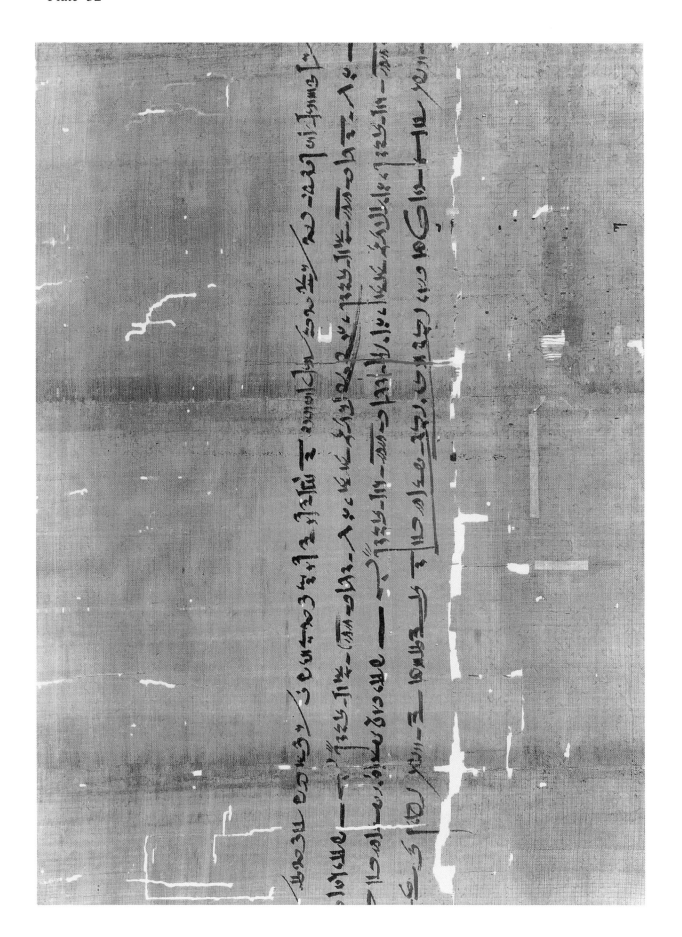

Chicago Hawara Papyrus 6 (P. O.I. 25388). Lines 1–4 (*cont.*)

Plate 33

Chicago Hawara Papyrus 6 (P. O.I. 25388). Lines 1–4 (*cont.*)

Plate 34

Chicago Hawara Papyrus 6 (P. O.I. 25388). Greek Docket and Demotic Signature

Plate 36

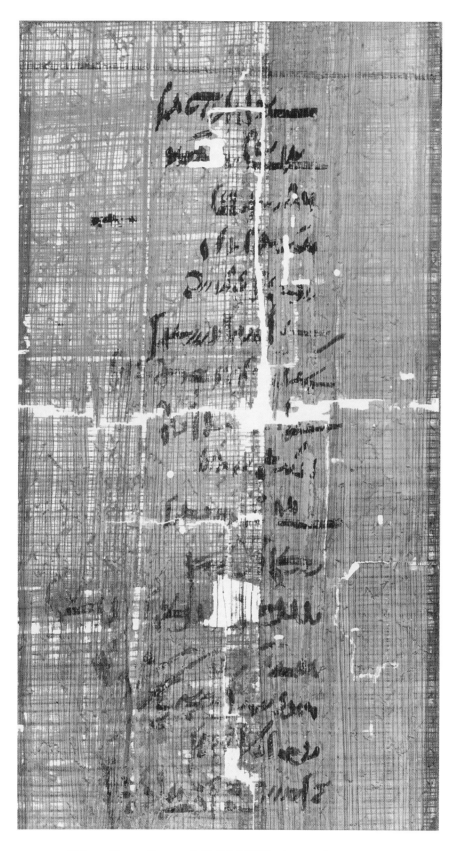

Chicago Hawara Papyrus 6 (P. O.I. 25388). Verso. Witness List

Plate 37

Chicago Hawara Papyrus 6 (P. O.I. 25388). Two Views of Signature on Verso

Plate 38

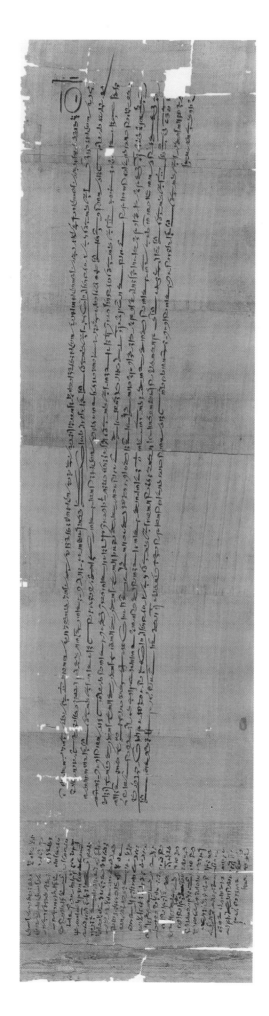

Chicago Hawara Papyrus 7A–B (P. O.I. 25255)

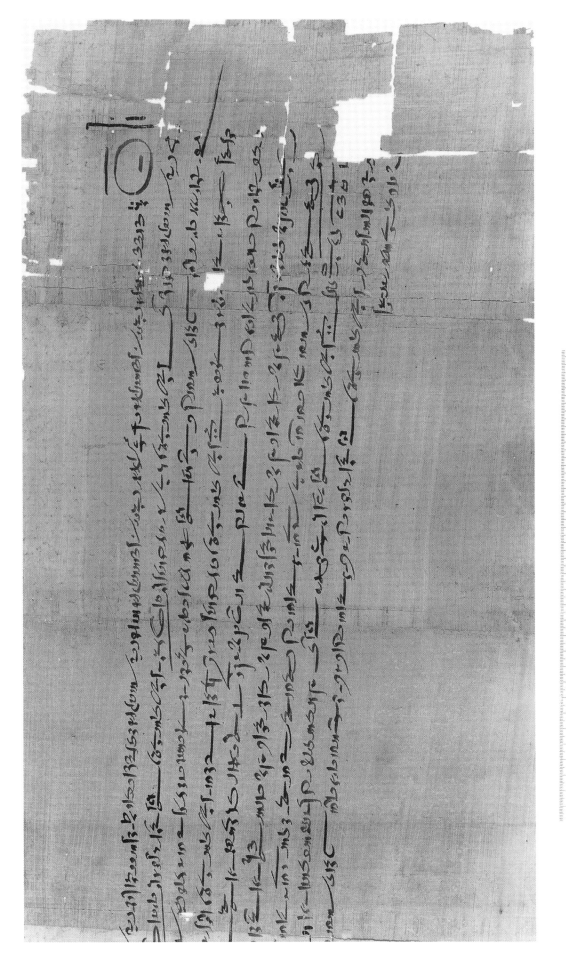

Chicago Hawara Papyrus 7A (P. O.I. 25255). Lines 1–10

Plate 39

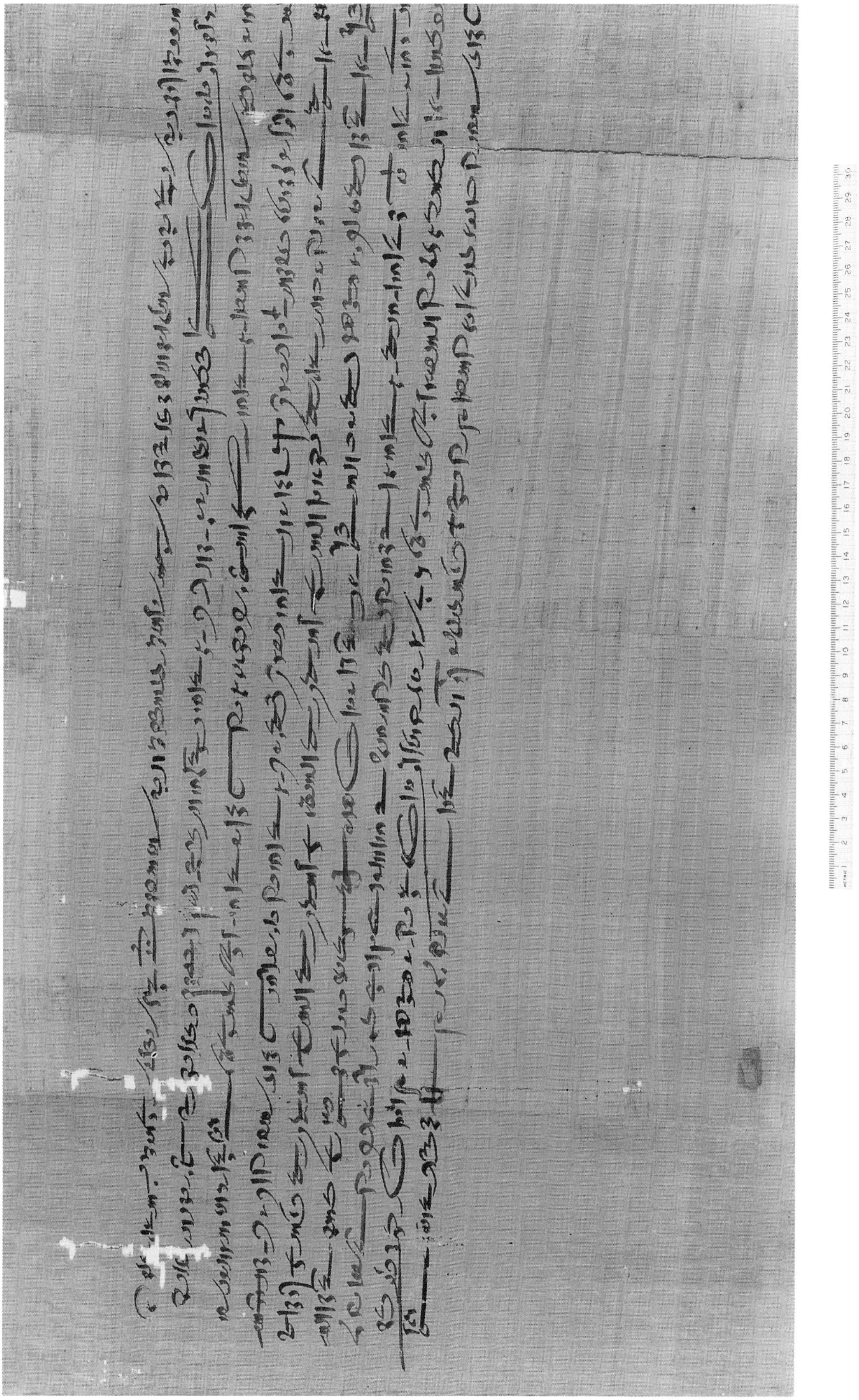

Plate 40

Chicago Hawara Papyrus 7A (P. O.I. 25255). Lines 1–9 (*cont.*)

Plate 41

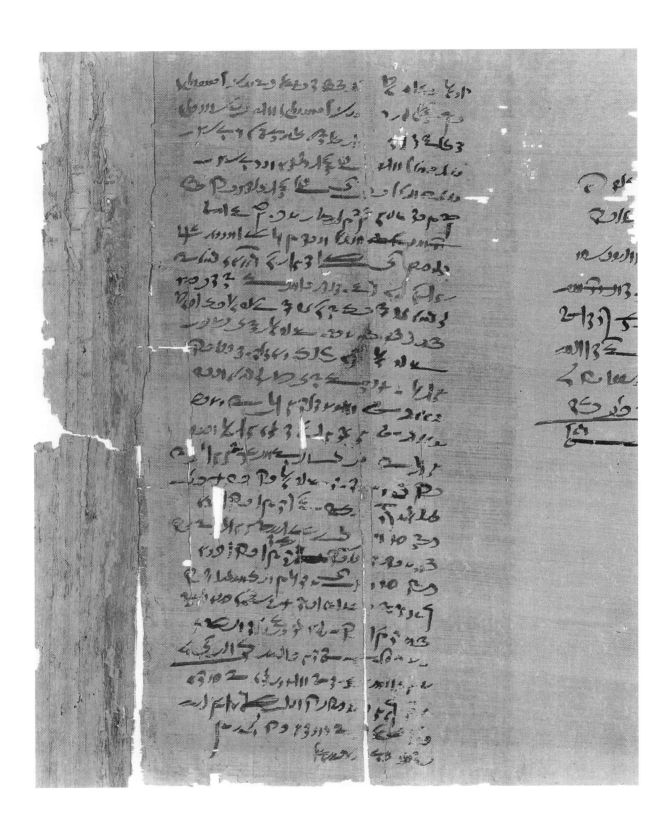

Chicago Hawara Papyrus 7B (P. O.I. 25255)

Plate 42

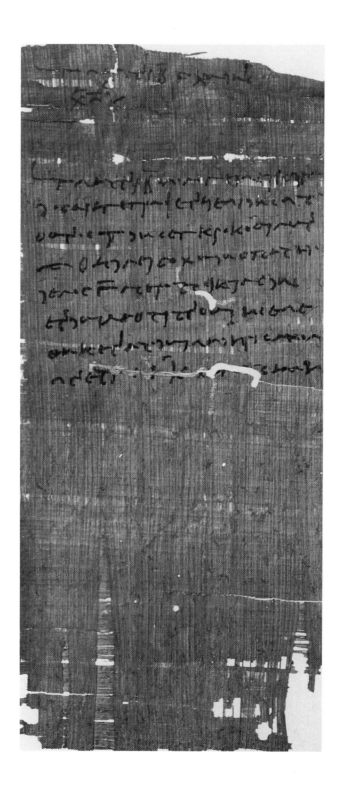

Chicago Hawara Greek Papyrus 7C (P. O.I. 25260). *Scriptura Interior* and *Scriptura Exterior*

Plate 43

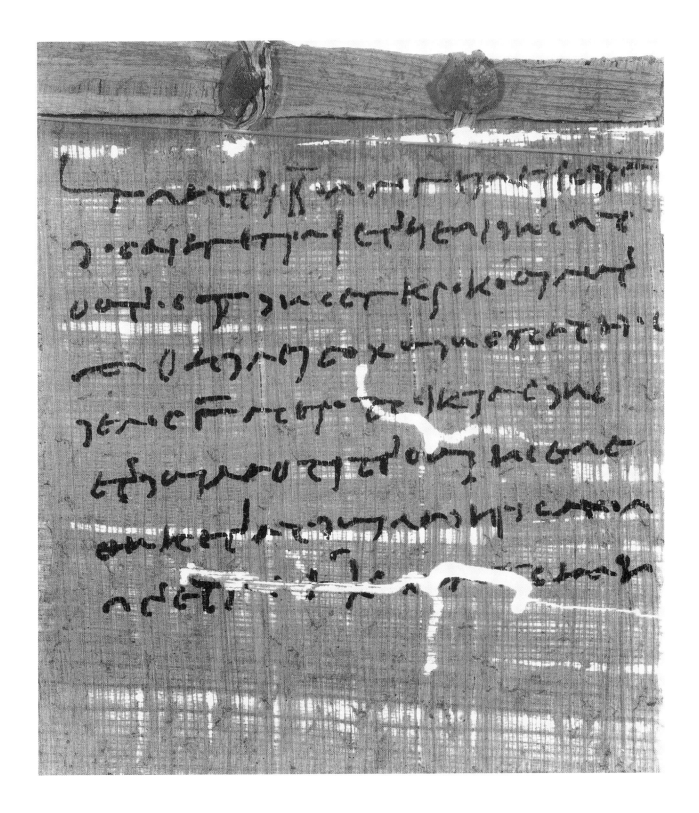

Chicago Hawara Greek Papyrus 7C (P. O.I. 25260). Detailed View of *Scriptura Exterior* with Seals *in Situ*

Plate 44

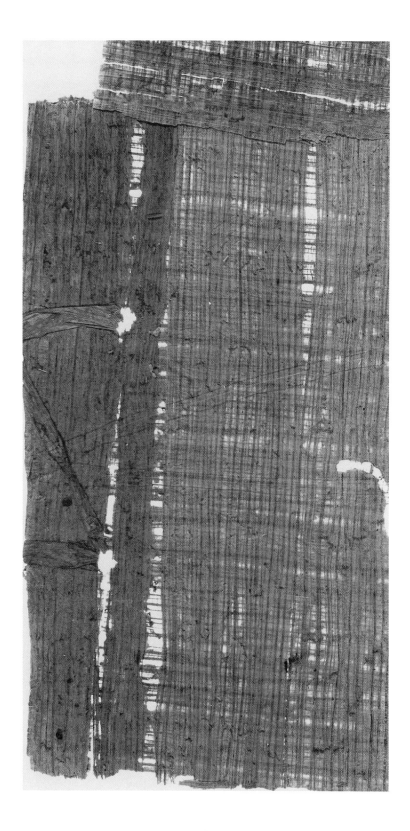

Chicago Hawara Greek Papyrus 7C (P. O.I. 25260). Detailed View of Sealed Portion of Papyrus (Verso)

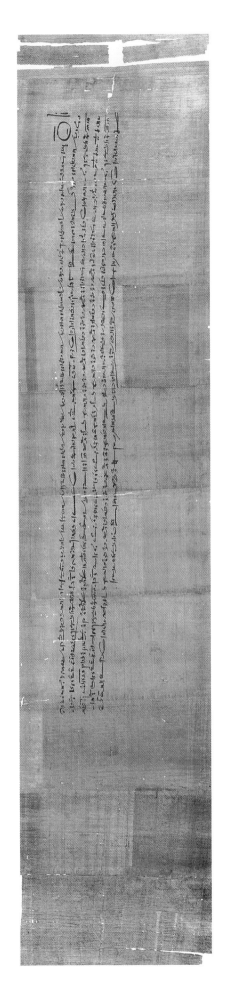

Chicago Hawara Papyrus 8 (P. O.I. 25256)

Plate 45

Plate 46

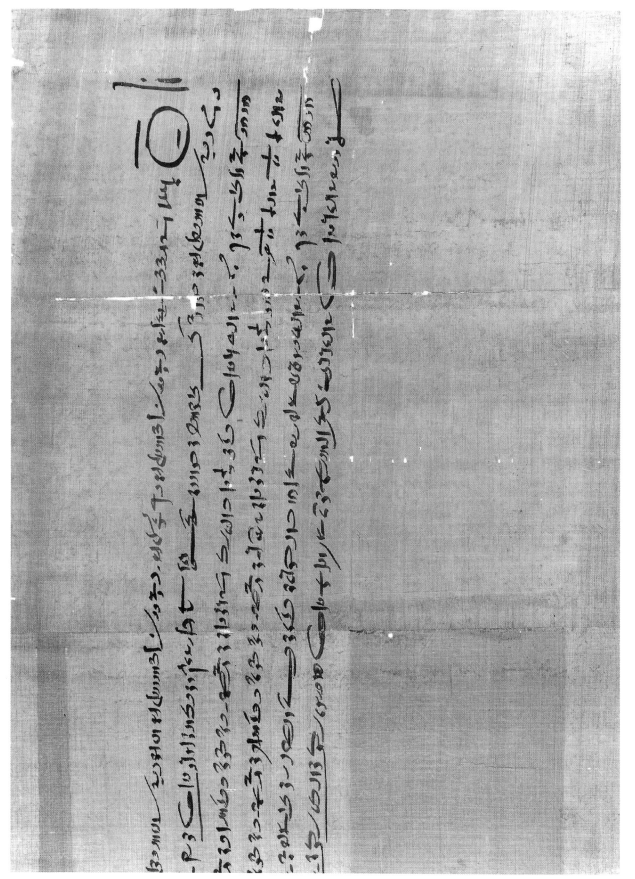

Chicago Hawara Papyrus 8 (P. O.I. 25256). Lines 1–6

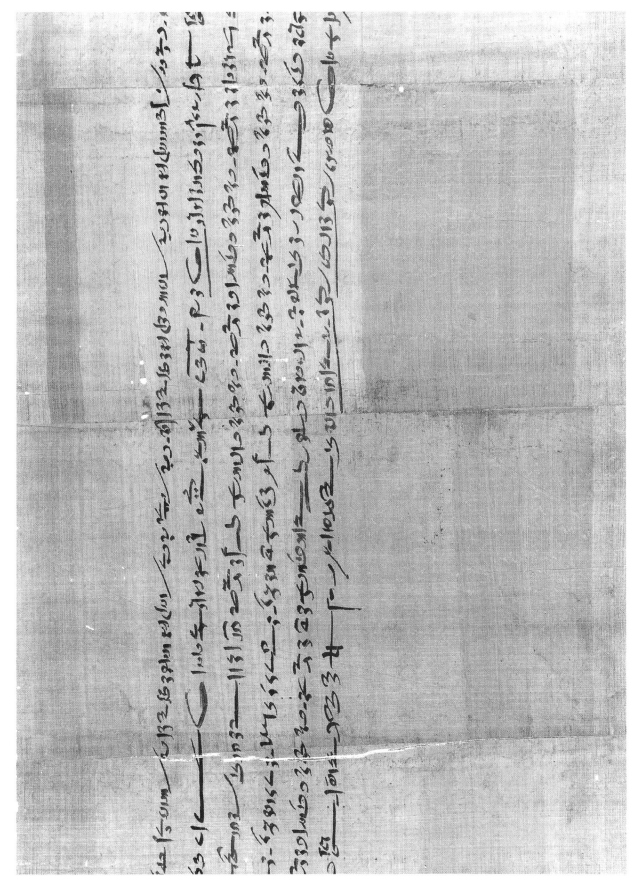

Plate 47

Chicago Hawara Papyrus 8 (P. O.I. 25256). Lines 1–6 (*cont.*)

Plate 48

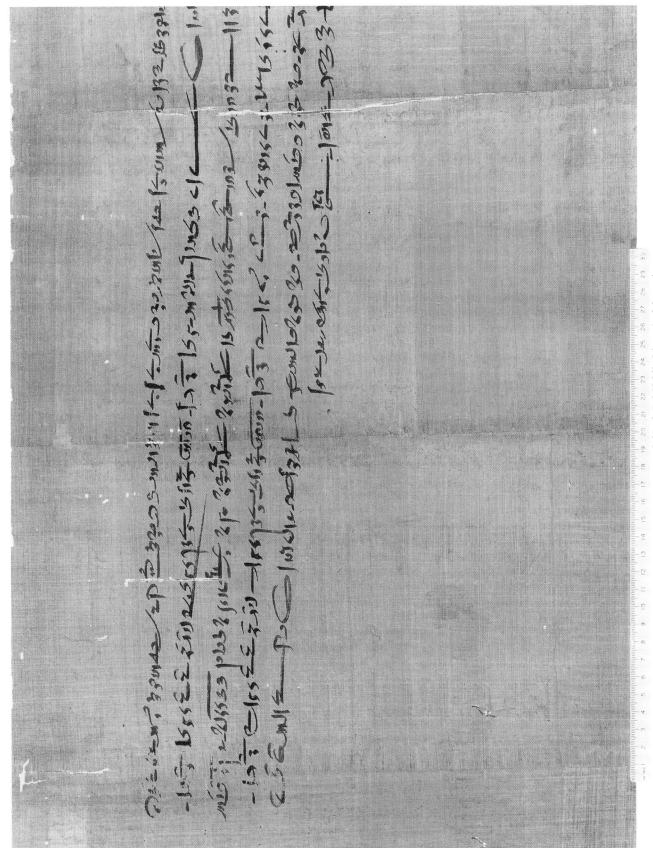

Chicago Hawara Papyrus 8 (P. O.I. 25256). Lines 1–6 (*cont.*)

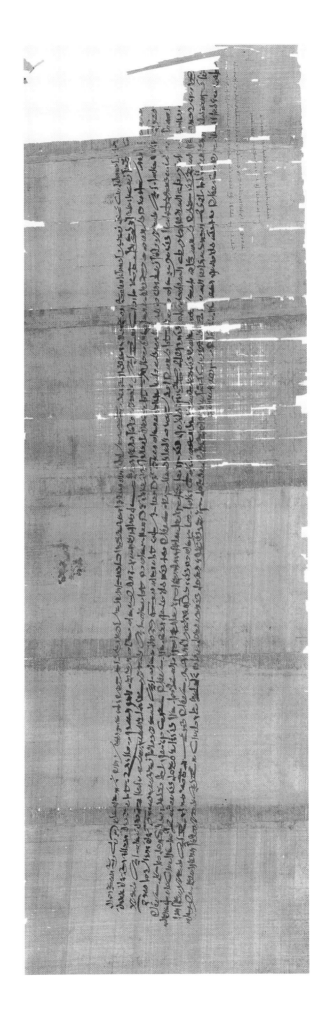

Chicago Hawara Papyrus 9 (P. O.I. 25263)

Plate 49

Plate 50

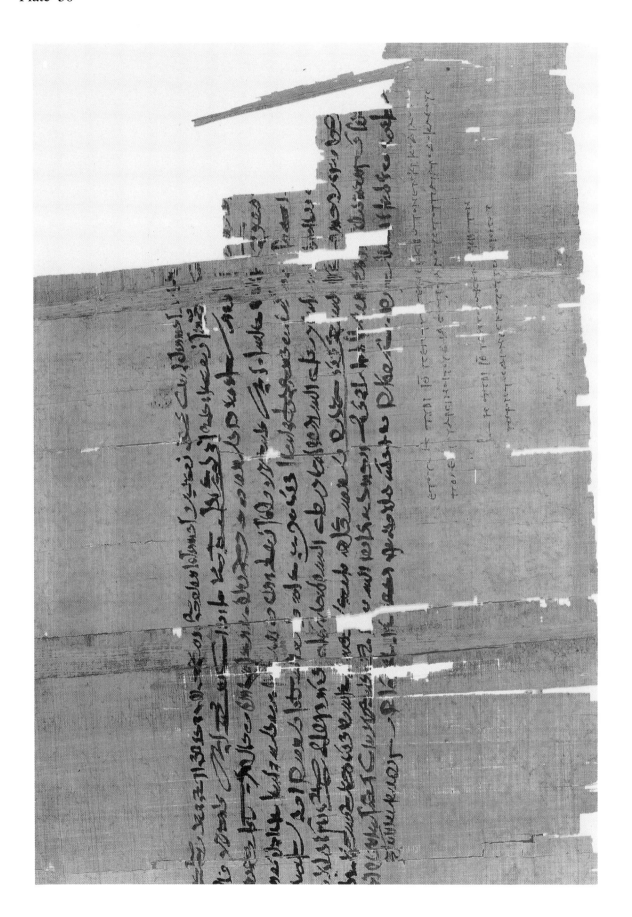

Chicago Hawara Papyrus 9 (P. O.I. 25263). Lines 1–9

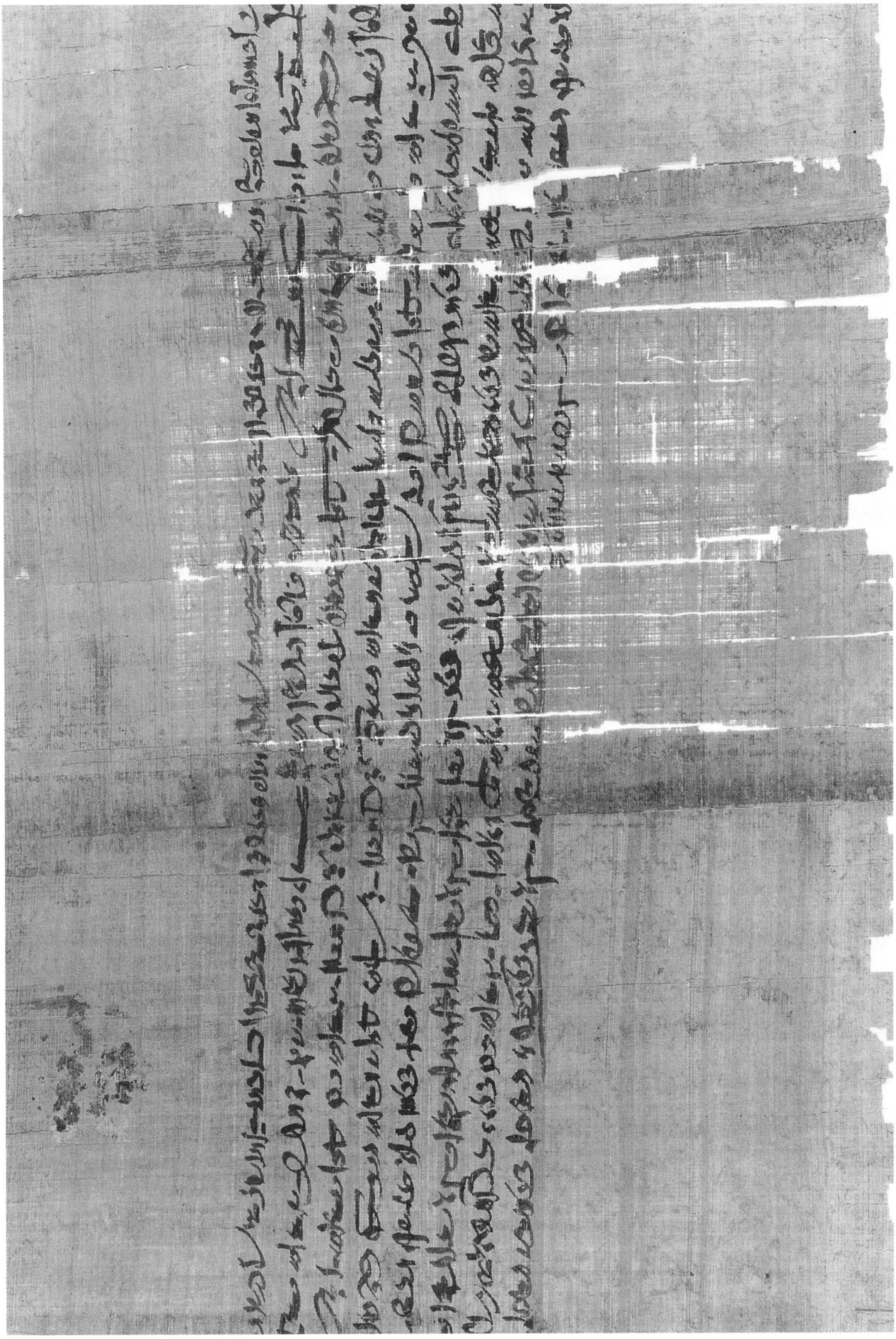

Plate 51

Chicago Hawara Papyrus 9 (P. O.I. 25263). Lines 1–9 (*cont.*)

Plate 52

Chicago Hawara Papyrus 9 (P. O.I. 25263). Lines 1–8 (*cont.*)

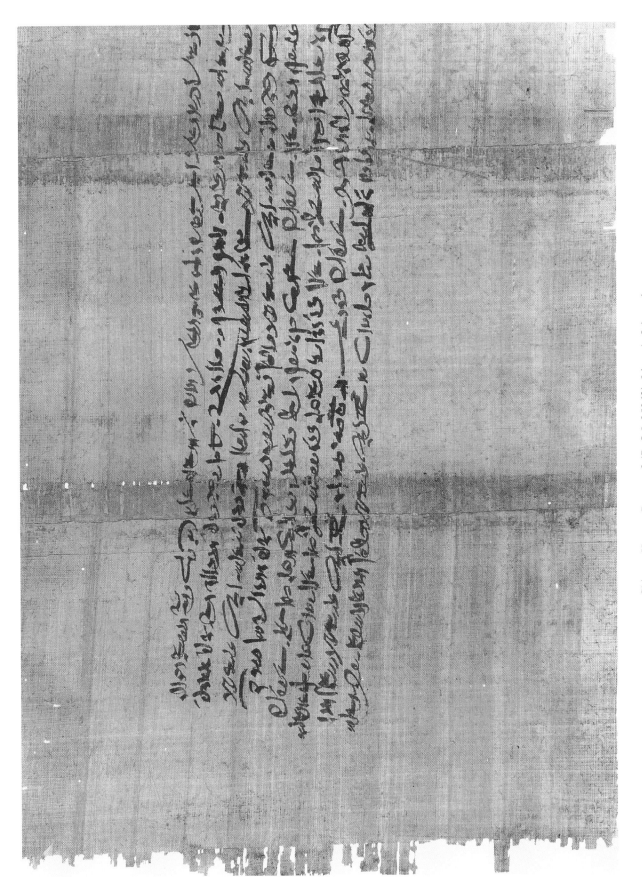

Plate 53

Chicago Hawara Papyrus 9 (P. O.I. 25263). Lines 1–8 (*cont.*)

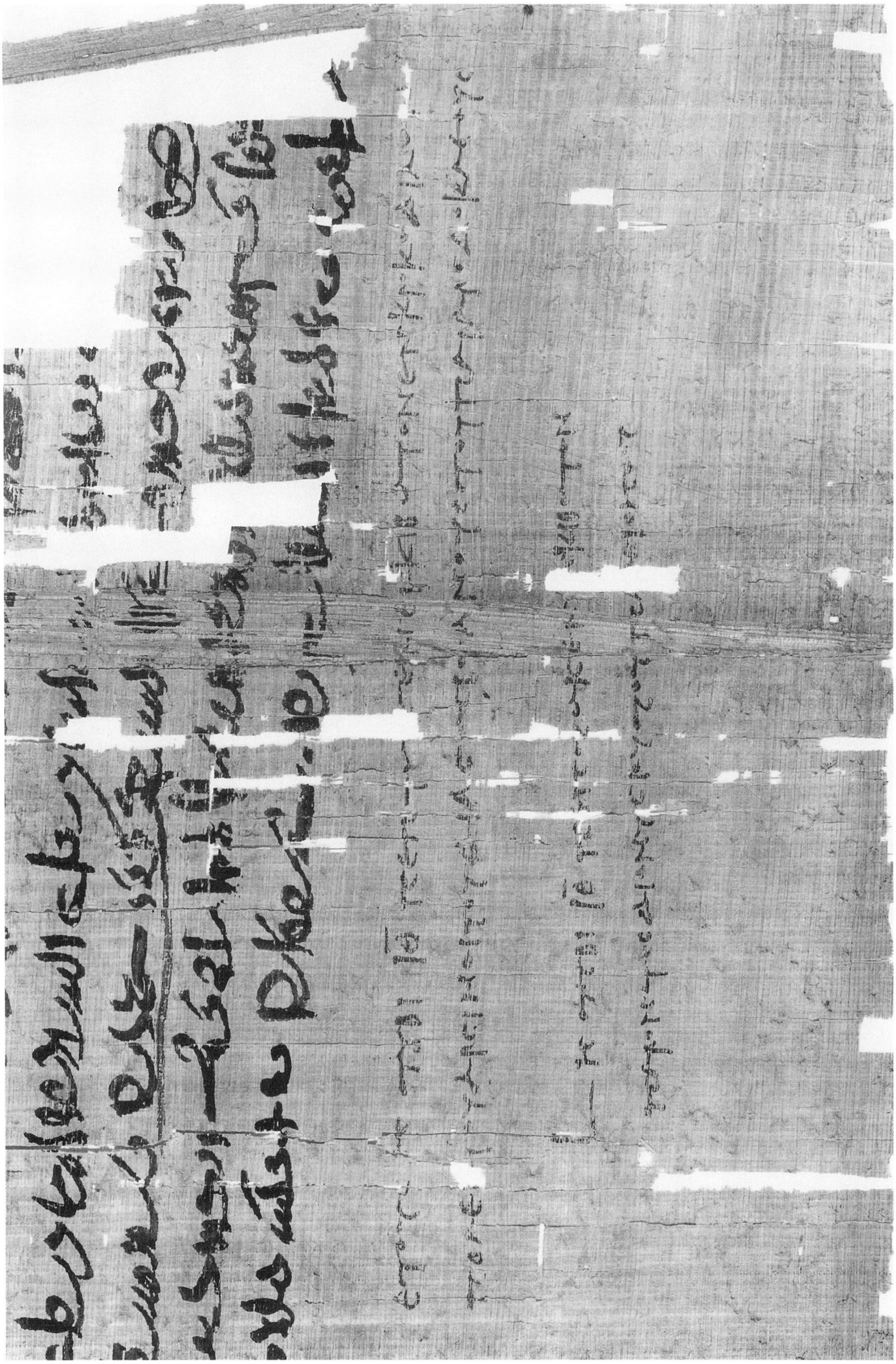

Plate 54

Chicago Hawara Papyrus 9 (P. O.I. 25263). Greek Dockets

Plate 55

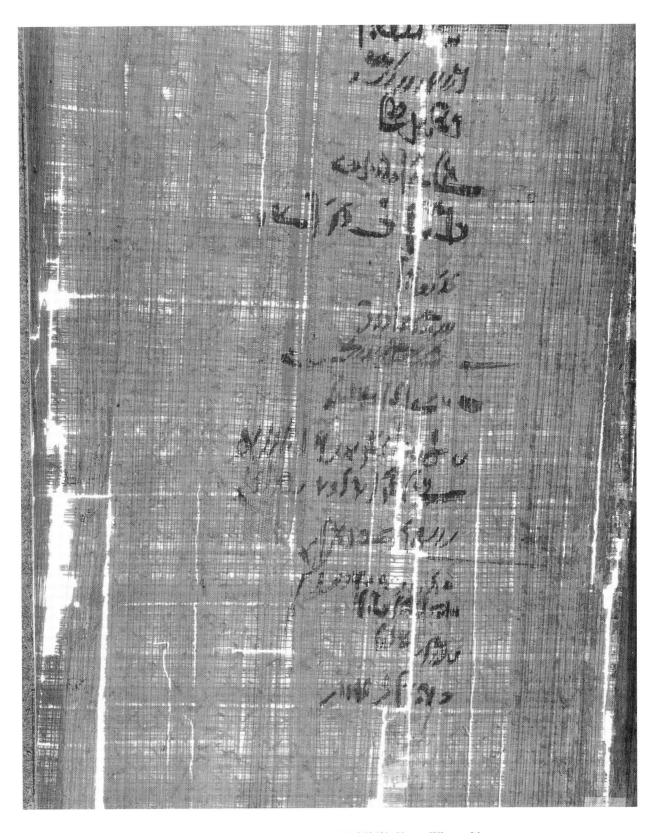

Chicago Hawara Papyrus 9 (P. O.I. 25263). Verso. Witness List

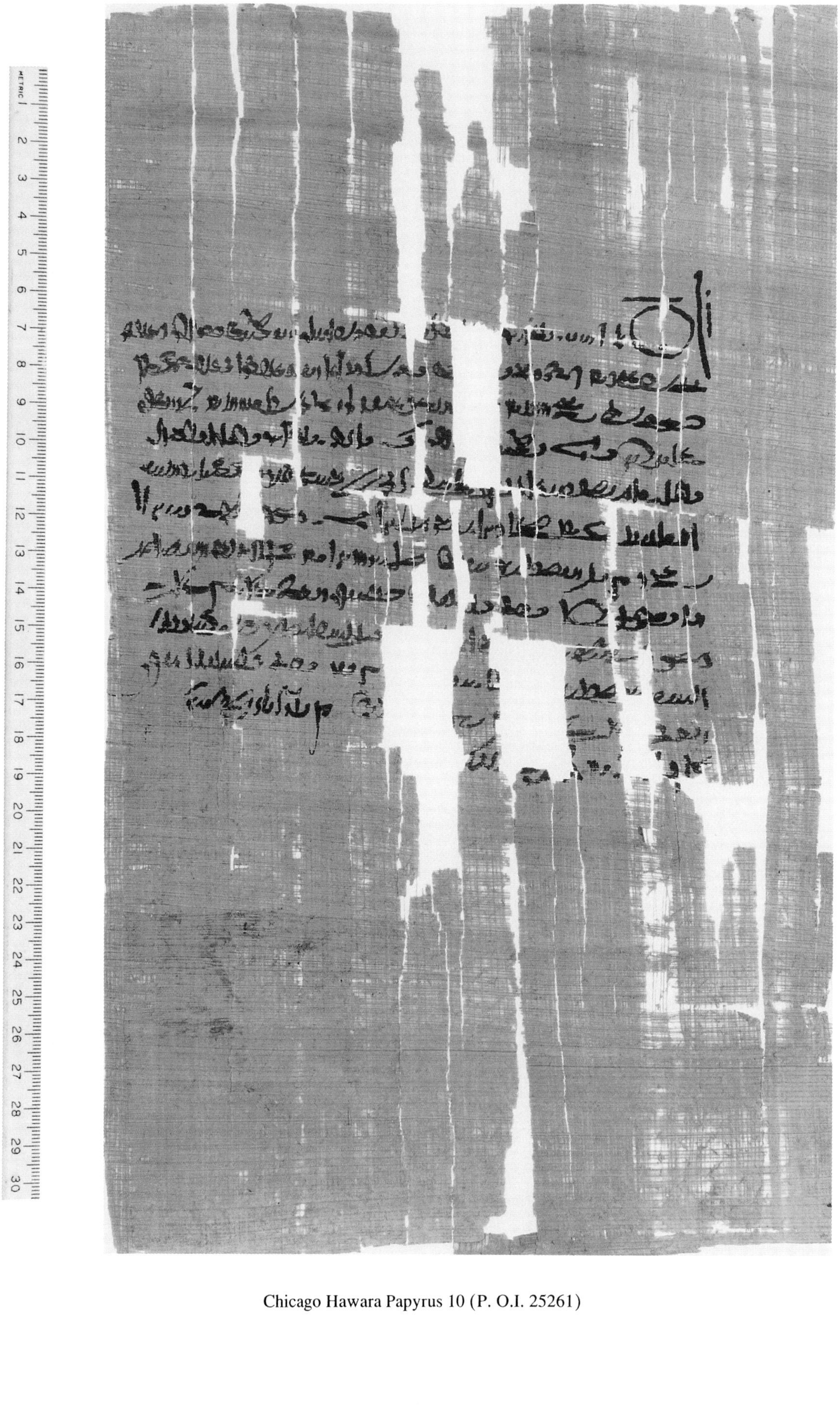

Plate 56

Chicago Hawara Papyrus 10 (P. O.I. 25261)

Plate 57

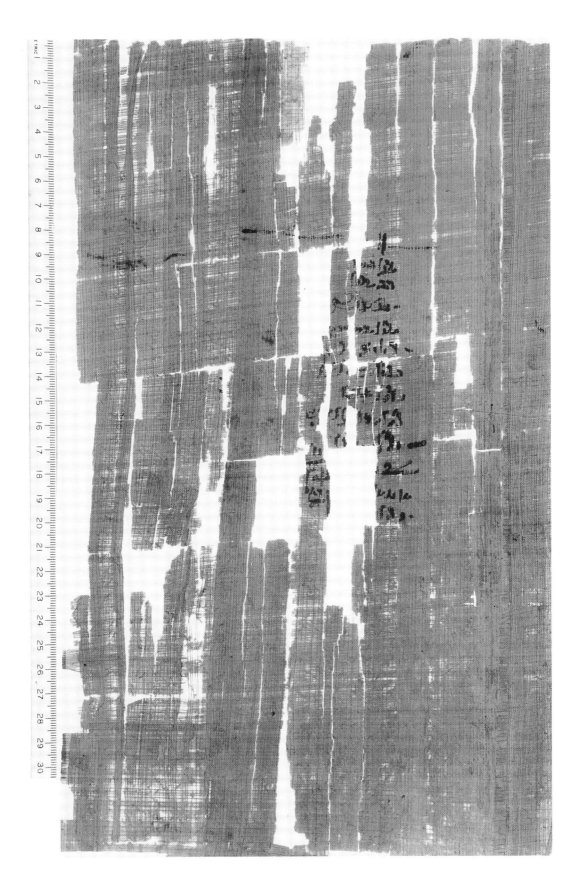

Chicago Hawara Papyrus 10 (P. O.I. 25261). Verso. Witness List

Plate 58

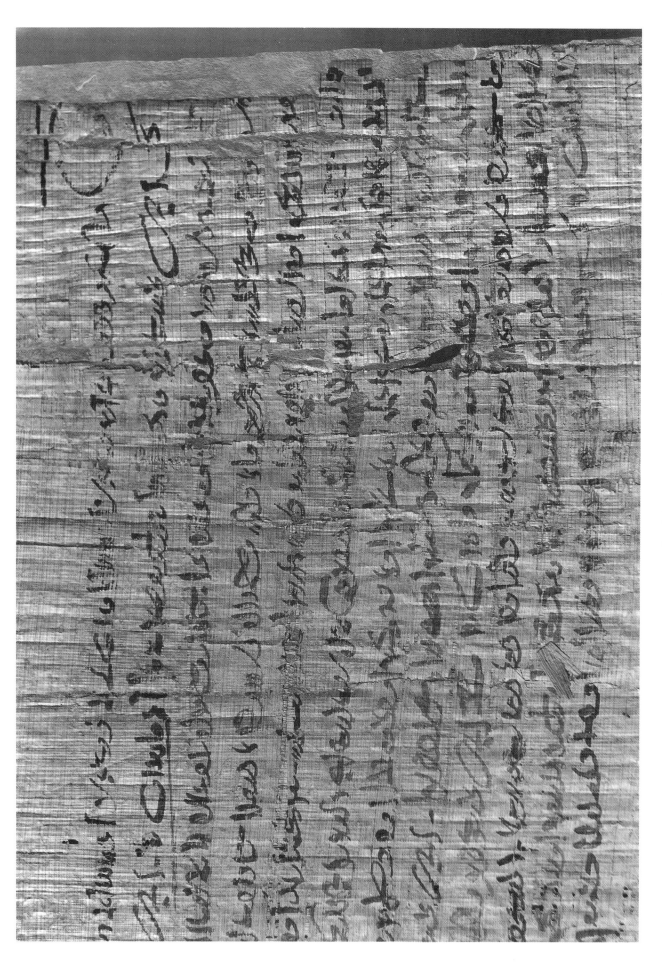

Rendell Papyrus. Lines 1–12

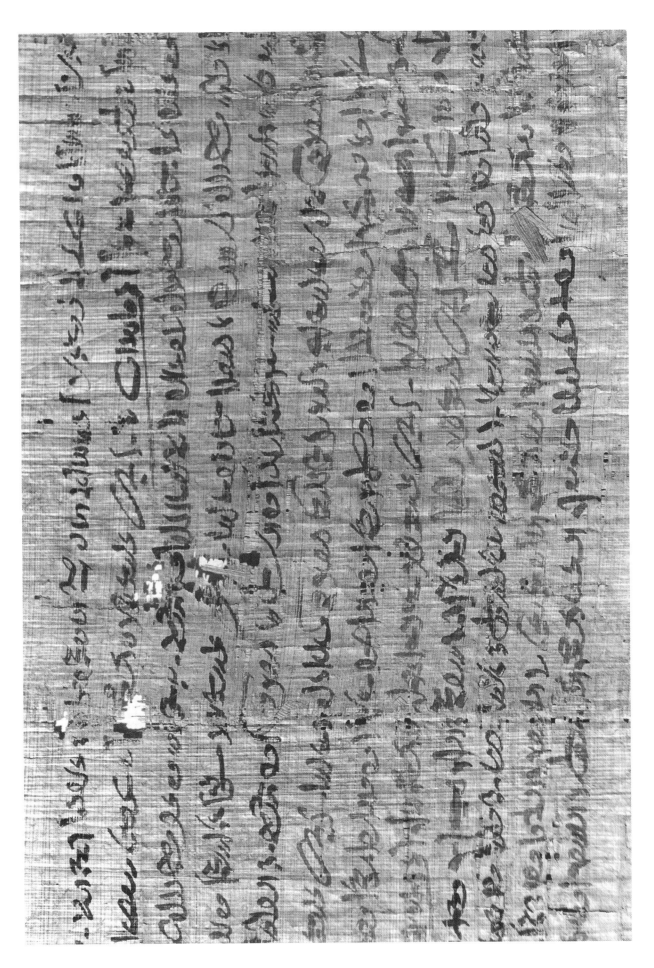

Plate 59

Rendell Papyrus. Lines 1–12 (*cont.*)

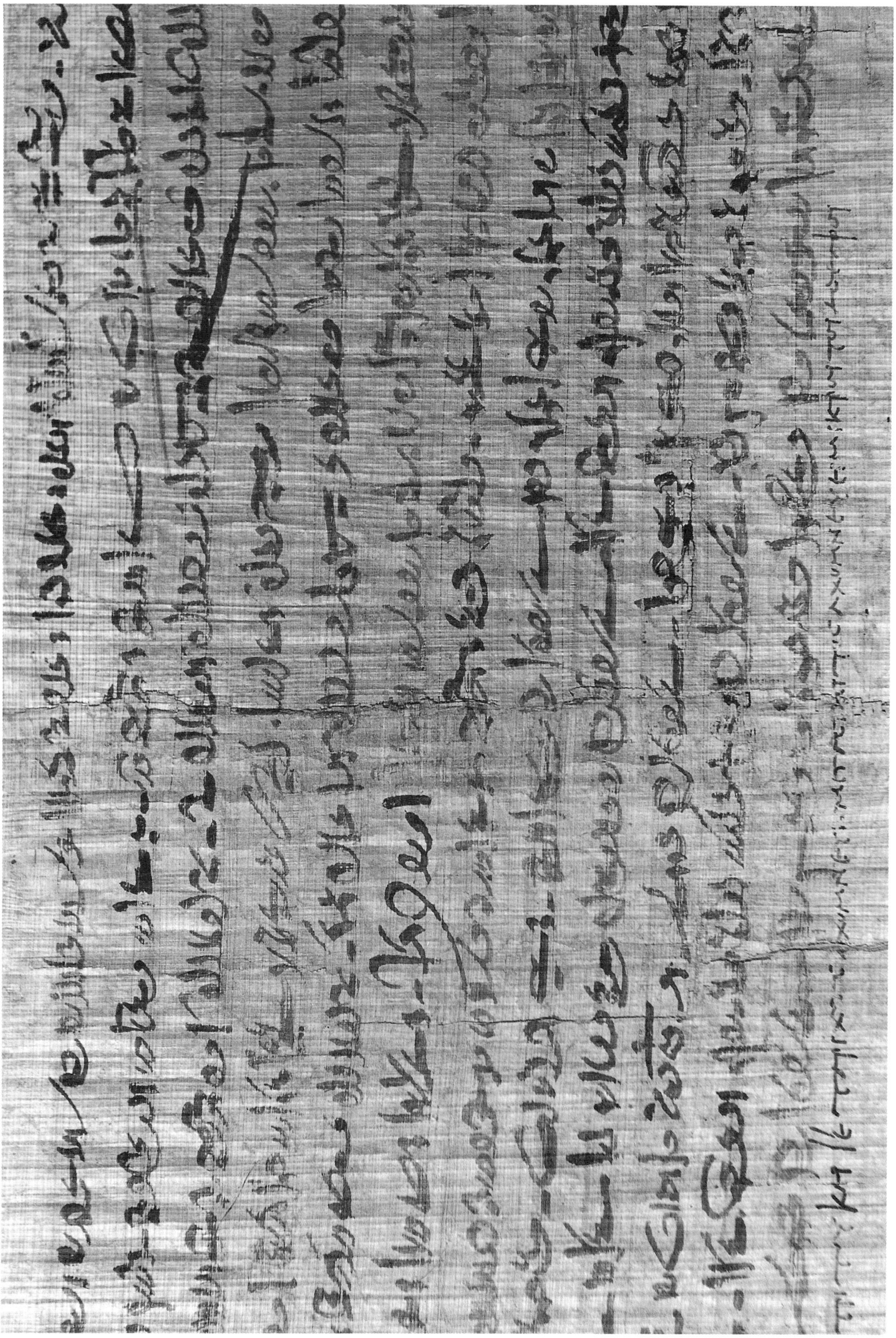

Plate 60

Rendell Papyrus. Lines 1–12 (*cont.*) and Greek Docket

Plate 61

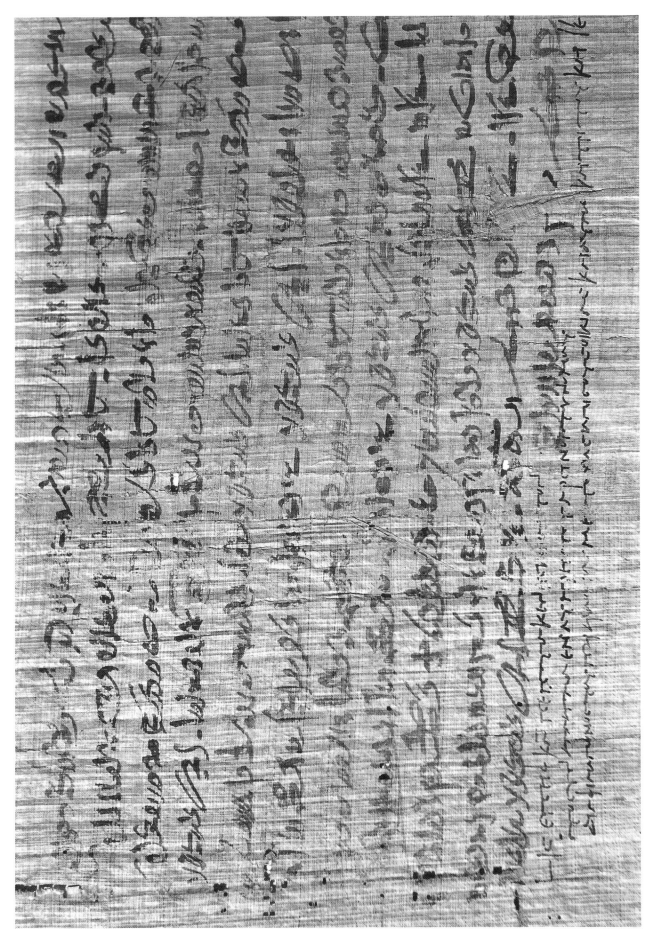

Rendell Papyrus. Lines 1–12 and Greek Docket (*cont.*)

Plate 62

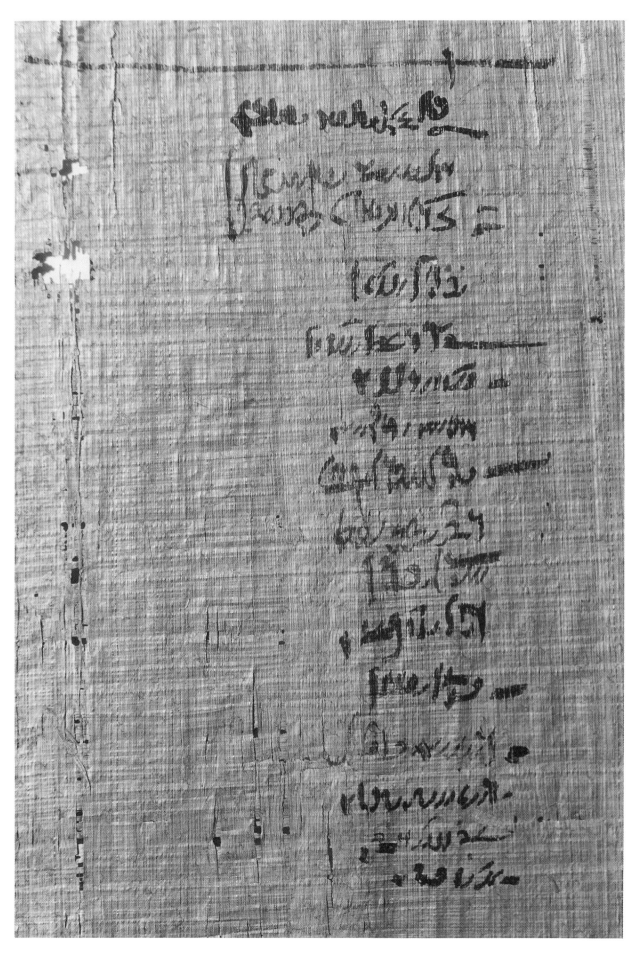

Rendell Papyrus. Verso. Witness List